# Albino Peacock
## Stories Of a Southern Jewish Girl-Child

## Lynn Strongin

Plain View Press
P. O. 42255
Austin, TX 78704

plainviewpress.net
sb@plainviewpress.net
1-512-441-2452

Copyright Lynn Strongin, 2008. All rights reserved.
ISBN: 978-0-911051-48-3
Library of Congress Number: 2008937008




Cover photo by Deborah Munro.

For Anam Cara
& in memory of Roman Vishniac's
*Children of a Vanished World*

## Acknowledgements

Thanks to my publisher, Susan Bright, who had the foresight to embrace my vision of *The Albino Peacock* and the artistic mastery to find the print form of it. Thanks to my copyeditor Pam Knight who lived up to her name and saw me thru the final stages of the book at the eleventh hour.

Thanks to *Artistry of Life. Confrontation, storySouth, New Works Review (in which the title story appears), Riverbabble, Centrifugal Eye, Greatcoat (inaugural issue,* and *storySouth* ChiZine (http://chizine.com), Cricket On-line Review *in which some of these stories first appeared.*

While these stories are inspired by real life, the characters are imaginative composites.

# Contents

| | |
|---|---|
| Forward | 11 |
| Author's Introduction: Indigo, Child Of the New Millennium | 13 |
| Threaded Characters | 17 |

## Champion Of the Spelling Bee — 21

| | |
|---|---|
| *Filling up the Dance Card: Hardly Know Ye* | 23 |
| *Spinal Tap* | 30 |
| *Paradise Gas Works Or, "Reserved for the Local Spelling Bee Champion"* | 31 |

## Natural Bacteria — 39

| | |
|---|---|
| *Natural Bacteria* | 41 |
| *Coda* | 46 |

## Broken Toys — 49

| | |
|---|---|
| *In Recurvatum* | 51 |
| *A Draft* | 54 |
| *Bag of Toys* | 54 |
| *Beneath My Wings* | 56 |
| *Let up* | 60 |

## Morning Glory Jeans — 63

| | |
|---|---|
| *Morning Glory Blue* | 65 |
| *Lionheart* | 67 |

## Audubon Wallpaper — 71

| | |
|---|---|
| *Stilled In Flight* | 73 |
| *Akimbo* | 78 |
| *Leap* | 82 |
| *Impaled* | 83 |

**Polio: A Girlhood Novitiate (Pooky and I)**     85

   *Poverty, Chastity, Obedience*     87
   *Small Forest Shrine*     88

**My First Polio**     95

**Going to the Bayou: Rockets Overhead**     101

   *Curtains*     103
   *Bayou City*     105

**Murder Ball: Butcher's Wife and Carnation**     109

   *Killa Ball*     111
   *Body Memory*     115

**Acting Ugly: Spin the Bottle Kiss Me**     123

**Alissa's Baby**     137

**One Dark Valentine: For the Children Of the Blitz**     143

   *Fatal Morning*     145
   *Valentine Meeting*     149
   *Ichabod Crane*     152
   *Home-Run*     154

**The Sad Little Abyss in Every Home**     159

**Undertaker Bird**     165

   *Keeping the Undertaker Bird Away*     167
   *Extending the Undertaker Bird an Invitation*     171

**Cry Me a River: A Musical Romance**     179

   *Prologue*     181
   *Largo*     181
   *Allegretto*     186
   *Sarabande*     192
   *Coda*     195

## Music To Get You Out Of the Pews, Dancing     205

    *One Step Nearer November*     207
    *Paralysis*     209
    *Fancy Plugging Your Ears*     210

## Ebon: Old Age     213

    *Edge*     215
    *Last Love, Last Loss*     216

## Cuffing the Boy's Shirt     219

    *Conti-Crayon Drawings*     221
    *Doll-Face*     228
    *The Angel In Question Is Rosario*     234

## North and South: Nickel and Diamond Store     235

    *Before the Loan Expired*     237
    *After the Loan*     242
    *Back Home with Interest*     245

## Whips: A Family Story     253

    *Whips: A Family Story*     255
    *Incantatory: Triangle Island*     257

## The Kind of Day to See an Albino Peacock     265

    *Peacock Weather*     267
    *Nectar Drops for Nerves*     276
    *Shut Shop On Emotions*     278

## About the Author     285

Marguerite Strongin, Portrait (1941), oil on canvas, 51 sm x 61 cm (24" x 20")

*Once, many years ago, in the garden of the church of St. John the Divine, in NYC, a peacock walked up to me and opened his tail. For a moment I thought to myself "Maybe there is a god."*
    Penelope Weiss




"Woe unto me when all men praise me."
    George Bernard Shaw's St. Joan

# Forward

Language is the tie that binds me to Lynn Strongin, and language is the heritage we share. Not language as people usually conceive of the term, as simple communication or shades of regional accent. Not even language as the system of symbols and grammatical rules which are now humanity's most powerful of tools.

No, what binds me to Lynn is a belief that under rare circumstances, language can be a window for seeing the world in new and unique ways. For delving toward unspoken truths. For creating life where previously no life could exist.

I first encountered Lynn while editing storySouth, a literary journal focusing on writings from the New South. To me, the concept of the New South is a celebration of the immense changes the region has undergone in the last few decades. The Civil Rights Movement, the influx of new people to the region, the dying of agricultural traditions and the boom of industrialization—all are aspects of the New South.

Lynn is in many ways a model example of a New South writer (although to pigeon-hole her as mainly a southern writer is to do her a great disservice). While she isn't native to the region, having been born in New York City in 1939, during World War II, Lynn followed her psychologist father across the South as he worked with injured soldiers. Living in what she's described as isolated hamlets and small hardscrabble farms, Lynn saw her own unique vision of the region. Lynn's father used to say, "It hurts to see too much, but we are what we say and we say what we see." Following that advice, Lynn has recreated what she saw in *Albino Peacock: Tales Of a Jewish Girl-Child In the South*.

Lynn's nonfiction reminds me in many ways of the writings of anthropologist Loren Eiseley. At first glance this comparison sounds strange—after all, Eiseley was a prominent scientist whose essays focused on explaining complex theories to the general public, while Lynn is primarily known as a poet. However, Eiseley's literary skill lay in what critics call his hidden essays, in which he combined poetic meditations with deep explorations of life. Perhaps nowhere did Eiseley rise to greater literary heights than in his memoir *All the Strange*

*Hours: The Excavation of a Life*, in which he looks back on his life from old age and attempts to make sense of his journey.

The stories in *Albino Peacock: Tales Of a Jewish Girl-Child In the South* echo Eiseley's proof that language can create the most profound explorations of life. In the startling rich language of *The Kind Of Day To See an Albino Peacock*, Lynn details her search for both the story's avian namesake and the tragic loses she endured during her childhood in the South. In the masterful *Audubon Wallpaper*, the image of a bird, not the real creation, is the focus of her attempt to understand the divisions which mark her life: "married versus divorced; South versus North, walking versus paralysis, homeland versus adopted land." Other stories explore her experiences with racism and childhood polio.

However, everything isn't painful in Lynn's stories or life. She often uses laughter to break through the tears, much as Flannery O'Connor and other southern writers used dark humor to arrive at deeper truths. And while Lynn sees the pain around her, she also sees the good. In *The Kind Of Day To See an Albino Peacock* she writes, "When you have been a child in a hospital, when you have had boils on your buttocks at age twelve, and seen children take the drip—nothing as benign as nectar drops for nerves—before you turned a teen, you turn toward anyone who takes you in with Kind. Kindness. The southern kind? No, the human kind."

And that's at the heart of Lynn's explorations—an understanding of the Kind. Of human kindness. Of kindness even when the world outside is cruel and hard and unforgiving.

If you, the reader, come to this book desiring a simple matter-of-fact accounting of a person's life, I suggest you look elsewhere. Yes, the life details are here. Yes, the accounts are accurate. But Lynn Strongin is first and foremost a poet, and her intent with these stories is to create new and unexpected understandings. To avoid what Eiseley called the "loneliness of not knowing, not knowing at all."

    Jason Sanford
    Editor, *storySouth*

# Author's Introduction:
# Indigo, Child Of the New Millennium

Indigo, first named after the sky, but finally seeing herself as child of the new century, narrates *Albino Peacock*, autobiographical stories of her sojourns in the South which create a tapestry. The surface at times is ruffled. At other times, the skin of the story-telling should be mirror-quiet like a green bayou. Revelation runs underneath. They are deeply southern. The weaving of a life is stitched using different colors. These stories trace the three major crises, or turning points in my early childhood.

The first was girlhood down south during the final years of World War II. As a Jewish girl-child keenly attuned to the voice music of conversation, to nuances of emotional overtones, I heard the horror of the Holocaust echoing and reflected in the voices of those at home as well as saw its reflecting fire in the *Warner Pathe Newsreels*. I remember standing on a dirt playground close to a roundabout made of piping, one of the early ones before they were created colorfully as toys.

I stood apart from my playmates thinking, "Will there be a time life without war?"

Our father was an Army psychologist testing boys and men for where they should be placed in the service. He wanted to keep his young family, a wife and two daughters with him. Ironically this plan failed. We lived on Golden Beach in Florida when Miami was no more than a dusting of palm trees. Despite our best efforts to remain together as a family, my parents divorced. Such stories as *Audubon Wallpaper* and *The Sad Little Abyss In Every Home* reflect this era. Language lifts Indigo over the wave. Its music is both message and miracle. No nectar drops exist for nerves, there is only reality.

I have ordered the stories in approximate chronological sequence although there are glances back and ahead to reinforce the imagery and emotional flow of any one story. A song of the South, the peacock keeps moving forward. *Champion of the Spelling Bee*, which opens the collection, occurs during mid-childhood. A word-child, I was obsessed with books and language. They made me feel as if I'd gone over the top, been sent to heaven and died. I learned early that they could construct their own world, confer their particular epiphany. This was during our second stay South.

During my second major life crisis, the divorce, the ground in Europe was still smoldering. It was the winter of 1947-48 when sole grounds for divorce were adultery had to be proven with a camera. Mother took us girls, age four and eight to Sarasota this time and enrolled us a small school near the beach, *The Out of Doors School*. The inspiration for *Acting Ugly* occurred during this time. Ecstatic and elegiac tones alternate as the sorrow of parental schism sink into Indigo, the protagonist and the writer, who is I, and yet she is given to bursts of joy. *Audubon Wallpaper*, which comes a bit later in the collection, reflects the deeper melancholy, the chiaroscuro of a family in the ominous pre-shadow of divorce. A disharmony, a profound sadness runs underneath its waters imaged forth in the delicate and brilliant birds drawn by John James Audubon, which my parents could scarce afford, but hung on the dining room wall. Such words as *Chiffarobe* and *vestibule* transported like garments up north form my sojourn south. I came home, my memory bank replete with images of girls wearing hair bows big as a country church.

At the same time, the rural South presented me with images of children in houses of secondhand lumber, corrugated tin roofs, sagging porch on which kids stood ragged, in overalls, biting in their upper lip with bashfulness. The girls on Sunday looked like peacocks, swanked up chickens, in thread thin chiffon hand-me-down party dresses.

The third crisis of my childhood, polio, occurred in the North. During that half year, on my back in a children's ward, I had ample time for reflection upon my past, which included the lyrical exile to the South. Now we lived in starched and numbered state hospital gowns. *My First Polio, Morning Glory Jeans* and *Polio: A Girlhood Novitiate* deal with this time when I became one of the ward gang in upstate New York at a place called Haverstraw. We developed a ward language. Just as lyricism and exile conveyed emotion in the South leaving blaze marks on trees, in the hospital our hopes and fears flared in words. A third language, the family language, was left behind. Here in these chapters which detail the experience of polio to a child on the cup, I give voice to the voiceless, paralyzed children. The body contains, heart and lungs, bones and blood retain their own memory deep within. I try, in the hospital to body forth a world now gone. We had our own moxie, our slang. Our lingo was the common coin of language in one of the last epidemics, 1951. When I came home, never to walk again, my bonds which were solely with women deepened.

In midlife Indigo meets her soul mate, Simone, a tall gifted Canadian in love with the writing Indigo has had published. *Sweetheart* is a Northern soul like Pegeen. Pegeen, *Anam Cara*, dear one Irish, born in Dublin, migrated to England, survived a childhood during the Blitz, then came to Canada. In multiples ways she was a survivor, she lived beyond breast cancer and the paralysis of one arm, the loss of any means, the loss of her son to an overdose of Angel Dust and the loss of her husband to alcohol. Ultimately, the marriage goes up in the flames of divorce, a bonfire to light the remainder of Pegeen's life. In the stories, *One Dark Valentine* and *Alissa's Baby*, Pegeen (Peg) appears most vividly in *Albino Peacock*. Like Hannah earlier, and Grandmother Tisanne, she is one of the women Indigo admires, emulates, and learns from in life. The darker stories in the collection *Undertaker Bird* and *Murder Ball* are infused with British dialect, so particular and vivid like the distinctly southern dialect of earlier stories. Place matters, as it does earlier in *Nickel and Diamond*. My subtitles are meant to convey meaning of their own. *Paradise Gas Works* and *Spinal Tap* function in the opening story of the book and *Bayou City* in *Going to the Bayou* and *Curtains* in the same story. In the specific colors of language, dialogue and dialect, these stories are of the American deep South. Using the vernacular, sometimes Indigo expresses herself in loving swings, as in the story *Spin the Bottle Kiss Me* or in sacrilegious rebellion as in *Music To Get You Out Of the Pews Dancing*. At other times, this hyperbole is expressed in the grotesque as in *Undertaker Bird*, or *Murder Ball.* The stories which revolve around polio, *Morning Glory Jeans*, *My First Polio*, and *Polio: A Girlhood Novitiate* use the language of middle lyric for the poet Indigo.

For Indigo, perhaps it is not far from curtains in the late story *Ebon Old Age*. Many times in the book one *Fatal Morning* has nearly occurred. Now the chorus of voices in the home for those of no memory brings time closer to the final call. I end with that startling creature, the ivory or albino peacock, anomaly of nature. Like a blazing match, he surges up against the drab, the mundane. He is also a source of magical inspiration, named as he is after *Alba* dawn. Yet a peacock is merely a swanked up chicken.

Flannery O'Connor lived with her mother in the rural South, Milledgeville Georgia. The novelist was a poet too, deeply spiritual and an observant Catholic, she raised her prize peacocks even when she knew herself to be dying, like her daddy before her, of lupus. If the family is harsh in such stories as *Whips: A Family Love Story*, in the final title-story, *The Kind of Day To See an Albino Peacock*, clemency is voiced. Leniency, even love and tenderness are expressed toward Marcelle, who has died that very morning. Epiphany, revelation always near to hand becomes larger than life as Indigo and Simone decide to take a picnic the very day of Marcelle's death. They have their picnic in front of the children's zoological garden. Like morning glory, the male peacock unfolds his resplendent tail, a startling blue. Like the thread of the sane battling the insane that runs throughout the collection, summing it up, he utters his inimitable cry, a shriek like that one imagines in an asylum. If it is a shriek it is also a wake up call to get up out of the pews dancing, to come one close nearer to the great beyond, it is both fatal morning and home run. Heart on sleeve, the alarming bird screams. Wake up, Indigo. Child of the new century, it's sunrise. The heart goes over the top: Glory Be has come.

Lynn Strongin
August, 2008

## Threaded Characters

INDIGO: the protagonist, a born storyteller, in every way exemplifies her position in the family as eldest. Indigo is a girl of whom one of her mother's guests said, "If she were mine, I'd dress her out of Holbein's paintings." She is fair, willowy, a gymnast who can beat all the boys at the race. The protagonist is a Jewish girl-child destined to become a poet and to become paralyzed by polio at age twelve. She is very much a child of the mid-twentieth century and toward the end of the century to become an Indigo child: intuitive, high-wire electric. Crucial periods of her girlhood are spent in the rural South. These occur in 1944-45 toward the end of the war when her daddy, an Army major and a psychologist are stationed in the South. Left unable to walk, Indigo becomes a maverick in many ways: child of divorce, Jewish girl in the deep South, a disabled girl stricken by one of the last infantile paralysis epidemics of the century. A tree climber, she remains a whippersnapper, dubbed "Silver Wheels" by the ward kids. She is winner of the local spelling bee. Less disabled than trapped, Indigo is twice alive. She is morning glory blue jeans, versed in several tongues: the Jewish language of home which is the family language, the ward language, and wordsmith in the South. She is a person who believes that if she is not standing at the rim, she is taking up too much room.

MARCELLE: Indigo's mother, divorced in 1948, is a pariah too because then divorce was such a stigma. She was still a beautiful young woman, one who broke hearts at Cornell and had her portrait painted on porcelain by an artist. A tragic figure, she wanted to be an actress but her voice was not strong enough. A daughter of wealth, she married poverty. She was a painter who studied with Alexander Archipenko but gave her career up to raise Rachel and Indigo, whom she adores. But she is also torn by ambivalence in a love-hate relationship. She crackles with withheld energy. Unfulfilled in love, disappointment clung like a veil. Once best all-around camper, she said, "It's not for nothing the lord gave me broad shoulders."

RACHEL: (also Chel and nicknamed "Pooky" in one story) is Indigo's younger sister by four years. A budding dancer and violinist, Chel is Indigo's one sibling. Deeply affected by her sister's paralysis,

Chel is in many ways in denial, a prodigy, a survivor who spills out her grief and bonds with her older sister in piano and violin duets which sing, a crucial part of their communication.

SIMONE: (Sweetheart) is Indigo's soul mate. Soft-voiced, not like modern girls, gifted in writing and the visual arts, she is taken by some to be a Catholic, even a nun. She is nine years younger than Indigo. Dark-haired with an English background, Simone has a peaches and cream complexion, in contrast to Indigo's dark blond. Simone is a northern soul.

PEGEEN: (*Anam Cara* occasionally called Peg) is an Irishwoman in her late sixties. Indigo clues in at once on her verbal abilities and her poverty. She hires Pegeen as research assistant for a year, culling and editing Indigo's late husband Jake's letters. Like all the women in *Albino Peacock,* she is a survivor. She has lived, one of seven kids in the family, during the Blitz as a child in London having emigrated from an England where the children went to nursery school in the Duke of Norfolk's Garden. She looks upon herself as a princess come back in the wrong skin. The list of what Pegeen has survived is long: breast cancer, loss of the use of one arm to surgery. Death took her only son thru an accidental drug overdose. Her marriage ended in divorce. Marked by her swinging, paralyzed left arm and her strong voice she is a sort of maven in the neighborhood where Indigo and Simone live in their fifties. She has lost her money but not her pride. Her malapropisms score the text about her: she goes to dentists "spasmodically," her voice cut a shaft in the London fog. Her sense of humor laces the collection with bravura, a touch of the bawdy and Irish dialect.

JESSE: Rachel's elder daughter, sister to Lily-Amiel (the prodigious dancer) helps her family thru the trials of a self-mutilation addiction in Lily-Amiel. Jesse is a great all round kid.

LILY-AMIEL: mirrors her mother, Rachel. In the book she is an adolescent in a love-hate relationship with dance. Exotic, beautiful, confused she plays one of the major minor characters in the collection. Britta, the European woman with the Northern European person's reserve figures here. She is from Bavaria. She is confidante to Indigo, one of the strong women woven into the background of the tapestry which constitutes the book.

NYRENE: is Indigo and Rachel's first cousin, a bright girl who is a companion to Indigo during her childhood. The girls are two years apart.

TISANNE: is Indigo and Chel's maternal grandmother. She rolls her r's. She is a Romanian born woman of exceptionally fine looks, is somewhat vain, and has been a wealthy woman due to her husband's brilliance. She is imperious but kind, colorful, having been pampered by her professor-husband, fond of expensive clothing and jewels, in every sense the matron of the small, now fatherless family. Although Rachel, Indigo and Marcelle are diminished by the loss of the father in the picture, the loss is largely compensated for by the largesse, and vibrancy of Tisanne's voice and vision. Her presence in a word, is lustrous.

NABEELA: was a girl who lost her leg and died in the ward cot right next to Indigo. Forever imprinted upon Indigo's eye and heart, she makes a brief appearance in the cast of characters but cuts a deep impression.

PRUNELLA: was one of Indigo's several girlfriend soul mates at the age of nine down south in Florida.

ALISSA: plays a minor role but comes at the moment when Indigo is adjusting to her move to Canada. Here, the camera pans back and forth looking back toward Dixie and ahead toward the North, with Canada her final home although she continues to see herself as profoundly an American writer.

JAKE: Indigo's husband, a Puritan Jew, is disabled in a freak accident in his own country, his spinal cord severed in maneuvers, putting out a small fire in a small pine tree. Ironically born on the Fourth of July, Jake epitomizes that independence which marked, perhaps scarred, the fathers of American literature whom he taught and adores. An Americanologist with a Ph.D. from Harvard, his letters are later turned over to the brilliant Pegeen to edit. He loved Hawthorne and Melville best among American novelists. He also taught Ichabod Crane, Washington Irving's *"Legend of Sleepy Hollow,"* and reminds Indigo of the Hoosier schoolmaster with the long dancing legs, spaghetti-twisted.

JOSHUA: is Rachel's husband. He is an archeologist deeply committed to his wife and two daughters.

*For Maura and Jim*

# Champion Of the Spelling Bee

*Ye haven't an arm, you haven't your leg,*
*You're an eyeless, boneless, chickenless egg*
*And you've got to be put with your bowl to beg*
*Johnny, I hardly knew ye*

"Maggie, I hardly knew ye"


"Even my loneliness is organized."
Maurice Sendak

— Herein we witness the importance of a spelling bee down South. You could either sit out your dance or fill your dance card. A ruffian, dirty blond, with "Coke-bottle green eyes," Indigo sits out dances.

She engages in life, in the battle with her mother who tells her to wash her mouth with soap but also gives her the spark to become a writer in this story in which the nine-year-old girl declares, "I don't want to marry."

One looks ahead to polio, back to earlier childhood but is essentially located in the spelling bee era although afterward, after infantile paralysis, putting her hands to her formerly wash-board thin chest, discovering small knobs, she knew she was blossoming.

## Filling up the Dance Card: Hardly Know Ye

Lapped in white wavelets of a Christening gown wasn't how her Annie was born. Taken to children's court, her mother at age thirteen had stolen some hot cross buns.

She also became champion of the spelling bee in that particular Magdalene Laundry in West Ireland. I was a spelling bee champ (fourth grade) too, but fizzled out—too much standing in front of huge crowds of people for me, and all my spelling came from reading, and now they wanted me to study spelling.

I came of age both in the deep South, the old South and Jewish immigrant New York. My name, Indigo, derives from that good stout American cloth of strong dye and character.

You could either sit out your dance, or fill up your dance card in the South where I did my first growing up. My first cousin, Nyrene, was the sort who'd fill up that debonair card swinging from her wrist at the Cotillion. Not me.

Winning the Bee was a badge of intellectual achievement, filling a dance card was a badge of social achievement. Of course, I was born later than Cotillions happened but I am speaking figuratively. Emotional patterns were more subtle up North, where envious of her confessions and ostensible purity, I'd told a Catholic girl she'd die if she ate a red berry. Her dance card would be filled by admiring beaus, but not mine. I was cross-eyed and Jewish. My card might as well have been eaten by the dog.

I'd pressed faith into service once again down south asking a Catholic girl to pray for me that my parents get together again. None of this worked. My dance card was a blank, but my toes never stopped jigging. I'd press the shiny red Coke machine in Alabama and the big red button would deliver me an All-American Coke, its glass bottle beaded with ice. I'd sit on the bench opposite the Coke machine, dangling my legs like a latter day Huck Finn and take swigs from the bottle in a very grownup way. It was a dark world whether the weathervane pointed up or down. Writing was an iron whim. Solitude was highly organized.

A ruffian, a hooligan, dirty blond, Coke-bottle green eyes with a squint, I'd worn a patch which made me appear menacing in my earlier childhood. Dick Deadeye. I also stood out like a bent nail because I sang both places. In northern nursery school I kept the other kids awake at naptime by regaling them with song. In the South, walking alongside brambly bushes, I sang to myself, my personal *niggun* (maybe an echo of the songs my mother sang, but has forgotten — the nurses told her about them, the night I was born.) Always accompanying me, the song the Jew sings to herself for hope and inspiration, or later in life for consolation. My relationship with my mother was fractious and difficult. My life was filled with marital fractures. There was a palpable sense of excitement even as a world slipped away. Even when I was again cloistered.

"I hardly know you, Indigo," Mother would say out of the blue.

She had an over the top manner in both regions though my true name in my early childhood was Indigo.

"I'm pregnant," I announced to Mother at age nine.

Knowing me, she didn't raise her eyebrows. She'd often said "You're a changeling, Indigo," or "You're a *dybbuk*."

This was the dislocated soul of a dead person believed to have escaped the Gehenna.

"The faeries dropped you," she smiled.

"I am with child," I repeated solemnly pointing to my head.

She swung me round by the wrist and thunked my rear end with the *Sarasota Daily Gazette*.

I remembered that threat my friend from South London had told me her mother hurled at her head, "I'm going to yank off your arm and hit you with the bloody stump."

It wasn't that violent between us, but it was edgy. Cottonwood leaves flickered like little pocket knives shot out from cases, or like flames.

"Keep talking like that, go wash your mouth with soap," Mother would say.

I figured I was only telling the truth about my life.

My lover Simone stares the same grieving way at my mouth now to indicate my lipstick's on crooked.

I composed and composed and composed carving lines on birch bark in my dreams. The same way I did on the old Underwood the summer I was stricken, when those quaint circular letters bore the weight of my passion. My uncle Phil had given us his old Underwood, on which he'd written *Truth or Consequences* for Ralph Edwards in Hollywood's early heydays when there was a great wave of Jewish immigrants. Later yet, it became the electric typewriter and now the computer at whose feet I am careful not to spill copper pennies due to the magnet. When I could no longer keep the toddlers awake in nursery school down at City & Country—they needed the nap, I didn't—I regaled campers at overnight camp. The girl in the cot beneath mine wept the first night.

"What's wrong?" I asked.

"Homesick."

"But we only left today," I said.

It felt as though I'd gone to heaven and died. This was the case, I decided when I woke up Christmas morning in Sarasota, 1948, and there were palm trees pasted on a blue sky like shaving brushes rather than the fir trees which shaded us in our sheltering North of white chapels and needle-steeples. Yes, this must have been heaven: wouldn't the first activity I'd take up in heaven be bouncing my pink Spalding ball counting?

It surely would, as I swung my right leg over the high bouncer, *One, two, three O'Lary.* Or, *My name is Alice and my husband's name is Al. We live in Alabama and we sell apples.* You knew your name, your husband's name, what you sold, where lived and your life would be right. I'd lay out my jacks and scoop them up like silver berries twinkling in the merciless sun. I had a sudden sharp learning curve thrust upon me when I arrived with my kid sister and Mother in March down South, where chinaberries gleam mockingbirds sing and the magnolia has its small indentations of cigarette burns just two nights before Christmas. First I was pregnant and then I delivered. I'd tell my stories in the hot fly-infested evenings to them, my baby sister and my mother. We had not only the black-tailed flies but the blue-tailed ones. It was all in the details, I figured, how you got things right.

We dragged our diminished family of three through little, one-street towns down South seeking out hardware stores. Mother was Mrs. Fixit. I loved hardware stores. Mesmerized, hallucinating, I'd lift each miniature sprocket and those graduated nails in enticing wood cups.

"Leave this hardware store alone, Indigo!" Mother would warn, "I'll have to pay for what you maul."

"Not mauling anything," I lied.

I was just re-organizing nails and washers graduated large to small nests of silver. Just as in the earlier benighted pilgrimage down South when Malka was baby-Chel and transported in a laundry basket, we'd seek out farmhouses to heat her formula.

"Now you go on ahead. You're the family presenter," Mother would shove me out of the old tan DeSoto Plymouth. She always had the answers.

I recall the fight between her and daddy over Chel's diapers laid out on the steaming lid of our car that led to the argument which precipitated the divorce. After polio, I got smart and tough about my orthopedic aids—knew how to find a Phillips screwdriver to tighten a bolt.

"Give me a Hex driver to give my self a good screw," I'd say, poker-faced, not batting a lash to the hardware store man.

After all, wasn't I the woman who had had the dancing girls erased from the mural over our fireplace in our grand beach home?

"You could never work for the government," my lover honors me.

Back in the old southern days, crumbling bits of *Swibek* stuck to everything. These days, it's Chinese fortune cookies which I still read although I swear I'm not superstitious. I know hardware stores inside out. After all, my legs don't carry me around. I carry them.

Great houses reflected in back of my retina from the one grandfather had built in Peekskill up near President Roosevelt's country home, Hyde Park—leaded glass diamond panes caught late afternoon sun at the same time as that bullet sun ignited the Waterford glass holding his sherry. Yet here I stood before a used lumber shack white washed, screens busted and letting flies in. These were the two parts of me— poor and ok.

"Indigo, mind your manners because one day you will come into this,"

Mother had both warned and smiled scattering imaginary sand around from her hand as though it were gold dust. Yet, *accustom yourself to your new surrounds,* she'd contradicted herself in the next breath when we hit the dust that December, 1948, to obtain our freedom papers, the divorce.

Here the world stepped to a different drummer. I learned to march in a paper soldier's hat, holding a stiff small American flag at a girlfriend's birthday party when we were stationed in placid, salty seawashed Atlantic City. But I frowned.

"It's a consequence of your eyes being green," Mother said, "but wipe off that frown. Nobody will marry you if you scowl."

"I don't want to marry."

Mother shot her eyebrows up. Like any kid, I hopped first on one foot, then the other when I had to pee, but most of the time I was quite poised. My mother might have been in emotional turmoil within but she was never in emotional disorder without, although I felt my childhood job half the time was cheering her up. The other half, I enjoyed life with her as one of us kids. After all, she'd painted the toy boxes, she made us midnight cocoa and laughed over it like a child herself. Marry? Maybe in her secret heart she knew my colors and that I wouldn't want to marry. I would be a Wack or a Wave dressing out the soldiers' bloodiest wounds.

"You're standing," she once warned me, "on a precipice."

I shuddered but I spun on my heel into the house and picked up the book I was reading. At times I felt I shouldered the weight of the separation and divorce by myself in girlhood. Some scenes we would cut off at the moment of high drama like an ancient projector snapping celluloid right in the middle of the big kiss.

Mother could be mannered. I was startlingly unmannered. People said so—natural. Mother was melancholy often but she had her ups.

She did thumbnail sketches in charcoal of shoeshine boys in Manhattan, kids jumping rope in the country. The *Book of Flying* and the *Book of Fire* were composing themselves in my mind. In Iowa people lived at edges, I remembered from our long drives during the war. In New York, people lived in the throe of things. Flash cards, intolerable to a bright child, had been the feature of first grade. I already knew how to read. The South was a balancing act along a gasoline pale but volatile line. It was the steel paw in the velvet glove. The dispossessed southern belle still floated thru that world and somehow ruled in 1944. I could cast my eyes down and hardly speak when introduced to someone. I was not afflicted with a stammer, my limbs were long and swift, but I had been cross-eyed. This made me self-conscious. I was sharper than most kids my age. I had peculiar tastes: I liked my rice saffron.

"When I have a daughter," I announced one day, (totally bypassing the issue of marriage), "I'll call her Saffron.

"Oh," Mother said. "Will she be black?"

"No. Blond like me but hair curly. Eyes hazel."

Saffron and I went thru my mid-childhood together. No skip stone Jenny-Ann. I'd crossed the river. I loved wading nude, the water sheer silk next to my skin. Saffron, leggy like me, waded with me but always followed on the bank, second. I led. Other times I think she was determined to dazzle like when I did win the spelling bee and she wouldn't take her hand from mine, right there, in front of everybody in the classroom. Would I win that afternoon? The light was slant, dust motes whirling in its golden shaft: cathedral light. With my linear tendencies, I was aware of the baroque miniatures in the classroom. I wouldn't know till the end if I'd win. By then it might be too late.

Jeannine was second best. I loved her the way girls love each other. We used to hug under her covers at home. I was sweet on her and she was jealous and sweet toward me, voicing her mad music. I'd get under the quilt and see the light: a quilt-like citron-to-orange glow. But the white light was something special that came only when I was alone: I shuddered the length of my whole body. All of a sudden my optic nerve (my eyes which had given me such hassle) would be struck as though crystal glass were struck and caused to chime.

Many schisms characterized my life. Emotion came in a new dress: transparent yet shabby. True feeling came in the most direct addresses I'd ever heard.

"Child! Put that spoon down or the devil'll get you."

Down south one could act ugly—pulling the hair bow out of one's hair in an assembly. Up north, one was expected to have a Yankee cool, a steel backbone. I wasn't old enough to know that the dead are not really dead. I mean, state hospital scared me into the knowledge that children really do die. But that was to come. Nabeela had frosty copper hair and died at only nine. The girls I loved had the traction of insight. Nabeela, who had one wooden leg, went swanning around in panties, she was a vamp. Saffron, tall, a beanpole, gymnastic like me, was the real McCoy. I saw the angel of death raise his sword above my cubicle mate. Her childhood fevers had come to an end.

"Reserved for the local Spelling bee Champion" was the chair I automatically appropriated with a grin the winter I was ten. Bees under glass, the blue stumbling blur of winter ice.

The devil, who was already rich, was getting paid more. The devil already had met me, I figured so I lay down on the clay and, trembling, prayed. *Lord, if you'd only lay me down . . .* In the tinted grass, I was bighead. My heart, in reality, was thud thudding like a trip-hammer.

I turn the pages I am pregnant with over and over. Rachel, whom I called Chel when she was small, and Malka (which means wheat in Hebrew) as she ripened into adolescence, Malka and I, both reticent it turned out, had been fed confidence with our mother's breast milk. In later girlhood, we associated with children who were artists, real workers, Trojans.

I hadn't mentioned Saffron for some time, I realized one day copying Bach chorales. She had not so much died as burned off like morning fog. Now in burnishing winter sun, the world of work, of worth and hard core study of musical composition had taken over. That niggle inside me like an ache in the shoulder blade from time to time might have been the ghost of Saffron twitching, fine as lung-tissue, a spirit, a wing thing.

## Spinal Tap

It's hard to concentrate when you're lying on a plinth waiting for a spinal tap. I remember that, New Rochelle, 1951.

The nurse whispered into my ear afterward, "You're the first kid who had a spinal tap and didn't cry."

I'd spent all my tears the night before.

The light was the color of dark milk after the spinal tap. I flashed back, during that hour, to the South. The South, the old South and new, so often both comfort and corrosion to me. Many things were corrugated down south: washboards, roofs, corduroy roads. They were smoother up north where ribbons of concrete turnpike in slick black licked the miles. I have ransacked my memory bag to find just where I caught the polio virus, but find no real evidence. I ransack my southern memories for solace. What is coming of age? When did it begin? Why do I often date it then, my ninth winter rather than my far more dramatic twelfth summer although both were vivid and dramatic. Minor grief is somebody else's grief. Did I prefer sitting on the sidelines? My handwriting I learned up north. My white body-light I definitely learned up north. But didn't it begin in the South? Casting a premonition shadow down among the bayous and the cotton?

How did we travel? Getting down south, we did, well strapped, with our luggage and meager wardrobes, in the metal and wood box of the train—oxygen and ozone consumed, chemicals locked into our sleeper, our Pullman. It was as if I traveled between my native New York and my adopted South like a Brit commuting between his native Ulster, Ireland, say, and adopted London. A sophisticated child, rain-thin, I was dexterous, fresh and deft. I loved my mother to a fault and, through an act of her will, my world was cracking.

"Girls smell like the ocean," Prunella, one of my Black Southern girlfriends leaned in and whispered in my ear, her hair ribbon torn yellow fabric which flapped in the breeze.

I knew that and liked the salty smell. What did boys smell of? Probably matchsticks and rails. The homes in which I grew up had some staffing issues. There were always women but no men.

I wear my Sibyl pin, a copy from the Sistine Chapel ceiling, and folk stop me and ask, "Is that your mother?"

Mother is now 91 who never wanted to live long; who smoked up a storm giving herself lung cancer. Marcelle, who threatened suicide often to her children during her frequent and intense bouts of melancholy. Yet she hangs not by a thread but by a steel cable.

"There goes your inheritance," says Malka. "And yours."

## Paradise Gas Works
*Or, "Reserved for the Local Spelling Bee Champion"*

Air was the color of dark milk. Bees were big in the South. Not so big up North. I'd begun grade eight in surreal surroundings, wearing a white hospital gown in the hospital. This wasn't a brief interlude. As it turned out, I went from eighth through twelfth grades and graduation mostly at home in our New York City living room overlooking roofs and water towers and the Beekman Hotel. I studied at my mother's desk, the foot of her bed or under our Steinway Baby Grand.

Time for change, my parents decided in grade nine. We hunted. We thought we'd found a good school. Mother enrolled me in a liberal private school up in Harlem, where there were mainly brothels. It was The New Lincoln School. A problem arose: I had no contemporary clothes. Only a purple-brown checked dress from Rappaport's. In biology I studied my wrist where the cufflink met cloth and grieved for the girl, who only a year ago, ran. Getting in and out of a blond wood school seat now was hell. Then I had enjoyed the easy swish of smoothing my skirt under me with my hand, seating myself and rising, books casually gathered in the crook of my right arm. Now everything was formal. Every step took strategy.

A returning student at the New Lincoln saw me from behind. "Daphne!" she exclaimed. What happened to *you?*"

I turned around and her face registered surprise.

"Oh, it's not Daphne."

It was only me. The fact that *I* was on crutches signaled no disaster but had it been Daphne, it would have been a catastrophe. I remembered Paradise Gas Works down in Tennessee in order not to cry—those brown summers, dry-goods stores on a plot of dirt, lobbing fastballs over the dust.

My twelfth summer, on top of having had polio, there was construction on East River Drive. Each blow of the pneumatic drill rose. Every jackhammer in the street twelve stories below my room in New York Hospital seemed to be going. I could not foresee eighth grade hospital schooling in an ancient institution with old Geographies hauled out of hospital cellars. Brown summer had curled up and turned into parchment autumn. These scarred atlases featured water-warped maps of old Russia. Asia blurred before my eyes on their shiny clay-based pages which were faded and which accompanied me into that wet, godforsaken Autumn of 1951.

When I got home, I missed the ward kids. The return to school proved an unmitigated disaster. Even after arduous hospital regimes, the normal school day was too much. My legs were sore from braces by the time I got home. Home life was more fatiguing and downtrodden than ever. I pored over *The Salting Book of Hours* with art by Simone Benn (1483-1561) *October–Ploughing*. The sense that I had lived before as a boy in the medieval times swept over me.

I wrote on my stomach at night in bed, our lights out, my pencil flashlight moving, arching my back as I had in the hospital on rough sheets. This made my lordosis in addition to my scoliosis more severe causing the jack knife in my spine to double. Nothing equaled like the hospital's autumn chill. Parents were allowed to visit Sundays.

Whatever nurse was on duty brought me my one linen blouse smiling sternly saying, "Linen is an iron bunny."

I had nodded, yet smiled, when she slipped it over my head. Not long ago I'd been doing cartwheels and climbing down trees. Fabrics, wools and cotton, touched a nerve. The sweater in which I was brought home haunts me to this day like a bucket full of stars or embers. I recalled the silhouettes we'd been taught to draw and cut on black construction paper in grade two.

I had the clear profile of a Roman child, androgynous. So often I felt inside the notion, the body-image even, of myself as boy or girl. I wrote as if writing could save me from my darkest self, could save my whole family. Never mind the dark Rorschach blots on the sheets. The pain I'd brought home was both shadow-child engulfing me and skeleton-girl supporting me. Icarus, Daedalus' son in more than one drama, my inventions both saved and seared me. (In some dreams, I'd light a torch from the fire and bring it to the barn. The sheep rubbed up against each other since the fire had gone out. I dreamt of writing on a table of splinters. Mother had drawn me the small desk that awaited me at home, pale and sad in an ash cloud.) I lived among children who were ill and dying.

Right-angled hospital corners: I remembered them. Folded wood linen or iron cloth.

After my sorrow-filled six week tour of duty was done at the New Lincoln School (days in which I often thought of Abraham Lincoln in his rock like endurance and stony isolation), the old Polish woman who worked in the cafeteria gave me Gogol's *Dead Souls*. Why? I didn't understand that the souls referred to the count of citizens in the Russian town Nikolai Gogol satirized. I thought it referred to me as a dead soul. I took it home, thanking her, and turned the book, spine to the wall, gold lettering on black binding. It was a Modern American Library Everyman's edition. Would retreating from school world keep me a child forever, wrapped in warm white flannel out of a warm bath?

"Everybody," said a friend years later, "loves the underdog.

And when the underdog is a child. . ."

But we were nudged with rifle butts—were direct targets for the staff's sadism— child reviled. Who was to give account of what the child suffered? It was the second of my many returns home from the big world to the convent, home. Dark sexuality was the sexuality we felt toward each other, the silver robes of the family. When my glance inadvertently fell on the Gogol book, I saw the dead souls of children in wards. Twisting round and round on my jacket, the sibyl brooch, as if it were a button from the Sistine ceiling, I tried, once or twice, to actually open the pages of *Dead Souls* and fall in but failed.

Only last spring, at age eleven, I had once gone ballroom dancing in seventh grade. I was being held in Aiden's arms, me the girl with hazel eyes, in sneakers and dirndl skirt, reflecting in the polished gym floor, laying my hand on his shoulder, searching in vain for his lead. We ended up, sidelined, two fervent Jewish children in conversation. First boy love. First loss. We were both champions of the local spelling bees— I, a bit more often than Aiden, which was symbolic of being able to spell out our grief and elation in life. Right now, sidelined, Shanghaied at the junior high dance, Aiden and I were burning the field of our childhood sexuality until it crumbled to ashes in this new light.

Despondent that fourteenth winter, homebound again, eight stories above New York City's snowline and the teal Hudson broken by ice-floes, one night I held up the hand mirror and saw the girl with the coke-bottle green eyes and thought like the girl of the soldier in the old song, *Nellie, I hardly know ye*.

I felt eyeless, boneless, moody. Suddenly plunged into the *Muldau*, I missed my legs, I missed the ocean. I saw that hot dusty road churning with cars down South, Paradise Gas Works, the thin piping built on the horizon to house the fuels. The children I knew I hardly had had time to say good-bye to. Crowning my bitterness was the strident echo of that girls' voice first day back at school mistaking me for Daphne. I never learned who Daphne was. The impress remained gouged into me. If I'd been Daphne, it would have been a disaster, what happened to me. I visited with my German friend who had stolen candles form the dead in Bavaria and been reprimanded.

"I'll tell your parents!" said the cemetery guard who caught them. He relented, "I'll wait and tell them next time. But for now, know the dead will come after you at night."

Magda had run home and told her mother who said, "nonsense, dear, wash that out of your hair."

I thought of her and identified myself with the Irish Magdalene who scrubbed away a fierce lather in the laundries, the incandescent light of sadism which burned against girl-children.

Those objects stashed in the corner were wooden crutches, not wings. There is a time beyond rise and shine, when you lie down: then memories of the unknown may—can accost you and the little ice age return. How can you burn the field of exile and betrayal which is in your spine?

"You need a Hex screw," Simone says.

"Then I'll get one. And please give me the old family photos."

"They have a lot of dust on them."

"Good. They're old. Let them look it. Dust and revelation under glass."

"I'll need some time."

*Dust and revelation*

*Rise & Shine*

*Alabama Light & Power Company*

Revisiting my girlhood, I see Marcelle tossing into the laundry one of my socks. Pure as the driven snow.

"I'd give anything to have them filthy," she said.

The Alabama Light & Power Company stood down south near that abandoned theme park. It was helium that made the balloon of the little midway down south miraculously rise, tilt, then explode. From the first floor of the state ward, I could spy a brick yard, a black wrought iron fire escape. It reminded me of the ruins of a crematory oven construed by my vivid, though childlike, medievalist's imagination—but it was a common incinerator. Able-bodied folk, in the whole of their health, have more fun. Disabled people know the ecstasy.

What became of my dance card? Torn to shreds, scattered to the wind.

Of course, I haven't stopped dancing, running circles around this or that roadblock, reeling with a surfeit of sheer high spirits to which I alone in the family am prone.

"You're a *dybbuk*, Indigo, the faeries have dropped you at my door."

The bees are done, Vergil's drowsy blunt-faced bees. Life is a *tabula rasa*. I am baroness of the trees, the bird-woman flying, rook-like cadged in the shiny mirrory leaves. Dying of unlived life? A jewel looking for a place to shine? When they all went to the beach I stayed home. A small body of surrender, mine.

"You are a giant," Mother Marcelle said, scoffing in the next words, "Rosie the Riveter." She always went for the jugular.

The three graces. Life threw us one curve ball after another. We stepped up to the plate. The war ended and divorce occurred. The divorce was accomplished and polio hit me, Indigo. It was my kid sister Chel who caught the curve ball and matured to live her life a survivor's guilt and inborn grace.

"If I could give you my legs," Mother said, "I would."

Radiator banging beneath me, paint on which I sat chipped into little countries—Europe, Brazil— there I stayed on the windowsill overlooking Riverside. Champion of the local spelling bee (I goaded myself), spell your way out of this one. If I craned enough, I'd glimpse a swatch of the oily gray Hudson where the tugs and barges slugged away and the great ships docked. Below — the boat basin where I made out with boys on warm August nights. The Hudson was my Pacific, my Atlantic. If you cried me a river, it would be this one on which ships of unfulfilled desire blew in and which I caught like thorns. They lodged in my breast covered with the wool vest. Northern Ironworks caught the cold sun. Sky rolled over like flattened steel, Bethlehem, from the Bessemers in Pennsylvania (land of chocolate and the Amish.)

Like teal ocean-waves, air currents billowed, like a priest's robes and lifted the sooty gray organdies in our bedroom windows. Having begun in my war-childhood, the taproot twisted, made earth swell like elbows in a Gothic fairytale. The sap was rising on a gasoline-hazed city skyline. It climbed throat-red though thin veins and branches. Our grandmother visiting the Autumn I was fifteen, when she was back from France with her steamer trunks and pearls, eyed me in a new strange way.

She turned me round and said, "While I wasn't looking you've turned into a woman."

Time was a quick-moving mirror. Time was a river. Spin the bottle and kiss me. My older cousin who filled up her dance card, she was always bringing home a new dress in a frosty green paper and going broke.

My washboard-flat chest had developed hard knobs, then pear-shaped breasts. Tisanne was home and like the young orange trees, I was blossoming.

# Natural Bacteria

— *After the divorce, Marcelle and her two daughters drive back to New York from Sarasota. They stay overnight halfway back in a third-class hotel where Indigo is taken for a beggar. She's offered a coin due to her blisters from three kinds of poison (ivy, oak, and sumac) which make her face look scarred. How to complete the trip? Mother Marcelle considers flying her elder daughter home, a rare event in the late forties. She cries out at her mother, "You're the death of my childhood," as the two strong characters, Marcelle and Indigo, tough out how to make the trip north with this heinous and pitiful condition seemingly scarring Indigo's face.*

## Natural Bacteria

About halfway back from the deep South, mirroring our profound sense of location and dislocation that year, I broke out in poison: oak, ivy and sumac, all three. By that time we were in Georgia, staying at a turn-of-the century brick building in the middle of some town whose name I can't recall. I'd gone down from the brown hotel room with peeling paint, for a dusty breath of fresh air at five in the evening. The street was still sweltering. People swam and shimmered in the blue heat, buildings crumpled like cardboard. The scorching street came up to hit me in the face. I did not know this part of the world. Fire-swallows. The fire, which was prejudice, superstition going down the throat as perilously as the fire which was real flame.

There I was somewhere in Georgia, slapping at black flies, standing outside a crumby third-class hotel just to breathe without feeling my lungs were behind gauze. I thought I was invisible pressed flat and lean as I was against the side of the building. Suddenly, out of the blue, a hand reached toward me. It held coin! I, Indigo, was actually being handed coin by a passing stranger. Taken for a street-beggar. Horrified, I took a deep breath and bolted. I beat it so fast up the three flights to our room my calves were throbbing. I must have looked scarred from burns.

My mother cut up her silk underpants to lay on my face. We hung a wash line from the ceiling during the heat wave that stretched the several thousand miles from Sarasota to Manhattan. It turned roofs into corrugated tin and cardboard. It flattened, then bent and buckled my family, Chel and Marcelle. It blistered, it broke red brown in the Southern states, turned green as rich swamps in the mid-Atlantic States and finally cooled to azure, indigo, cobalt as we neared home.

"Indigo," Mother said. "You're a big girl now. I'm thinking of flying you home."

"Alone?"

"Alone. You're nine years of age."

The airlines were in their early days. None of us had ever flown in 1948. All the planes were warplanes.

"You're in such misery, you're spreading the *mizzables* around."

"I aint." I began to talk southern.

"I'd send you to Grandmother's, Indigo, she could take you to the doctor up east."

"I don't want to go home alone ahead of you and Rachel."

"Let me think on it overnight, Indigo," she said in her old mother voice, lower in pitch. She pulled out a pack of Luckies from the breast-pocket of her shirt and lit up.

I waved it off, screwing up my face.

"You're looking worse by the moment, that blistering."

"Don't be scared."

"I don't scare easy."

Then Rach and I started sassing. We'd had a tin of beans for supper again. Beans on the hot coil. And we'd gulped root beer out of its glass bottles. I squinted and saw three fiery coils. The light was endless and it was cruel. It lit up every mote of dust in that room, every coil of the burner heating. First I began to sing, then Chel.

*Beans, beans the musical fruit.*

*The more you eat the more you toot.*

*The more you toot the better you feel.*

*So eat beans with every meal!*

Always the tomboy, I was horsing and horsing, jumping barefoot on those beds with rotten springs. That wild body-energy that took me over at times, turned me into a wild child, *enfant sauvage*, my body-ecstasy overcame me and I sprang like a cat from one bed to the other, mine to Rachel's right across the room with wooden floor, that mean little poor bastard of a room.

"Stop it, Indy!" Mother raised her voice.

Then more quietly, she mustered her quiet, her thunder guns. "Here you are sick and all. You'll be the death of me."

"You're the death of my childhood!" I yelled.

"Think, just think of the natural bacteria in this room!" she looked scathingly at my bare feet, which were callused filthy, my hands breaking out now in this thing, this strange thing. "It's this dislocation we're going thru, Indigo, now act your age."

"Think of the natural bacteria"—as if there were any other kind—was a family phrase. It could bring us to laughter or tears.

I thought of that back bay Georgia doctor in the antiquated office she'd taken me to that morning. He shook his head. He was stumped.

"Never seen anythin' like it, ma'am. Your girl's got a cross between poison oak, poison sumac, and poison ivy. She must have bin swimmin' thru the stuff."

"Indigo?" Mother arched her eyebrows.

They were still dark, not singed by cigarette smoke like her lashes.

How did their cranky little southern doc, Dr. Lacoya, know I'd gone swimming through grass the week before we left Sarasota? I did it on a dare. I always won.

I was too miserable in that hot little office with the fans whirring but not cutting the heat any.

I hung my head like a dog.

This must have flashed back in Mother's mind while I was jumping.

"That's it! I'm flying you north tomorrow morning."

"I'm thinking of the natural bacteria in this room," I slowed the beating of my heart, jumped down off the bed onto the wood floor where I'd driven a splinter into my right foot the night before but not told her.

My father was the one good at removing splinters, shards of wood I drove into my running feet constantly.

"I'm thinking," I said slowly, deliberately ignoring by now three types of pain, the pain in the sole of my right foot, the pain in my face, the mounting pains in my heart and mind. All I could focus my soul upon was that I didn't want to fly north in the morning without them. Nor did I want to let on I was scared. I turned the tap on till it ran tepid, down that rusty little runnel in the old battered soapstone sink. The batteries in the radio were shot. It was dead silent in that room.

"What, tell me, Indigo, are you thinking?"

"I'm thinking that the pain's easing some."

"Truth?"

"Truth," I crossed my toes mentally.

She looked at me with that hard look of—you're my child, not my friend, which presently softened to—I'm your mother, you're my child. That she with all she had instilled in us of pride, self-sufficiency, should have her child seen as beggar. She, above all who taught me get back on your own two feet, you know who you are—if she should learn this she would be annihilated, or worse, would annihilate.

"Then you won't need these," Mother folded the silk panties she'd cut up the night before. "Nor will I ever wear them again," she said bitterly.

I remembered that bitterly. I felt the way I did the day she walked in the door and said, "I'm allergic to my children."

I was thinking I could overcome anything by not wanting to fly home in the morning. I began lifting that bronzed knocker I imagined existed at the door of my soul. The sun had set. The room was bluish-white outlines in black liquid night. Rachel wriggled under the covers nude except for her cotton underpants, and fell asleep in twenty.

Mother read a Daphne du Maurier mystery novel and smoked in the window's last light, blowing out smoke-rings, wearing her man-tailored shirt whose breast pocket always held her Luckies, the sleeves of the blue shirt rolled up below the elbow. It was a trouser role she was playing. Instinctively, I knew that even then. I wondered, was she going to come and kiss me goodnight. It was a long time before she rose.

"You asleep?" she called from the window.

"You know I am not," I said, beginning to smile through the pain in my cheekbones.

"Well," she rose, came over, my heart was a trip hammer. "You're too sore for me to kiss you goodnight, Lynn, but I—"

"You do anyway in your heart and mind."

"Got it." She snapped out the light bulb by the chain.

When I was in my forties, Marcelle reminded me, "You remember that trip down south when I cut up my underwear to soothe your blistered face?"

"We were heading back north. How could I forget?"

"Well, that's when you began to be the tough person you are today, Indigo. Don't ever put your boxing gloves on the shelf."

I noticed how pale our mother looked then. Last year, she'd got on hands and knees and scraped down one room in the attic of our big old colonial home we bought post war.

She said, "The more you scrape, the better things get, Lynn."

She'd told me then about *Pentimento*: "It means scraping away one layer to get at another one."

Even though she was the death of my childhood, the death of all vibrant fun-loving things, in that split-second I cried out as I saw another rip appear in the mattress ticking, and burst feathers had gone flying.

From that time of heightened longing and quickened senses in Georgia, down in Dixie, slave-land, I go in my mind when terrible things happen. Silently lethal things occur in merciless heat. The kind that blinds people and makes objects swim.

## Coda

I lay awake 'til I swore it was the midnight caboose—not the ten p.m. train slicing the night.

I knew she wouldn't be flying me home alone in the morning. I imagined by the time we crossed the New York State line my skin would be clear and smooth as a newborn. That was the turn of events crises always took in my life. Except for one. But that was three years later. I would be twelve then.

No radio played. The batteries had given up the ghost.

It was blackout like the war.

I wondered about my father.

Now that we had the divorce formally would the two be split by a knife?

That entire drive home I was to imagine we hauled a small casket in the trunk of the car. It was glass, it contained my childhood. During that momentous, yet monotonous drive when hills were anonymous like rain, and the town which is so memorable for my having been taken for a beggar, began the sole time in my life. The town forever remains without name, during that drive I grew by leaps and bounds. Mother always at-the-wheel, in command, up through sweltering Tennessee, up into the North Atlantic states, it was visible in my mind's eye, every time I blinked: yes, the death of my childhood in a casket of bright light formally laid within—that very night when I'd been taken for a beggar and told no one. As I felt my body-panic coming on in a wave, I calmed myself thinking of all the episodes where I was strong, Rachel less strong, and our Mother's predictions wrong.

It began with Lox and sturgeon which are too strong and rich for a little kid's stomach. But Poppa brought them all the time. I'd whittle away at the chunk left in the fridge after we were served our dinner or breakfast helpings.

Oh yeah? I thought: *Not this kid.* So I'd take an extra bite of each when Poppa brought them over. I was four or five. Then we graduated to plum pudding.

"Because we're in this dislocation," I told mother soberly, "I need more of the things to which we are accustomed."

"Girls," she'd say again, sometimes breaking down and laughing at herself, "this is far too rich for a child's stomach."

My ears perked. I smiled at her from one side of my mouth. I got myself into a brief feverish sleep—my face was blistery and burning—realizing how few times she'd lied to us, our mother. Thinking of Mother and Father. How they were dissolved forever as a team. Thinking of the two of them, two black construction paper silhouettes like those we made in first grade when I was even more lonesome, when the war was still on. Then suddenly something shifted, maybe Rachel in her sleep, maybe only another hotel guest coming in late in the hall, but I wakened and couldn't get to sleep again. I dreaded seeing the blue light of dawn, the first birdcall. But sometimes that's the way it happened.

I didn't tell her someone had thought I was a beggar. It had never occurred to me to look in the mirror. I thought I was my same old belle-laide, dirty blonde.

I pulled on my hermit hood again.

I was the Prisoner of Zenda, I dreamed. That's where I located myself in my dream.

I was blond Ingrid Bergman, St. Joan.

The shape of the black typewriter, the old Royal Underwood, would ghostly loom, was in and out of my dreams as it was on the long drive through our Dixie States, which were death, up into the North, which was life. This was the Confederacy against the Union, but the Union after the dissolution had welded our nation—that long, heart-rending, blistering drive home. We were going back to the Union. Those glossy southern mornings, those white, cruel noons.

What of those boys stopping outside Garbo's apartment in Manhattan? Did they never, ever get a glimpse of her radiance?

Me as beggar one more terrifying second flashed through my mind, then I zapped it with this transcendent power I'd developed by age nine to mentally stop things dead in their paths.

I went to sleep alongside Rachel thinking of my life as a doorknocker, a sombre heavy one, of bronze with a woman's face. It was with this heavy knocker that the visitor must knock to enter the door of my house, my soul. The light was dusty 'til way past twilight outside that window in a hotel someplace in Georgia. Location, dislocation. The flies clung to the vivid yellow, oily flypaper suspended from the ceiling. One light bulb shone over the old clothing hung on a line. I hadn't read about skid row. Not yet. When I did I picture it flowing out from, beginning in that room. When Rachel reached her hand out to mine I caught her hand, then slipped back into bed, and noticed when I woke way past midnight so intense was the pain in my face, observed I did, that Mother and Rach wrapped up in their pale bed sheets as though the sheets were water, looked like two drowned persons. Once I closed my eyes, I likely looked the same.

# Broken Toys

*– The South is compared to broken toys, and compared to Indigo, stretched after polio that felt like being a broken toy. This story introduces Indigo's Canadian sweetheart, Simone and compares the water land of the North with the South. Up north she lives in a railroad apartment which triggers memories of the tubs of her girlhood when chains lifted them as though in prison. It is a transition between a deprived girlhood year and the coming down of living at first up north with the northern soul she has chosen for her life partner. It ends with solstice and the image of them being stretched, challenged by this new circumstance as far as they can be. In recurvatum the hospital term of her childhood returns: when a limb is overstretched and bent in backward, hence deformed.*

## In Recurvatum

The South can be symbolized by broken toys. My memory of the South which occurred first during War, then during the divorce, is connected with these busted gadgets. And with Christian girls.

"Jesus loves me this I know," the Catholic girls sang. "Little ones to him belong, they are weak, but He is strong."

There wasn't a cloud in the sky for comfort. It was summer, 1951. The calendar pointed to a new decade ahead. The past decade had left the world smoldering. Europe was still hot with ashes.

Just as I look about me now, in 2003, for signs of the millennium that have been good, I fasten upon the slightest, yet perhaps a significant thing. There's painted wood: painted wood carries the history of the object before it was painted—round wood clock, wooden chair—as well as after. Then after the paint comes the satin, the patina. I count the wooden clock with moon face, cow jumping over, two metal hands. There's a sheep painted on the burgundy *Loo* sign on the bathroom door, a small teal measuring spoon in our coffee, teal green-blue with white scrolls. The latest is a painted stool, a footstool now, but used by milkmaids in former times. How outrageous, how wonderful that it is has purple bursts of flowers on it!

What new object will come thru our door?

After polio, we were stretched. Over-stretched, our limbs—arms at elbows, legs at knees—would bend grotesquely backward, as though we were made double-jointed. This was called in *recurvatum*. I looked in medical dictionaries but at the time could not found this term.

"Yet we kids called out, "Katie's in *recurvatum*.".

"You're in *recurvatum*."

The strong Latin word carried import, the tone of surprise betraying a discovery wondrous as a crater on the moon.

Bent back, we felt like broken toys.

Which reminds me, in the South we had few toys during the war, and those were mainly broken. Susie Doll with her eye sprung out—

sproing! Hanging on its spring. The kitten flung from the shoebox into the field as we drove at 70 m.p.h. But although he whirled like a top, he was dead, that broken.

Not toys really.

Not fun really—being in *recurvatum*.

Yet those same kids sang. "Jesus loves me, this I know." Conclusion, "They are weak but He is strong."

Were we, the fifty of us, doll heads in a dim ward, weak or strong? The power of the child, the crusade of the children.

The South, of course, was a borderline. The hospital too, was a borderline.

There was a divine economy to both regions.

Call it paucity.

Here, in British Columbia, Simone, my love, and I live in ferry country. We wear stocking caps. They say if you don't like the weather here, wait five minutes. Everything's connected by waterways. The changeable weather, sunny with cloudy breaks, cloudy with sunny breaks, has an effect upon your mood. They say more suicides are committed on islands than other places.

We started out in a cold water flat, very northern, reminiscent of Buffalo and Rochester—those mill and mining northeastern towns where industry died, not southern at all. The flat was on Cook Street, sounding properly British and it felt as though all the British pigeons had come home to roost. We lived a Jacob's age on Cook. During those years, we drank too much, had few friends, and were broken, flying back and forth to keep up my visitor's visa. Simone worked as a homemaker for the elderly and homebound. I volunteered to make music twice a week with hospitalized children.

Nothing could have bent me backward more toward my early times. I knew no one, was alone eight or ten hours each day in the dim blue North Sea light of railroad apartment facing north. This, after the desert Southwest.

"Remember not to buy any art!" Simone sings out, as I wheel into one of our favorite haunts, a gallery on nearby Saltspring Island.

What she's really saying is—don't leave me out of any decisions on what we bring into the home. She too fastened her eye upon the cathedral-back chair. Her brown eyes lit up like lamps, my green like coals. High-backed, with three rungs, it is an old kitchen chair straight out of my girlhood—make that southern or northern—sanded over and over, then meticulously hand-painted with flower scrolls, ferns. Best of all—on the seat—the painting of a letter, the kind Emily Dickinson might have written in her incarceration.

"Dearest—I write you from the shadows of my love."

Hidden in that pulpit of prayer I habit daily, it is implied. Beside the letter stands a key on an old fashioned ribbon. All of this painting on the sea shines up like a mirror because it is covered with antique satin polyurethane, perhaps five times. I have also bought another milk stool, now a footstool—Simone can rest her feet on it—used formerly by mild maids, with handle to lift it and carry from room to room. This one is painted similarly with lilac flowers. Like the *Blue Dipper* tempera painting last year, which she first found boring. She will come to love these I think. We become more what we are.

At Pharmasave, I found tea-oil talc. There's a bath in this cabin but not easy to negotiate. The cabin challenges the imagination. The cutlery is strange, knives with curves like curve balls. Like the broken toys of the South, problems haunt us, multiply like rabbits, and follow. But countering these riling struggles stands art.

Art. The galleries—release!

A friend writes me she works on body memory in therapy. Really, does the body not hold any memory?

"Indigo," Mother's voice haunts me, "you'll wake the neighbors with your raving!"

And bang goes the window down that eternal night of July 1 1951. When it comes, catheterization is God himself.

I've never been seriously sick. She doesn't know what's wrong with me. I cannot pee, and keep returning in tears to the toilet, loosening the drawstring on my pj's. The nighties I soaked thru, that is both the first (pink) and the second (blue) ones. Will this night ever break in dawn?

## A Draft

Simone rarely complains but tonight when I bang open the window to our cabin, she complains, "My knees—the draft is hitting them broadside."

At our first lunch out on holiday, she mentions the house insurance. These are necessities to nail life in place for Simone, just as I place myself by freedoms. Wildly extravagant? No, but the purchase of some whimsy animal at the Rexall, just to say life, can still make us laugh. Some colorful stamps, a patterned pair of stockings—these are my wild flings. Her sobriety becomes more so, my carefree-core accentuates the vivid as we pass thru thirty years with their varied seasons. Until, that is, things are bent back too far, like fingernails, and we are all of a sudden, tormented, in *recurvatum*.


## Bag Of Toys

That bag of toys we toted thru the South was no comfort. No more than the cigarette-burned magnolia blossoms. The honky tonk tinselly glitter and pianos of those times. Dead kitten in shoebox, cat's cradle string Rach and I wove for hours on end scenting honeysuckle down in Sarasota wondering why it didn't take away the mizzables we felt inside, the grinch in our stomach and groin.

We waited for the evening breeze to come in. I still wake, when nights are intolerable with pain, memories of the past held in the body like burning splinters, and say to Simone picking up my restlessness, "There's a wind coming up off the water."

It was the water we looked to. In the South for certain, but also in Manhattan, those romances early in my life, my late teens, walking with Gordon who would wheel me to the Boat Basin where we might steal a longer kiss than was possible at the backdoor. Rachel got the trash door, I the front one to the West End avenue apartment that Mother moved us to after polio. Or vice versa.

"You get the garbage door tonight, it's my turn."

We could spy on each other from the bathroom. We'd pull the lid of the toilet down and look from the bathroom to the living room at a right angle, perfect for spying—unless the shade was snapped all the way down. But hot nights, around midnight, the temperature would drop imperceptibly. Puerto Rican kids ran when the fire hydrants opened, and Gordon and I would come back from the Riverside Drive Boat Basin down a ramp, a flight, to boats docking on the Hudson. But what comfort was to be found in Marfa, Texas? Or the Tidal Mud flats of Georgia? Wasn't I a mariner steering out of my loss, my parents having just split, as I am now on this Island? If we don't like the weather, we wait five minutes. Or we lump it.

Which throws me back to the release, the comfort of prayer. I know an Irish woman who as a girl wanted a chapel for a gift, a chapel with pew and window. She coveted this. How am I to explain to Simone that after polio I transferred to just such a chair for the bath? The white paint of course was cheap and blistered on that one. But the body memory of it travels up my buttocks, from the base of my spine to my neck, setting me tingling.

And baths were an issue in those times. It was a horrendous piece to work thru, our bathing having been done in huge vats of tepid water, flat on the floor of the bathing room, where grey winter twilight always seemed to pour in. Great chains operated by electricity called *Hoyer Heists*—a leftover for sure from the war machine—these lifted us on a canvas plinth, which could be immersed in water. I remember the waving of the plinth back and forth as it tilted like the pan to a scale of justice. Justice this had none. We were just entering the age of puberty, at our most vulnerable about our private parts, twelve going on thirteen. Orderlies would bathe us in the colorless light with a light sponge, then shivering with cold, getting goose bumps, we'd be lifted back, transferred to a stretcher whose linen was so woody it cut, always smelling of fire and the oven, and wheeled back to the ward. Back home, the self-consciousness carried over, like a poison it had seeped in. I'd been so young I had virgin veins, was certainly virgin, and had that open an imagination. I wouldn't strip for Mother lest she criticize my posture, altered by the disease. I didn't want her to see my feet turning blue as morning glory and dancing—feet, which had run.

"Indigo!" she'd mourn sometimes, "Look at these socks of yours. They're pure as the driven snow, spotless as the unborn lamb."

Well, what did she think? I didn't want them so.

Chel took to riding the rocking horse for comfort because, "You know why," she'd say to me.

I understood. I'd mastered the same secret in the ward as a matter of fact and it was one thing that kept my faith alight.

So this cathedral chair, which must make the ferry ride home, how hard would it be for Simone to like it? Like the rocking horse, must it remain a bone of contention? It's a horse of a different color to be certain but immersed in her childhood, she sleeps upon a bed, upon waters of thorns.


Beneath My Wings

After all, she is the wind beneath my wings. I steer, she rows. By the fourth morning of having put the money down on the painted and varnished chair, I'm smiling, recalling the sound of that strong voice calling "Remember, no art buying!" as if she could possible take my impulse and wring it by the throat, grind my desire to a boiling halt.

Now I consider the chair, in this light of finality, as a place to pray.


Each day in the subdued light of the cabin, I can count upon one golden star being illumined: like the lamp by the old gasman's taper. She will write a card, beautifully decorated, "Dear Mum."

Her mother, after many small strokes, has forgotten most things. Thinking of my own mother's bedside manner, I shiver. Then smile. I watch Simone weaving these last tensile bridges to her mother across the loss time will inevitably bring. This afternoon, Simone is out motoring, shopping on an island smaller than the one we live on. She dresses in colors quiet as those one imagines on a nun. But actually—I know some nuns—I recall Mother saying, Rachel has a tendency to look tartly.

"You don't dress that way, Indigo. God be praised."

"Where was the box for my typewriter ribbon?" she asked before leaving.

"Why, I tossed it."

"How could you be so—daft?"

She needed to draw the design. She bends over my typewriter of thirty years, frowning, beautifully calligraphed like those postcards and long letters to Mum. By now, these roundings are our almost breath-like morning rituals, these scoldings. By the time she's made it one mile down the road I'll bet she wants to phone. She will regret the chiding, but there is no way. The cell's back home. The cabin is without a phone. Out the kitchen window in Massachusetts, I'd often take refuge and draw comfort, like a blood transfusion, from a harbor deserted by all but lobster boats. I'd go out back, touch them. In one dream I went with my friend in a severe gale. A storm. The friend died of exposure. Miraculously the scene turned into a rowboat. We were two of those wonderfully androgynous fourteen-year-olds of dreams. Boy-girls. Girls before they flesh out, boys before their balls drop, their voices break, then hit the lower registers. My frozen partner died of exposure. I lifted him/her with my own blue lifeless hands. My fingers were bare to the bone on the wooden handles of the oars.

Waking was the only comfort of that dream.

I have to hand it to Mother Marcelle, when Chel and I comforted ourselves as children do, she never called it wicked. Nor did the nurses. Maybe they knew—the best of them—we ravaged children had learned this one comfort like a prayer and saved it for the dark alone. Rachel had no rocking horse when she was at the Riverside School, so her teacher complained to our mother that she played with herself all the time during story hour.

"Why not?" I heard Mother speaking to the teacher in our living room. "The stories are probably boring."

Marcelle didn't threaten us with the loss of our hands if we continued the practice. She didn't, like one catholic mother whose son was terrified say; "I'll stick a red hot poker up your ass."

No, with all her strictures she never held this against us.

Simone, I suspect due to an unhappy experience in childhood, sabotaged our sex life. She has held it against me, using my hands that I could cause her to have an infection. Once she did have an infection in her private parts but I don't think I was to blame. That was the summer we stayed with my sister in the mountains and indiscreetly, south of the Horse Unloading Station, drank.

No, it must be a shadow from way back when. For me, sex has been the one joyous thing. That and of course writing. My hands. Digitless health! I think my way back to that eleven-year-old summer's freedom as high intoxication.

Twice, I have spoken to my doctor about this problem. Despite the fact that she's a woman, she seems to have no sympathy.

She said, "We all have our own cross to bear."

I hadn't known she took to religion. I could not make her understand my loss. Perhaps she took refuge in the thought God is good, and this too would pass.

What wouldn't I give to have one day, one hour of my eleventh summer back again! I'd show Simone how I climbed down trees by my knees, upside-down. I must have been a wild child, enfant sauvage.

"Indigo, if you hadn't caught polio," said Mother, "You'd clearly have broken your neck falling out of a tree and been worse paralyzed. Whenever I'd drive back to New Rochelle, home from Manhattan, I'd be in for a rude awakening. I see a human shape, a girl's shape in the tallest elm, I think, my god that's my kid, my brat, Lynn!"

Bitterness creeps in. It tastes so like iron. I think of that nurse who once told me, "Imagine, a nice disabled person."

When I transfer these days from wheelchair to car, Simone says, "Well done!" I think, "You should have seen me when, woman!"

"I can imagine."

Can you? I wonder. These broken toys are, alas, our stash. Only resignation can bring us round to a point of peace again, to a point of loving them.

Onto our pattern of two women, I superimpose those evenings with Mother in the Jewish Alps, the Catskills, two impeccably done up Henry James' women. The nuance of handkerchief falling, teacup lifted, conveying all passion, imbued with ardor. But an undercurrent of violence roiled thru our night halls reminiscent of those down south, although we were in Gloucester, Massachusetts most often.

It was not such a bad marriage after all. Everybody knows about the sexual attraction of mother for child. A breeze would get up, then slough off. We would drink maybe a third cup of tea and call it a night, sleeping in our beds side by side. Could happier a couple be? Clearly it was a test of our mettle, the steel in our backbone, like seeing how long each of us could go under water without breathing. Go without love, sex, nuance and innuendo conveying subtle yet profound control each held over the other. All struggles are power struggles. Then the argument would begin. Pretty soon, it would get sailing.

We could argue late into the evening, but neither of us remembered the cause the next morning.

When Simone entered my life, I was thirty-six.

Simone was twenty-seven and Mother in midlife. Flaring like a radish, a rosebush, Mother had competition. Each against the other, played me off, turned me into the child— an intolerable position.

God must have had in store for me, harboring in my childhood's wings, that I'd catch polio, that I'd migrate North in a kind of exile thus fully realizing my Jewish destiny to boot. Perhaps I fit into a smaller boat, embarked on my own. Ambulances wail, sirens flash red spinners on the island highway. I worry when Simone will return. I don't normally worry about things. It shows lack of faith, seems trite, too much the ways of a woman. Digit-less. My God, if my fingers had been lost to frostbite in my dream.

## Let Up

If the worst happens and we come to grief over the cathedral-back chair, I mean out-and-out confrontation. I'll plunk myself on that austere yet richly decorated item and say, "Simone. Listen to me. You have the legs, the car and its keys, the train rides across Canada, the flight to see Mum, freedom to climb, to roam. I have my things. Stuff you might say, but it's not. Stuff is trinkets, stuff is party favors, and stuff is the condoms I found in my Mother's purse and thought white balloons. This is my anchor, this cathedral back means the world to me and you'd better not curse it or you'll pay."

Silence

"If I were you, I'd watch it," I'll finally say.

"Dearest," I will read, now underneath me, "the shadow of your love shades my life, protects me." Beside, drawn with scroll and ribbon, the key implies this is the key to my heart, this key.

I will remain taken, completely taken and in adoration by those broken toys of the South because they were not toys really but, like us in the ward, they were reality. A death kit? No, the kitten had the biscuit so was flung, and in being flung, began spinning out of control till she met her final rest. So at last, beloved, will you and I spin. The string cradles Rachel and I wove across the country, south to north, in desperation: two highly strung, highly imaginative and grieving children. Cradle. Yes! Now I see the appellation. The musicality even of the name. O cradle that rocks deeply, my hands have scoured smooth the palms, leathers, these hands, my only tool for love making who loved to be a child uncontained. My childhood turned into the knife I slept upon.

Summer Solstice has come From Sarasota thru Appalachia, the Genesee valley, the Allegheny hills, these hands have steered me. No one, absolutely no one, gets to call me crip, or busted, nor to warn me, "No art buying!"

We're all stretched to the utmost, to breaking point with light this long. I can remember back to that horrendous evening when, pitched above some cliff which drooped sharply to the water, Simone said, "Go ahead! "I'll catch you."

I held, as I hold, still.

Waiting for that first buzz of black fly. Was it the drinking glass? Did Rachel catch it first, then abort me, being a more healthy age? Mother crying out after me, "It was that broken mirror, Indigo. It was that scene we had that summer nightfall." But never, in all my born days did she cry out against Rachel or me for pleasuring ourselves. She knew where to stop. A child's body memory was her mystery, her privacy, her chapel.

When my freedom's bent back too far, *Jesus loves me*, I sing, at first taunting myself, then ending genuinely moved, not sobbing, but trembling, *We are weak, but He is strong*. If he is, he will show himself. Your love shadows me but I shadow our passion in my pen. That alone. It is still winter light in upstate New York first 1943, then fast forward to 1947, then hold at 1951.

Here freeze the frame—for this is where things change. For better or worse, forever. Now paralysis. Now 1951 is melting into 1952, like ice thawing, making an ugly mess of water with rainbow oil sheen. Those far away, mirror-haunting times when all hope of healing was flip-sided. Its reverse, the *Twenty Third Psalm*.

*If the Lord was my shepherd, why did I so want?*

*I couldn't bathe.*

*I couldn't carry out the bedpan.*

Was I becoming the little sister and Chel the big one. Was I being childized by this dilemma? Being stretched by one of a series of faceless physiotherapists many of whom, Jews, escaped from Berlin just in the nick of time. Instead of screaming, however, one winter afternoon back home having therapy I decide to smile.

"It's out of one side of your face, Indigo. It's crooked," Mother would say. "That smile will cheer no one."

But I go on, a Mona Lisa smile. I welcome my companion, raising my eyes to the mirror above the exercise mat and parallel bars we've rigged up. This girl blooms. Her crutches stand rakishly to the side like ski poles. I welcome her companions, the breath of scolding, mornings totally erased by the hand across the mirror steam. For the child has after-altered into a woman. There is a knife edge, true, an ancient elbow-dig of one more treatment. One more round. When is the final one? I am on the plinth; she has stretched me back too far. I shriek. I scream. Through half a century the echoes that scream: *Jesus loves me, this I know,* STOP! But I am suddenly out of wind.

I hand my voice over to him, the kid on the next plinth, the brat with the brown eyes, comes to my defense, "Let up on 'er! Bitch! She's in *rekovadum*."

# Morning Glory Jeans

*for Anne & Jim who know the cell, the release*

– Indigo reminisces on her hospital year at age twelve, so it segues the preceding story very naturally. She speaks of the once a week the ward kids are allowed to be dressed in street clothes rather than hospital gowns and takes morning glory jeans as her icon. This toggles her memory of being an able-bodied child in blue jeans who could run, skip, and jump.

## Morning Glory Blue

Often they straightened our backs with braces: with Stryker frames which turned the child strapped into a bed, like a pancake— now in this, now that direction. Reese jackets for extreme cases of curvature of a spine were a rod inserted into a body cast that held the backbone rigid from skull to toes. One was covered like a turtle. A girl's, a boy's face would peek out. Still, we hardly pecked at crumbs. We older kids took up smoking. My own spine was held in a corset with steel bones that cut my shoulder blades and made me think of Lucinda Violet, my aunt's mannequin.

She too had no flesh on her bones, "picked dry by the blackbirds," Uncle would gaffe.

These macabre jokes made me laugh in the ward, without blushing like a peony.

There was a certain milk-blue of morning glory that our jeans turned, not deliberately bleached but colored by wear and by the sun. This was a color badge we had to earn—denim mixed with milk paint, squatting, running, climbing, no hiding under a frothy hat for the likes of me.

Once in a while on the ward, rather than being slipped into my ash-rose gingham, or dotted Swiss, I asked for the jeans which had miraculously made it thru the fire with my lean twelve-year-old body the night I was stricken. On these star-occasions, which merited a marquee in my book, a Sunday nurse would draw them down from a wire hanger in the metal closets, reminiscent of a gym, which stood beside each of our hospital cots. On Sundays we were slipped out of regulation hospital gowns and dressed in whatever school clothes we had. Once in a blue moon, I asked for my jeans. The Sunday nurse had a rear end that was shaped like the bell of a gourd squash. I was a thin pear. They fit my lean-hipped frame.

These jeans were echoes, mirrors from the summer I had been eleven— faded hollyhock, larkspur, magnolia. I'd climbed the final house frames I was to climb, wearing these jeans. I pedaled over to the poor part of town and visited my dog, Skeezix (named from the comic strip). He had ended up there because I was commanded by Mother Marcelle to sell him for ten dollars.

"He has eight holes in him."

He'd got in a fight again and was cowering under our parents' desk. It had belonged to both my parents until the divorce. This desk had a deep knee hole and tooled gold-green leather on top. Mysteriously, and indicting me forever, the first two letters of my name had appeared, cut with a letter opener in the right lower-hand corner of the Italian leather desk.

How was it that my blue jeans were not burned? All my clothing was there when the house was fumigated. It was as if they took the child's flesh but left the skeleton standing. I'd worn those jeans for Math tutoring, for scouring the country club which would not allow Jewish people to join.

"We'll get even," I incited the other kids and we did, tobogganing over all the nicely sculpted gold ruts when blizzards came. I was light as a grasshopper the leanest kid, so I rode on the end and always flew off amid gales of laughter.

But with this virus there was no way to get even. I was not the type of kid who'd carp and grow bitter. I was wiry and still leaping hedges in my heart when I read the headlines from my hospital bed which spoke of the earliest vaccine coming in just the summer I was stricken. We'd jump the great divide between the ill and the well. Mother was standing firm, the ranks were closed. Now I was a hospitalized child, but there was another state of mind where my imagination lived.

This state had the *Hallelujah Chorus,* survival meetings along river banks and it was my Mecca, the roof I might have jumped off in hospital gown—and flown.

Mother had given me an accordion file for letters so I could alphabetize all the get-well cards or sympathy notes from schoolmates. I became briefly alarmed. I was trussed, the war was over only six years earlier, 1945-1951— we played jazz songs. Currents ran through me live-wire, my body, a hot house with red currants, gooseberries and raspberries growing. Here was Maggie's card. Here Danielle's. But would I ever see either of those girls again? No kids were allowed to visit. The needle and thread of poliomyelitis had looped thru me and I was left untouchable.

Mother had got rid of the yellow clock I nightmared over. In my dream our family sat in a circle. My forever family was to change, and the clock circulated like a mythical animal behind us. At whoever's chair it stopped that person would die. I woke up screaming. When I actually came to die, I was silent. No white clock peopled and darkened my dream.

O squandered lambs.

Who was my forever family now? A brick incinerator that I imagined to be a crematorium stood outside my end of the ward. A desperate dash up the path was made by the dog, Livingstone. He was the exact color of blood pudding. The sky was white as lard, the earth dark as dung, dark that is until snow came, sugar powdering bushes, branches, buildings. I lay on the tilt table till my feet burned, itched to run. This was done to stimulate the circulation.

Agnes Peck, my favorite nurse, was in good health, tall and thin, had handsome legs, a haunting beauty about her movement, the type I saw coming for me 'til smash bang— the virus came and exploded all over me like lit kerosene.


## Lionheart

Hip-huggers the jeans, but boy had they ever circled my hips. I was a dirty blond. No Bearington Bears inhabited our world. I was parentless now. Nurses held the way stations. I was a child locked up beside a radiant ocean.

Mother and I used to chase each other round the dining table, I'd shove it up against the kitchen wall, scoot under. Very few children on the ward were allowed to enter a Griselda mood which might have occurred among pre-adolescent girls confined. Mother came to the ward once wearing her Beethoven wing collar. Was this to cheer me up? I was envious lying there with budding breasts in my white regulation hospital gown with numbers tamped inside it. I recalled with longing the glory days of our chasing one another round and round the dining table like numerals of a clock now totally ground to a halt—pulverized ash dust which blew away when I held my palm up to the wind puffing out my cheeks as though blowing a trumpet.

It was dark and late.

No one came, no footfall. The night was lace, cancerous, riddled. No escape. A dazzling light of being scrutinized was shone upon us children. Every freckle, wart, every curve of bone was seen by hostile eyes. Was it a bit like this in the prison camps? *How can I remotely imagine.* The shimmering colors swept me away.

That night, when I was lifted out of my jeans, I noticed the black and blue mark on my thigh.

"How did that get there?" the nurse interrogated.

I did not know. I shook my head.

"Was it the clamps, being measured for braces?"

"I don't know, I told you," I shook my head again. I went about my conquest in my own way. I could see that she liked me. Blue jeans were passion —and hayfields, tall chive grass. She smiled. This passion freed me. I remembered in a flash.

I'd swung myself by one of the bars in the gym, hoisting my skinny body up by my hands last week , and had fallen on the exercise mat in the railroad station, cathedral light of the gym on a late winter day, early evening, bruising my hip. I didn't feel much then. It was the most dire and extreme hour of all for me, the hour when my whole worldview, my *weltanshauung* changed. Parents picked up kids but never me. October had come and gone and it was clear that I would not get better to return home with my kin.

My forever family was changed. No more butterscotch, pencil-smelling schoolrooms with the snap-down maps I adored. The smell of old wooden rulers was still in my nostrils. The kids in the ward were now my block gang. I swallowed hard every Friday that last hour in the gym between four and five. I threw myself to the lions when I dared to lift my slender weight from the mat with my strong though thin biceps. Then was when the bruise the size of a grapefruit bloomed. It might have been a boy's hand in rape, my first orgasm behind the barn. But I'd handled that myself too.

"Green eyes," she smiled at me. It's true that somebody had dubbed them *Coke-bottle green*.

I turned toward the wall.

I would not, could not tell her although a stream of Joycean lyricism came to my inner lips and I must have been close to a grin myself. One of the children had cancer of the face and the surgeons could not figure how near her right eye it was rooted. This scared me. I saw the branches of innocence wrapped up in the arms of the children. I knew, however, where this fear was rooted, this fear of mine. I missed the hummingbirds back home dipping their needle beaks into red. Did I miss Chel? The world of the schoolroom was never again to be mine. I knew this although the ancient geographies they brought up on carts from the hospital basement made a makeshift schoolroom.

Out of my jeans, I realized they felt so good I'd frozen. I wanted to wear them again. Mysteriously, miraculously, I wanted to wear them in bed, knees pulled up to chin—I had to do this now with my hand. I burrowed my nose in a book as I had done when a walking child.

But now it was the silver wheelchair I wakened to every morning, went to bed from every night.

"Goodnight, Pal, old horse, stallion," I touched the icy silver. It, too, was the first thing I touched on waking.

What I had wasn't cancer of the spine as I first dreaded. It wasn't spreading but  lace was cast, a narrow net over the body with bowl haircut, heart-armor breaking, cupping each breast in one hand, budding in Ward C bed #9. I was called, *Jacklyn* because I loved painting with words.

I, who had taken away peoples' breath at the music conservatory when I performed Chopin, I, at whom they had gasped because I climbed out of fir trees upside down, I was paralyzed and my only claim to fame was that I *was* having a story, *Holly Comes Home for Christmas*, my dream fantasy, published in the *Ward Words*, the modest mimeographed publication of the hospital. I never saw the publication.

One night a bridge had broken, a dam had burst. One of the older girls was jackknifed coughing, she had a cigarette cough, at age fourteen, no longer little, and was crying. If I stopped now, I'd die. Where were the grammars and spellers now? I dreamed of those jeans being taken down, I longed for the stiff cardboard touch of them at first, then the pinafore-tender warmth of them encasing my legs.

I lived in a shoebox. There was no tree, no piano. There might have been drug dealers under my window. The veil was lifted, the ward in water had waves rolling over it, then became very still, mirror-still. I had begun composing stories. Lionheart, I was back in morning glory blue jeans. It was true. From the whip crack, I'd had stardust in my eyes.

# Audubon Wallpaper

– *Beautiful birds whose flight is frozen in time become the chiaroscuro of a family in the ominous pre-shadow of divorce. A disharmony, a profound sadness runs through this time imaged forth in the delicate and brilliant birds drawn by John James Audubon, which my parents could scarce afford, but hung on the dining room wall. Such words as "chiffarobe" and "vestibule" transported like garments up north from my sojourn south. I returned to my home in the North, my memory bank replete with images of girls wearing hair bows big as a country church.*

## Stilled Flight

The stilled bird, impeccably drawn in palest tones by Audubon is part of my American childhood in the South, water-colored, superimposed upon a dark wood carousel horse brought by boat from Europe, red painted saddle, black hoofs. One papered our walls, one we rode round and round. Both are grafted upon my eighth year. Horse and blue heron composed a double-spread in a fairytale book whose illustrations shone from glossy clay-based paper.

We'd never had a dining room so this was the room where symbolically and in reality we took our meals, where the heart began to be starved while apple-paper covered the walls with scrolls of fiddle fern and magnolia blossoms, with their small cigarette burns like those on the piano teacher's piano.

Forbidden to run our fingers along the elegant wallpaper, we'd put our hands over our heads, Rach and I, or behind our backs passing the aviary. But when I did break down and do the forbidden thing, I thought Indigo, my name, was the rebel's color. Looking to right and left, scanning the field, I'd catch the golden moment and I'd run my index finger from light-switch to one delicate blue heron and to him alone.

The search for air beyond the smoke of experience drove me.

There, in the corner of the paper he inscribed with the burin of a pen– *John Jacob Audubon* —with a flourish. In museums we were forbidden to touch, and in school we absorbed the message in the air from the older girls, *Nice girls don't touch*. But I touched now. This was alluring as an etching, a bas-relief, a sculpture. In the classical winter-light of our post-war dining room, those Audubon birds became the symbol of the unattainable, the gold ring on the merry-go-round, transfixed and transfixing.

Audubon, I'd read, was half-caste: part Creole, part French, which gave him allure. The touch of this spare era was upon our bodies. Divorce, like war, eroded a canyon in the land of our lives. I allowed my strange compulsions sway until, obeying them, I felt I fell into a state of grace.

But the next compulsion was more haunting, more inexplicable. Hillary Kronengold had had polio; she wore a brace on her left leg which was withered, icy to the touch, thin, and turned purple in the cold. I wanted to be the one to lace her old-fashioned boot on after she took the brace off for a nap. I wanted to be in on the mystery, which affected mobility and carried with it the cold thrill of icy steel on warm human flesh.

As it turned out, that was just what I was to inherit. Only my involvement was more extensive. I required two long leg braces, foot to hip, plus a corset when I was stricken in 1951. I was one of the last polios. Hillary must have caught hers around 1944. I had running for a longer time. A natural tomboy, this polarity between immobility—the birds—and revolving, the carousel horses was to become the pole on which you could place the pattern of my life— stilled toucan, or stork, or pelican, or racing stallion, palomino, pinto. I became each by turns. The decades were the demarcation.

Like the Mason-Dixon Line, the divorce further divided one part of my life from another. And I was the one who was to adopt two lands, immigrating, further drawing an ebony line, as though on a map reflected in water, upon that early geography: married versus divorced, South versus North, walking versus paralysis, homeland versus adopted land.

The Audubon wallpaper that was our parents' pride. We later learned they scarce could afford it. Our father had fallen in love with an old Colonial house in New Rochelle, a suburb of New York where he worked at the hospitals. These birds, pristine, exotic flamingoes, storks, and blue herons, poised like crystal, feathered and floated beside us where we ate on the old mahogany table inherited from Grandmother Tisanne. It was 1945. We were putting down roots after years of traveling.

During those long brown afternoons, I took Rachel by the hand. Sometimes I led her downstairs to the kitchen by the backstairs, *the maid's stairs*, to the lino-floored yellow and black kitchen. If, on rare occasions, we took the front staircase, we'd stop at the landing—halfway down—to look out the large window over our ragged back orchards. The colors of the birds were stunners: orange-pink for the storks and pelicans, celadon were green and thrush were fawn-brown. There was also, disturbingly, a tinge of blood in the eye lens of some.

Later I was to see with my own eyes the very deltas and savannas of the American South. Cypress and Spanish moss groves, moss green, were foreshadowed in the birds. Sarasota, the divorce which was forecast (although I hardly twigged then) by Mother sweeping another dinner off the table, folding the white linen and giving the birds a scathing glance.

"Girls, you know we cannot afford this." She went on with that southernism, "I am chagrined, you both rile me."

She took a symbolic journey with us on the romantic night-train, dark, smelling of raisins, with its wood paneling and black porters all the way from the North down into the South; both are real. We left the book of country Christmas crafts behind: teddies with button eyes, toy boxes hand painted by mother. In a profound sense, it was as though I, at eight, and Chel, at four, were leaving the first segment of our childhood behind, the enchanted part, despite the metallic cast war threw over our winters, turning to pewter the sky's lid. The light brought disenchantment because it revealed everything: flaws, cracks in the pavement, in the doll's skull, in the very construction of existence. I learned then, at age nine, that light is pitiless and grew to loathe and seek shelter from the scalding, blinding sun.

But the train was our last touch of old world luxury, with overtones, reflections, echoes of Rosenblum's Tudor estate because, with valises and wearing our best winter coats from grandmother and our bowler hats with elastic under the chin, we trained from Grand Central Station down to Sarasota, to establish residence, thus file for divorce in a state where adultery was not the only ground for it.

This was the promised land: this flat country off the Gulf of Mexico where the very air and land were anemic, toned down ten notches of color from the North. Adultery was out of the question in our case. It was a question of a deep rift from the start, emotional incompatibility.

"Does it have to do with being an adult, Mother?" I asked Marcelle the first month.

"Yes and no," she said. "Indigo, fold that clothing I've just ironed."

Thus she bit the thread short off the spool. But never did she say, "Indy, you're too young." No, not that. Not in a million.

Tallahassee, Sarasota—those names pinpointed the towns where our parents made formal the diction and the dichotomy.

I felt the blue in the air those evenings back in 1947. Something had caused the mechanism of our parents' marriage to be broken. The Army Post left colors upon my retina dun, dung, *merde*. I felt blue, strung-out cobalt with reverberations of my name, Indigo, like ripples from a stone shot in the air those evenings back in 1947 when I was nine and Rachel five. The years we'd just survived tended to flash in my dreams, or to illumine eidetic images upon my eye.

We lived in Permanent Military Quarters, P.M.Q, barracks, row-upon-row, haunted me, they were so like Dachau, Bergen-Belsen, and the Auschwitz I had seen on newsreels spooling off cellophane like oil separating from water. But they stuck, those pictures lit up by the dusty cone of whirling light the projector threw. The idea of a row, a queue was now a nightmare-triggering image. I had dreams of soldiers in trenches I'd seen in the Warner Pathe Newsreels. There I learned the meaning of the words optical illusion because I had a squint which obliged Mother to administer orthoptics to me, a small wooden stick with viewer and an early slide which caused the boy to leap thru the hoop by focusing my two eyes upon one thing. He really did become one boy, not two. I was being cured of astigmatism, which meant I wouldn't need eye surgery. But there was a deeper grief. There was no way I could marry my two parents again. They had established hostility so that by now, they moved thru a division of volatile hours during Army Post days, a schism, which would only end in total rending.

That's why the cream background of these birds drawn as if in water, perfectly reflected, was all the more astounding when it fractured, shattered as if the elegant birds were made of glass. We were forbidden, we must never, ever under any condition put our hands upon this wallpaper. If our grubby little mitts were found to have left tracery upon them. . .

I did it on a dare. I now see it as another of my schisms between turmoil, and calm. War and resolution. But in this case I provoked conflict. It was a compulsion, compulsive neurotic disorder they might call it. I had to walk five times from molding to light switch and drag my index finger along the cream paper with the tracery of birds. I'd run my index finger from molding to light switch in a beeline. Something was smoldering in me which made me cross the line. The evidence of my crime was clear: the faint and eerie gray smudge my finger had made.

We lived in winter brightness. There was a sunroom, all glassed roof and walls which let sun shine thru glass but was austere, demanding that I give my full and undivided attention, read and concentrate upon my grammar or spelling for hours on end. *Sunny* (Rachel) would give us one of her rare smiles.

But Marcelle would turn and say, "It's a severe brightness, Indigo, come to bloom."

So my art was destined to come to fruition in the cold, glacial North where my destiny had to be realized above the ocean. With the hindsight of nearly sixty-five years, I read the forecast now in those New England winter dawns. It hurts to lose anything you once had — youth, beauty, legs — but with age, you can almost look back upon it as somebody else's youth, beauty, mobility. I am able to read life with a more quieting love.

Homer's rosy fingered dawn continues to come. Feeling the old torsion of my life, all the same, on this teal crust over the ocean I dare to place an Audubon cardinal, or shall it be the greater blue heron? Thin as a pencil, the ocean-bird leans, tilting. With that amazing curvature of the neck which makes him look like an "S" he stands, almost imperceptible, immobile, his beak at the ready to prong a fish for dinner.

I live with fracture— Mother's portrait, perfectly oval, just that bit askew, thrown in its oval frame to make all her features appear exaggerated in her Byron collar, and peach coloring, Mother breaking hearts at twenty-one. Was she a man's woman? Or a woman's woman?

## Akimbo

"Indigo," Mother phones from Massachusetts, "It's bitterly cold here. There?"

I think of her as severe but with a bloom. It is foreboding, dark-thoughted as a witch hunt. A Puritan Rachel, down the road from Marcelle, asks me the same question, hinting at the melancholy which haunts our family. With other families, it is addiction. Full of life as a fresh dime, I feel. Blue-black, a night sky which is clear as crystal when I go out on the terrace.

Mentally, I have not left the issue of the suicidal child. I bring Rachel along in imagination where I go. Those phone conversations we had, they are carved in stone.

"It will pass," I told her, "Rowena's a ballerina, used to pain, she's not necessarily suicidal. Maybe it's a cry for help."

Where did she burn herself? I thought, immediately when I heard, that it must be her wrists. But, no, it was directly into her abdomen. Some twenty-two little cigarette burns looking like tiny nails to a coffin. Blood-orange, it brings back to my mind's eye the wings of Audubon which I flex in my imagination picturing, lifting, then folding in that classical glass-clear light.

How could she jolt her child from this frame of mind?

She tried the South of Spain where she and Row went into exile as a dyad. Here the streets with their sidewalk cafes exuded sensuality. They were sultry, sexual. An enormous undertaking, she sold her home and left Texas. It was then that it began, my haunting by the vivid southern birds (perhaps the way Jerzy Kozinski was haunted by the painted bird of the Holocaust, bearing a boy in basket on his back.)

The first time she came to me, her wings were not dipped in blood, but in ink, like a pen. So much of my childhood is steeped in, based upon impressionism— a robe with arms on the wash line frozen, its pockets turned inside out, a bit of laundry blows, frozen, to my feet. The white sheets I step out of the morning I have polio are drenched, cling to me like dead birds. I shudder. I have no more tears to spend.

"How will we ever get over the ballet?" I wake at night to find you sobbing, your chin curled to your knees, your boom box on, Rowena. "How will I ever get over walking?"

Head down, counting pirouettes (at which she excelled) under her breath, Rowena in the last days before she took up the razor— she crashed with the uncontrollable sorrow of a child over what she does best and must forfeit, emotionally exhausted, burned out at fourteen. I, on the other hand, was just getting going, into first gear. I too had grand ambitions. In modern dance, leaps were my greatest joy.

The autumn before she went thru the wall, before they discovered that Rowena, like Rachel, had inherited scoliosis, curvature of the spine, Rowena heard her Mother say quietly, with dignity and pride, reined in, "Row, you realize you have passed some of the toughest national ballet auditions."

Rachel stood in the doorway arms akimbo. She imagined Row was lighting up, behind the flimsy wood door, smoking, scarring her lungs, darkening her teeth, crushing out the butt, turning the boom box on again. But it was silent. (She was recalling herself at the same age, fourteen, traveling to the Mozarteum in Salzburg.) She lists the ballets: Bolshoi Ballet, National Ballet of Canada.

"They have you fast-tracked for prima ballerina at the Houston, you know."

"I know." the child piped back from behind the bolted bath door. Blue-black, the girls' hair shone. "It got too heavy, my bun," she smiled, "So I had to keep cutting it. It was like cutting my belly by working on my abs."

At night, Rachel would hear a voice in Row's bedroom, "To whom are you talking?" Rachel asks.

"Myself, Mom."

Rachel turns, quietly closes the door, and goes down the stairs to their linoleum-floored, Austin kitchen faintly reminiscent of the kitchen in their New Rochelle home. It has the overtones of another life, the early life with the Audubon wallpaper, but this was a pale comparison. A ghost of the former time. Texas.

Why did they ever come to Texas where air burned like dry cigarette paper being ignited? Houston, beginning of their tragic days. It was hard. Hard, when Rowena first began working four hours a day, at age eleven, on her abdominal muscles. But Rachel bore it because like me she had been raised in the arts. It would pour, a pelting southwestern rain, then flash flood. Then it would stop and they all would go outside, stare at the cottonwoods as dry tired-gold, dusty-gold as though no rain had fallen at all. Rowena developed thrush, and entered puberty, showing small knobs of breasts, a Botticelli Primavera. The second summer. There were only to be three before the great undertaking of leaving that no man's land for the land of green New England commenced once again. Three summers in hell. It was hallucinatory, as if Row were moving in a dream.

Could Chel remember back to those clear days like lagoon water, when this child with the silken skin, Asian blue-white, and hair blue-black had moved untroubled thru her hours toward the ballet with which she was to engage in a love-hate embrace?

Spain, Barcelona.

It rained and rained.

"I'm devoting my life just to get her beyond thirteen," you said.

Rachel, you urged your child to observe the discipline of ballet, and in another language.

"I was born to dance," the child laughed, and did a pirouette or one of her fabulous extensions.

She wore her backpack like all the French children. Thursdays and Tuesdays she went to ballet lessons. Her mother made a chignon of the black hair and pinned it back. Mother and daughter made a special trip from Barcelona to Madrid to buy toe-shoes.

Back at the memory box, I, at Row's age, fourteen, was in traction in state hospital or having my leg stretched by the physiotherapist in what I felt to be the sort of light which pours thru prison windows.

These five centimeters of snow don't simplify life for the postal carriers the first full workweek of the New Year. I see snow, its purity, the Audubon birds, and Rowena's scars.

Flashback. It is the second winter in New England.

Rowena has gone into the bathroom. The clock on the kitchen wall is ticking loud as a gun. The fields are cream white background color for Audubon's birds. Rachel, you stand outside the bath door, heart in mouth.

"What are you doing, honey?"

"You know what I do when I feel trapped, Mom. Hey, I didn't burn myself, when I was dancing."

Chel, you go back thru the hallway to the kitchen where, as you always do, you lay your head forward on your arms for a moment, then you pour yourself morning's black coffee from the chipped enamel pot. You have brought your broken child, your prodigy, to psychologists in Europe, psychologists in New England and now back home. Bank accounts are all at the bottom. You take a second mortgage on the benighted home, the godforsaken plot of land where you have come to so much grief. You are thirty grand in debt. You took her to Yoga masters, chiropractors—sometimes they asked, "What has happened to you?"

"I burned myself," she would reply, ingénue, in that singsong of a child, now in her fourteenth summer. Autumn is full of panicked parents phoning the child psychologist late at night. Then it becomes winter again.

New England.

Icicles hung from eaves and trees. Your house in Texas is on the market, but is a monkey wrench. You cannot unload it—ten months, eleven. You make a bid on a small Colonial on a side street, a *cul de sac*, and hold your breath. The most expensive neighborhood in Vermont. The deal comes thru. You will be in the red for years. You do not love the home, but it will suffice. What marks must it leave on a mother's body when a child self-inflicts? Is it not like living a birth backward, cutting away to an abortion of what broke the heart by breaking the flesh?

## Leap

"Happy New Year," I say to Rachel.

"I don't believe in New Years," she says.

"You have been thru the years in hell," I reply.

"All times, to me, are one."

Age has made me more tolerant, though still the lion of rage can wake in me and roar. Like me, Rachel has that touch of that post-depression era upon her body. Economical light *with a bloom.*

Things are pristine up North. I imagine that I stand in a Creole-clear dawn.

Feather-by-feather, they never fly. As soon as I close my eyes, those pink-orange pelicans, explode, first into white snow, then into a firebird. It is Rowena at Lincoln Center at age nineteen.

As I stood in that diaphanous, ethereal dawn down South, yearning for the solid, the opaque birds on the real bough of the North, how could I realize it would be precisely this torsion which would drive me in the direction of my life—writing. Did I realize that this was propelling me into that faith which is the challenge if one is to carry the soul's dialogue with God from one year into the next?

*Port de bras*, floating, Row moves, feet cushioned by lamb's wool, but still forced into toe slippers with wooden toe which will leave her feet bruised black and blue for years, with these points, she hardly brushs earth. Look closely though. She has caught fire! How sweetly she smiles as she burns. The audience, horrified, rise to their feet but they cannot smother their flame.

When Nijinsky made his leaps, they said he was a madman. Although I was only eight at *Jacob's Pillow* the *elan* was not lost on me. I remember the floor plan of that theatre as I remember all floor plans. The exit was to my right, that meant stage left, and it led through wooden doors onto forested ground. The pen, which drew that, too, was dipped in blood.

*Impaled*

When you hovered in the air, you were a hummingbird, Rowena, against those burned out Texas evenings of sad-eyed junkies and porno strips where cottonwood leaves were so dry they rattled like castanets, made their music in the wind.

Considering a white latticed front porch, I decide, "A southern belle having dreams of the North." A neurotic, compulsive child—or one twice alive, driven?

The stilled impeccably drawn bird in palest tones is superimposed upon the mahogany or oak carousel horse brought over from Europe, red saddle and all. Both are impaled.

"I'd give you my legs," Marcelle said.

I, too, went thru the wall. One thin foot strapped in leather and steel brace comes down to touch floor. It tingles as though it is on flame. I reach out, Rowena, to take your Pavlovian hand and pull you out of the flames. We close our eyes. Over snowfields as over bayous, and deltas, we float. Snowbird and firebird, the paralyzed and the dynamo, the extra energy kid whom everyone swore would be the next Pavlov and the kid who climbed the highest mountain in New York State at age eleven.

"I have a temper," Row laughed, "like Grandmother Marcelle."

Rowena had been known to break every object in her room. When I could no longer hike, I trashed my wolverines. Nijinksy's portrait on the wall curls to white silent ash. Crematory. One expects to hear crackling.

But all becomes silent. In a stage whisper I say, "Dance! Just once more for us."

Fawn-colored and rose birds gaze with eyes like black mirrors, eagle-sharp. I touch one more time, the blue heron, compulsive-neurotic child, twice alive, South-steeped, North-born, driven.

It feels delicious with its eggshell-cream background, for these birds are both sharp-eyed toward the earth and hinting at that which is beyond.

January 2004

# Polio:
# A Girlhood Novitiate
## (Pooky and I)

— *Indigo sees the onset of polio in conjunction with her love for Rachel (Pooky). She creates allegorical characters: Poverty, Chastity, and Obedience, listed as the qualities the hospital inflicted upon the kids, those exacted of a nun. Indigo allegories here making "Mrs. Olivia" the wind, "Mr. Scar" the fire, "Weightless" water and "Grit-Soul," the earth. Yet another look at the experience of polio, this story, which imagines Indigo as a novitiate into the nunnery also, is an elegy for her parent's marriage.*

## Poverty, Chastity, Obedience

I now see in how many ways my journey through polio resembled a novitiate's passage into nunhood. I came of age in the South. And in the North. In the south, I was a southern Jewish girl-child, a pariah always. Sacrifice came first— childhood activities such as running, walking, climbing, then worldly things, and reconciliation last. I was left a tin cup and a plush bunny. When our father went to fetch my things from the state institute up north, all he brought home with him were my blue bunny and two new shiny steel long-leg braces, for which I'd just been fitted in the German brace shop that was run from the basement of the hospital. I remember the feeling of being below earth, in the bowels of the institution where my sleep and waking had occurred for that half year in my life—braces fit out with leather knee-pads, small circles in them, and straps.

Poverty. Chastity. Obedience.

The hospital inflicted upon us poorness in possessions, and the price of disobedience was Matron. As for chastity, we kids learned a way to surmount that restriction. Wealth and disobedience were out of the question, chastity was straddled.

I was challenged from early childhood to set an example for my sister.

"You're the eldest, Indigo," Mother commanded. "Don't set a bad example."

Was I setting a good example by going away, so far away that I might have been in a nunnery, riding on a horse, disappearing deeper and deeper into a snow filled woods, serving a novice hood this twelfth summer of my life when Pooky was only eight?

Pooky and I did almost everything together. We sang songs, played games, culled pennies in a tin can, hiked, played *Little House on the Prairie* on snowy days. Plus, I showed her movies in bed, holding a flashlight over the back of the quilt, causing a light to shine, creating circles of light in the pea soup khaki blanket, garnered, leftover from the war.

Pooky, whose given name was Rachel, became Pooky one Halloween when she was three. Things that scared her, they were so 'pooky.'

It stuck. She was the one to whom I told things. The shoe wouldn't fit. My ninth birthday shoes were too tight when I was ten.

"Pooks, think of something to sub for a shoehorn."

"I can't." Then, suddenly I smiled and snapped my fingers, elbowing from my favorite position, knees drawn to chin.

"A soup spoon. A soup spoon!" to ladle my foot into the hush-puppy.

In the twinkling of an eye, fast as greased lightning, I ran down to our kitchen.

That was in New England. Later I was to learn the ways Canadian kids would play while mother was away. They made Reese's pieces out of chips of nuts and cocoa. They watered the molasses.

## Small Forest Shrine

"What's it like, Indigo?" Pooky asked me as we sat side-by-side on her bed my first weekend home after polio, a weekend visit.

I told her everything, but *this* there was no way to tell. "I watched the little lights," I said, "from the hospital in the rear-view of our father's car mirror recede. Then we drove into the thousand lights of Manhattan." I saw her eyes widen.

"What was it like?" she demanded again. I thought of telling her about the twenty cots lined on each side of the ward with cubicles of plastic separating us.

I said, "You see, we each had our cubicle-mate. Karenine was mine."

"Did she get to go home this weekend too?"

"No." I answered.

"Why?"

"She died."

There a silence fell between us, black, black as ink.

How could I tell her about the mornings which felt like the war was on again? After all, Europe was still smoking, 1945 to 1951. I recalled, lying in the ward waiting for the gray cruel light of dawn, being wakened to meet our daddy at the railway station, Mother throwing my coat over my pajamas. The body has a memory. I moved feet which were leaden, struggled through dawn toward the light, but it was eerie, a half-light only. I was learning, even then, the sacrifices required by love.

But this sacrifice had nothing to do with love. They were sadistic toward us, the nurses who were holdovers from when the institute had been a military hospital. In every way, we were treated, not as patients—certainly not as children who were patients—but as soldiers.

I wanted to let Pooky know it all felt like a faded photograph with thick grain like our winter coats or our cream of farina in morning, a faded photograph left in a bureau drawer, or a lock of hair. But in her soulful way, Pooky would cloud over if I told her. Besides, she couldn't relate to these things, war awakenings and photograph albums, since we were four years apart in age and that four years almost signified a generation. I recalled, in addition, the way she mustered her bravery. She would sit for hours in the window seat watching for me to come home from elementary school.

She'd cry when I played on the piano one piece from Peter Pan, *Who am I? Did I ever live before as a mountain lion or a fly?* The sense of who she might have been in another world haunted Pooky. I didn't want to wake this fear, this haunt. There was no way to get through but by getting through. She wore coal black bears on fire-red pajamas at age eight while I wore a blue flannel nightgown at age twelve, my legs dancing.

My mind was on getting back to the hospital in 48 hours or, "Yer bed'll run out," the ward kids warned.

It was one of the ways the home-going kids were taunted by the bed-bound ones. We were given to know that the State paid exactly seven dollars per child for a bed and that this pittance was a great favor granted us, the sick kids, a favor which could—like the loving touch of a mother—be withdrawn.

So much had been withdrawn.

"What do you want?" Pook asked.

"I want every ordinary thing, some extraordinary things."

But Pook was only nine.

She jumped up from the bed to get something in the living room and for the first time it struck me that I could not jump up any longer but must transfer to my wheelchair, loaned from the hospital. This took longer, and required care, a skill I'd just learned. Being rail thin, my body was not difficult to swing from seat to seat. Suddenly my heart was racing; it leapt into my throat. I was fearful of being transferred from this sagging cot to the wheelchair. It wasn't like the firm bed at the hospital. I had to call Pooky. I'd never needed her.

"Pook," I said.

"What?" her dark head appeared in the doorway.

"Give me a hand."

"What?"

"Just hold the handlebars of the wheelchair. My brakes are on but they could slip."

This was to become an image of us together which haunted me for years. It was dominant—the smaller Pook behind me, Indigo, pushing the chair up treacherous hills, holding the handlebars while I was transferred. This was the younger sister who always followed me. I must now be in her ken.

The hospital had granted a weekend pass to go home, yet no one had prepared me for life out of the hospital. How do I to handle the bathroom when I'd only used the bedpan for the past half year? How to handle strange transfers? By early Sunday morning shadows of the yellow-brick prison house again darkened my scene. It reminded me of our schoolhouse down South and I shuddered, covered my eyes to block its lightless gleam, a glare if ever there were one. My bicycle, what had been done with blue bicycle? I only thought to ask this later.

Hardly anything was retained from my past: all my clothing, books, keepsakes had been burned when the room was fumigated. We were in a new city, Manhattan. The green stucco house with the mock-castle details was left behind. The Tudor roof in sleepy little suburb, the upstairs *castle* room Mother swapped with me when I passed my twelfth birthday was gone. The half flight of stairs was gone, and the curved balance on which I dared myself to lean forward, catching myself on my fingers my last night walking – my body already heavy as lead, my spine on fire. I'd leaned forward to catch my body's weight on the thin fingers of both hands. Always a daredevil, I'd never posed myself a test like this. Now that too was like a photograph, half a year behind, fading.

"Pooks," I said, when she came back into the room, "What's it like at the Riverside School?"

Her school had switched with the move. Mother had now enrolled her in The Riverside School round the corner from us on West 73rd Street.

"Mother had to hold me down so I don't get blown away by the wind."

That was how I must have felt to her, blown away by the wind.

Although I knew our father was married to Nurse Anya, now our stepmother, in my child's mind I wanted my parents to get together again, now that I was paralyzed. It hurt that my parents separated at the door. It was a magical fusion, them driving that one hour home from the hospital. Despite my might and main of prayers, our father left to drive back to his pregnant wife, about to give birth to her first daughter while I turned in daughter-darkness toward my two women, Mother and Pooky, all of us being initiated in the dark baptism, and the even darker novitiate of polio—life after the sieges.

Poverty. Chastity. Obedience.

We were sufficiently poor to please the Lord. We had nothing but our furniture from Europe inherited from Grandmother, our polio insurance which had been used up in the five days during which it was thought I would have to enter the iron lung. That part of the pilgrimage, however, was spared me. We were chaste. There was no sex, no heartily longing alive and stirring except in our young girl imaginations, and Mother had an aversion to human touch. But were we obedient to these charcoal gray days, these twigs curled in a conspiracy with the secret life of dust?

It was winter. Outside our West Side Manhattan brownstone, filthy sparrows hopped in the courtyard. It was during these hours that I became aware a little ice could return. Became aware of how medieval winter is essentially, and most particularly in a stone city. The cold went thru my legs till five hours after bedtime I was still trying to get warm. It was then I dreamt myself in a medieval dungeon.

Pook? She was fast in sleep, her eight year old head held in the arms of Morpheus. Was Mother asleep down the hall or dealing with the thousand things on her mind, how to educate a paralyzed child at home? Was there any possibility of bringing me home, wresting me from the iron fist of that institution whose horrors were only revealed to her in flickers, certainly not by my tongue? We were not bowing down. We would rebel against what boxed us all in.

But these were only early stirrings.

An ash-feather of smoke climbed the city skyline of the West Side. My God, it was already morning and I still had not got warm. That death-click of another day beginning nudged me as it did at the state institution. Pook was sound asleep in her fire-red pajamas with coal-black bears on them. There was not a sigh from Mother, asleep in the living room, the foot of her bed under the piano. I was keen to navigate my waking alone.

No nurse barked, "Bedpan, Strongin!"

I knew the roll call of the children by heart, beginning with our one toddler, Joanne. No cart rattled with tin cups and thermometers breaking the silence. Branches the color of the crucified Christ shone. Although I am Jewish, I have some Catholic traits, my earliest bond being with a Catholic child, my bonding with those in cells, disciplined, celibate— those thin thorns of light. I must transfer and scrub my face and hands.

Last morning at home, only the second. I thought of calling Pooks but then, double-checking the locks on my wooden wheelchair, lifting first my left foot, then my right to place them square on foot pedals. Stouter in courage this morning than yesterday morning, I swung my self from bed to wheelchair taking all the weight on my right arm. A faint glimmer of dawn came thru the bath window's frosted pane.

I laughed at myself, despite myself. As I wheeled down the hall, willing to wake no one, I noticed a silence. I moved, obedient, pure of heart, toward the milk pale light which was coming thru our windowpane, magnetizing me, pulling me through to what was full, free and reminiscent a gypsy child.

Before I was paralyzed, I wanted a small forest. I would kneel at the shrine, I would make rows for worshippers but they would be invisible although I would assign a name to each one. Mrs. Olivia would be the wind. Mr. Scar would be fire. Weightless would be water, and Grit-Soul the earth. I got lots of grit-soul in my shoes my last year walking, lots of Mrs. Olivia washing over my limbs and always in my hair, I became Weightless over and over again. Mrs. Olivia exchanged roles with Mr. Scar. Strangely, they were all southern where the freak was the norm.

Androgynous, they slipped swiftly into each other's skin, though I thought little about gender then despite the pears developing to replace the raisins, the small knobs on my chest. I was twelve years and four months. It felt as though my future was behind me, as indeed I was folding away like bright linens my dozen years and several months walking. Dizzy I was standing at the helm of my uncle's boat which had docked in our small Westchester Suburb. I had never been on the water in a boat but now I felt like a torch of fire riding, riding the waves.

Only when I wakened in the middle of nights, climbing down my last five stairs, could I feel the column of fire my spine had become. I reached out my arms to Mrs. Olivia, but she had died in my arms. There was no more mirroring wind, she was a shadow, a heavy one. I looked up to the sky but she too was heavy and in my arms. Grit-Soul under my feet had betrayed me too turning into quicksilver. I did not hold her/him, but he/she sucked me in as though I was being sucked back into the birth canal, becoming smaller and smaller till I fit again into the womb of she who brought me to earth.

My parents' marriage had dissolved, now my four worshippers were dissolving. It was like beholding your own death. Perhaps like Kera feeling her marriage, becoming the child who died in her arms.

# My First Polio

*– First legs, then God. The story flashes forward to Pegeen. Here, she asks the crucial questions: Is she southern or northern? Is she Catholic or Jewish? It is resolved in terms of her spirituality by her pressing the Star of David into her sternum forever and by feeling this is a forecast of curtains in her life, as it would have been for Pegeen had the bomb dropped overhead, the plane cut its motors.*

## My First Polio

How could a mother name her child after a polished Siberian stone, *Lapis-Lazuli*, the densest, most opaque and saturated blue? To live up to my name, I had to reach the sky. Alias Indigo, a bolt of cloth dyed that peculiar blue-violet of early American Indigo. Given a heaven, we imagine it to be blue. I was taken aback when someone once told me to live up to my face. It was the name I could not fulfill. Either I must reach up, or like indigo cloth, the famous strong homespun fabric, shelter and clothe the young, the wounded around me. Rachel, my kid-sister, was simply Rach.

"Lynn, we are all measured, cut to wear the cloth we are given." Mother spoke in measured terms, like a solemn music, firm, but not severe.

Once I met a nun who said, "Before you had legs. Now you have God. You are selected for Daughterhood, a servant of the Eternal."

*Bird Ambulance* is overdue, I reminded myself (while she spoke, both of us shadowed by leaves which danced over us like mirror-reflections). Must return it Monday or will have a fine.

Up North, dawn glazing to pewter, or down South, daybreak bruising into saffron. I should have known when the angel was knocked off our mantle, her right wing severed from her body, that it was to prophesize our lives. I caught her reflection in the mantle mirror the split-second she broke. There was a bead of *Lapis Lazuli* from Siberia for each of her eyes.

Home was wherever Rachel, Mother and I were together. My mother had sung all night the night I was born, in New York City, at the end of the dirty thirties. She herself had been born in Boston, a daughter of New England which revolves wholly around water, a water star radiating in many directions like a pin-wheel round its pin, a carousel round its music, its horses whirling, and its glistening brass ring.

I cut my teeth on Mozart and Chopin etudes which she practiced late at night, in those loneliest days of her life when she no longer was in love with her husband and was trying to figure out how to divorce, while her father, Rosenblum, the brilliant research chemist who bore the same name as our father, Israel, was still alive. Her father, the brilliant immigrant from Romania, research chemist even then had won the family's fortune and had predicted the marriage would come to grief. Rosenblum had a cutting edge to his tongue and my father avowed was the most brilliant man he had ever met. My grandfather — I remembered mainly his stunning silence and his velvet gardens, a home with leaded glass panes, diamonds, the kind of glass that wrinkles.

The marriage did end in ruin. The angel's wing was shattered, that with which she would have flown; her hand severed, that with which she could have written. Yet the recording angel in me was wakened.

Down South, the sky at times was parchment, was magnolia-fine, bone-ivory or like Irish lace. Up North, the sky was a shell, out of Pieter Brueghel the elder(to me, the leader), that teal frost of a lower heaven which interchanged the word *heaven* for *winter*.

"You were born to be torn in half," said Mother.

Through all the moves, the distances, the trauma of the past fifty years we have been singing back and forth to each other, three women, the *Three Graces* we were called from the mid-forties on. Wherever we were, the compass pointed home, whether Mother set us up for one week in a Memphis hotel room, or we sunk our stakes into another Army post on another godforsaken outpost of New York, the city which intersects my life.

Overflowing with energy, I'd thwack sign posts, when I was four and five, leaving them resonating, their pipe ringing until I was out of earshot. These were lonely rig towns, mining and mill towns. Bricked-in linen mills began to haunt my dreams — the boarded-up windows, nailed against the red, thread-thin color, the heavenly hue, of old brick which I was to perceive later in seventeenth century Dutch artists. Those were our rooms! Their gloom was ours — their penetrating shafts of light, their mirrors, their quiet heartbreak which nonetheless spilled over young girls and women making lace, reading a letter, intense absorption: that was what we had as adolescent girls.

"The graveyard is full of irreplaceable poets, Indigo," Mother said. "Write."

These patterns of choir were set up from the cradle. Mother played *Ravel* at night on the old black upright piano in the hallway. Playing, she tells me I would come down and play the exact same music in morning.

This was a constant, like *The Settlement Cookbook* with its happy kids trailing a mother to the bake oven on the yellowed cover that was part of our lives. It stood in every kitchen we ever had, "The way to a man's heart is through his stomach," it said.

The *Cheerful Cherub* came out in the newspaper every morning during the war urging Americans to show the British trait of a stiff upper lip. Mother turned to us, me especially when I looked at war headlines.

"What can one do? You can't leave town." Then she put her arms around me and said, "C'mon, Lapis, c'mon, Indigo."

I'd smile.

I was the only one with green eyes in the family. Neither lapis nor indigo but I wanted them to be. I coveted the eyes of angel like those of almost all our dolls. Non-brown, that's what my eyes were. Mother called me a dirty blonde, a natural blonde.

Rachel would look up to me in those early times, and say, "Keep good care of me, Lynn."

The cathedral-radios of our early girlhood dignify the background, playing, playing It amazed my mother, my playing on the piano precisely what she had played the night before, same key, same notes. My ear had recorded it, memorized the melodies. It assuaged my pain, helped mend my sadness, like lace, over our father being gone. The war.

I have vignettes of my father. He did put in cameo appearances during the war when he was on leave.

*Baruch Atov Adonoi*, the gentle, slightly gravelly voice would say. He took me to the Russian Tea Room right beside Carnegie Hall. The war had been over only a year. In the air, euphoria. In this historic tearoom, with its dark burnished wood, its buzz of activity from musicians who came in before and after concerts, there was a custom of presenting the prettiest girl of the day with a rose.

That day, a tall mustachioed gentleman came over to me, "For you," he said extending his hand with a pale pink rose.

"Me?" I held it. I smiled all the way on the drive home — my rose cheeks, my dirty blonde hair, my grin. What would mother say?

She'd say, "It wants water," and plunk it in a mayonnaise jar filled with water on our oilcloth kitchen table.

Looking at Mother one evening, I noticed what a beautiful breastbone she had. Sternum she told me it was called.

"Remember that, Indigo."

It was near the heart. It was the body's most vulnerable spot, where pain was lodged.

Julys and Augusts during the nineteen-forties polio epidemics raged, whole families of children carried out on stretchers into ambulances with it. The dread of catching the virus ignited parents until panic spread, wildfire. Sidewalks buckled and rippled like a washboard. You could see the heat shimmering off cement and tarmac. You could pop tar-bubbles with your toe and chew them. Still your parents would not let you go to a public swimming pool, a movie, even a grocery store to buy nickel candy. You might get paralyzed like Hillary. That meant wearing your leg in a brace, not being able to run like the other children, to climb trees, hike ever again.

In winter, ponds in New York and up in New Hampshire and Maine froze silvery cobalt. You could almost touch the frost, ice particles hitting air like your breath. We lived in upstate New York, 1945, on a chicken farm. The glacial Northern skies under which we lived when the war ended were reflective of the pale bayou southern skies. The songs of comfort about Jesus which our black nannies sang to us up North when we couldn't sleep reflected the spirituals we had heard chain gangs of prisoners sing down South.

We were Jewish, but non-observant. It became crystal-clear to me that I had formed some mystical religion of my own.

Some voice said to me: "When you pass through the flames you will not burn. When the waters circle you, you will not drown."

# Going to the Bayou: Rockets Overhead

– Behind something as simple as a curtain can be a misunderstanding between family or friends, or layers of time, geographies, moments of war, holiday, peace or pain and fear. Pegeen and Indigo have much in common so each can project onto the other characters and scenes from the past, clouding and informing the present. When one moves from North to South, from continent to continent, everything one has lived through comes along.

## Curtains

People dug deep inside themselves for humor during the war.

"When the Germans sent remote-controlled bombs, if they stopped over our heads, we knew it was curtains."

Terrifying it must have been, to shut your eyes to the explosion of the world crashing like so much glass about you. More terrifying to look up into a sky of fire, at age nine, as Pegeen must have done many times.

Many times she has looked for help for her vision, our mother, eighty-five, with macular degeneration and then a cataract milking her better eye. She has looked for reading aids, looked into machines. It must feel to her as though it is curtains.

The Texas night is favored with rain, a soft grey veil, a lace of rain falling.

Legally blind, up to one hundred pounds, from ninety-five, she has finally made the decision to the move to the bayou. She is a survivor, like Pegeen. I see a spiritual courage in her, like Pegeen. She remembers those water bodies from her youth in the South, the marshy offshoots of a river that were man-made to keep a Texas town from flooding when it rained. As her daughter, I too remembered those pale water bodies that stood, down South, in the infancy of my imaginations.

Then, I superimpose upon our mother, Pegeen. We each live in our ironic bodies, parts of them paralyzed, heavy. Sometimes, what I imagine must be her pain digs into me like a hook.

Then—superimposed upon that is the child, cool, classical, the Catholic child who knew when remote-controlled German bombers stopped right above their heads, it was curtains.

She hurt her neck last week doing some typing for me. The florist stuttered when I ordered larkspur for Pegeen over the phone. I'd noticed she had a stutter, would sometimes try agonizing seconds to get a consonant out (when I was in the flower shop) only to blurt it out in an explosion which embarrassed her, I could tell. So now, when there was dead silence over the phone, I prayed.

"Sorry about this—" she finally got out, with great grace, "Sometimes I stutter over the phone."

Pegeen couldn't read because she couldn't hold her head that long in one position. I wondered whether to offer her the loan of my neck brace—it was the soft kind—but then reminded myself this was the child cool in the sight of the bombs. I didn't want to invade her privacy.

People reached deep inside themselves for courage during the bombs.

Sunday, yesterday, walking into the village with Simone, I'd made up my mind to look up—for the very first time—to Pegeen's window to see the vase she said she'd stuck in it for passersby the share her flowers. I pictured Mother, frail, gracious and graceful, engineering a slender birch bark canoe, a dream-canoe, thru the bayous of south Texas where she'd landed. I saw her maneuvering her escape from the cage of old age, starvation, both physical and spiritual, into the Bayou, a pleasant mansion where she'd have a penthouse apartment.

Not unlike Pegeen, who spoke little to me, if at all, of the pain in her left side. She simply said when the broom leapt out of the closet and whacked her, it would be her left side.

She said, "It gives me compassion I don't live in constant pain," and told me more of the Blitz over the phone.

By evening, even holding the phone causes anguish. "I was getting close to tears last night," she laughed. "Mind if I use the speaker phone? Now, what was the number of that Chinese order-in?"

While I take Simone out for a celebration-sushi—a job we've completed this afternoon—Pegeen orders in. First time in her life. Lemon chicken, I learn later when I ask her what she had, and shrimp with vegetable.

"You can have the rest for dinner tonight."

"No, that's lunch. Got rice for dinner."

## Bayou City

"Didn't you know this is Bayou City?" she asks in clipped New England tones.

"No. I've never been to Houston."

"Well, don't come."

"It's called this because when flashfloods come the city would be drowned, if they hadn't dug these bayous, totally submerged, which wouldn't be a bad thing."

Looking up is as refreshing as looking at fresh snow. Pegeen never takes me for prisoner. It is the forties again. I feel the emotional bond we felt during that time. I see the brown drapes drawn each evening, the circle of candlelight describing our home.

But where Pegeen was a child—it was curtains. Why is there a link between the Irish and those from the South?

Then, when I became a woman it, too, was terrible often, as if it were curtains. My husband came home several times in some one else's clothing. I tried to keep violence from the children. One mornin' I remember after I was awake all night, when they traipsed in at six a.m..

I simply said, "Now Kathleen, you're eldest. Pour a bowl of Cornflakes for you and Nick, then pour some milk in."

They were awfully good at two and four, good together, good for each other.

This morning, wakin' to violence again, I went into the lobby only to discover our problem tenant had slashed the two palms and poured oil in them. I called the police. A lovely policewoman came, she saw me hobbled with this lame left arm and now stiff neck, so when I noticed her limp I asked why—she was so young—an accident.

My marriage was totally loveless. My only one.

It was the sense that one's own flesh was being slashed that cut when the palms in the hallway were damaged. It was the sense she was saving her own skin and bones, the old woman, appropriately, respectfully wrapping them in the calmer cooler air of the asylum which was The Bayou Mansion. It is the feeling I hold more caringly, the skin around my body, my husk, by respecting the beliefs of my ancestors, by moving in ways that are considerate and tender towards Pegeen.

This is the year's overcoat, the end of my sixtieth year. Simone is down the hall laundering the pillows, feathers and all.

It will be a week, before the drinking tenant gets out— above her breathing, below her breathing. Only a week now to wait. Pegeen both leans on and feels the pressure of the public world. She is after all, a pensioner, an ex-Brit. She had the portrait of Queen Elizabeth hanging in her dining room in the old house on Apple Orchard Road before she lost everything. She phones the newspaper for the definition of a word, the municipality for advice on a lease, the police force for vandalism toward two plants in her hallway. She has a sense of public presence and personal heartbreak at all times.

The further I get from St. Valentine's eve, the worse I feel about the way Simone and Pegeen treated each other. I should have known they'd darken and block up their hearts to each other. I should have known they'd take refuge in discussions of this ministry and that ministry and the fiscal year.

Anxious over Pegeen, I phone one more time this evening.

There she is, a Catholic girl in a convent, the Jewish star under her uniform, pressing so hard on her breast it caves her shape in.

"I've taken a turn for the worse, and the weather's gloom itself again. I'm goin' to bed early—very soon."

There are many girls with ugly shoes. But only one who hides her feet behind flowerpots when her picture is taken, only one who lives to write impassioned articles to the papers in whatever province she dwells, urging social action be taken—for the poor, the disabled, the battered women.

It is a wine dark evening ten days after Valentine's Day.

Only one old woman, eighty-five, legally blind, is moving to The

Bayou Mansion, steering her small skiff of life meticulously to the end—my mother, mine.

I look up to the sky. Am I southern or am I northern? That is a question I ask often and turn like the taste of honeysuckle on my tongue. I am both, is the answer that comes to my tongue. Am I Catholic or Jewish? Do I wear a crucifix or star? I tried to dig up a Catholic girl's crucifix which fell off her, wearing her organdy white, the day of first communion, but though I clawed like a small wild red fox, nothing came to my hands. I am Jewish forever, the Star of David pressed into my sternum. Am turning in early too tonight. It is curtains...

February 21, 2000

# Murder Ball:
## Butcher's Wife and Carnation

– A tale is about being in the pews, young Jewish girls ironically, and southern girls more naturally being used to the sight of blood before their periods. It talks about the murderous aspects of struggling against a mother who called her child "Little Hitler," a Jewish child, and the struggles to overcome the effects of polio. It also flipsides the southern belle and analyizes the mother, Marcelle, whose beauty was equaled by her cruelty. The primary focus of the story is the lapis lazuli (from which Indigo derives her nickname) a gift mother Marcelle promises but never gives. Bitterness is the emotion at the core of this story. So goes childhood's celebration. Northern born. Southern raised. Indigo keeps losing and finding herself in this one, a microcosm of the book about growing up in the forties and fifties when the earth in Europe was still smoldering.

## Killa Ball

Don't move that dial. Glen Miller's Big Band is rocking the room with sweet sound waves, the brown room. Roll back the carpets. It is Florida, 1947. They're putting another platter on. These are the raw years of our girlhood, radio years rolling in, it is the 40's. Our hired help is reading *Dick Tracy* and playing soaps in the kitchen while Mother plays WQXR, New York's classical music station. Music becomes the supreme metaphor for stepping up to the plate.

"Don't loll about girls," she'd rouse us. "It's high time you got up out of the pews and danced in the aisles!"

Of course, we didn't go to church. We were Jewish children, but in the South spirituals ruled along with the Baptist Church.

When I was at sixes and sevens, Marcelle would frown and command, "Ok. Diogenes, go into the bath tub and have a think."

Never mind that our tub was a zinc, iron claw-footed one out of the Victorian age, in the top bath of an old farmhouse.

Southern girls should be used to the sight of blood—even before their periods, and used to the word murder.

When were we ever in the pews, young Jewish girls?

Sabbath morning, I wake sad and get this breathing machine into motion thinking of the final tip of the wave of my childhood, being taken to The Center of Anxiety and Depression at age 51.

"She looks young for her age," the psychiatrist wrote in the report which I hid from Marcelle. Gamine, yet the god of small things, beating his/her head against the wall—I was always younger having not lived in many ways. On the first floor of Meany Towers Hotel (its real name...like Dr. Pain when we were kids) was a breakfast joint, *The Cheerful Little Café*. Pink tee shirts were sold with this name on them.

The last I saw Simone was when I took a two-week break with Marcelle, a last-ditch effort to get well enough to come home, visions of the psychiatric ward I'd been in half a day still blazing in my mind, visions of Hell's Kitchen. Well, the moment Simone recedes and Marcelle enlarges. Simone is wearing The Cheerful Little Café pink tee shirt with the menu printed on it. A taunt if ever there was one.

Like the name Lulene. But this is to jump the gun. The murder ball set into motion with my part probably like a watch ticking. Where was my safe harbor? The asylum? The loft?

Radial Flyers and radios reigned king over other props of childhood. I loved hardware stores and shoe stores. The smell of rubber and steel in the first, the scent of leather and in the second. I loved looking thru the small Floorsheim x-ray thing-a-ma-jig and seeing my toe bones dance in red. I thought of our friend who grew up on the prairies and loved to squelch thru mud after snow run off.

"I packed my Wellington boots with bread bags."

How did our father know to get each kid in the children's hospital where I lived a radio? How was he to know what it would mean to me to wheel out at dusk—the Irish hour—and mail a handful of letters, feeling the cold, the snow on my cheeks after months of the ward, and drop the letter in the slot at the corner mailbox, then hear the metal mouth clang and bang. A boy during the Depression, he could find his way to a discount of anything. Later that year, my first Christmas in a wheelchair, it was to be a tiny diamond ring, small as it was, still loose on my finger, so thin was I. He found a discount-diamond dealer somewhere in his home-borough Brooklyn.

My taxi-driver to the Manhattan School of Music up in Harlem, Jo Abramovitch, once said to me that Mother Marcelle had the patience of a saint. He'd watched over and over our routine getting in and of Checker's cabs with jump seats, first parking long wooden crutches under the seats on the floor, then unlocking my knee in the long-leg brace, then sitting down.

"Don't ever do anything to hurt her," he told me.

Yet this petite French-looking woman was the one who accused me of looking like a murderer on the cover of one of my books. And how can I deny she called me *Little Hitler* at age five?

She affected Rachel and me wildly. Radio music played most of the day, while she was ironing, stewing tomatoes, mending. She always stuck out her tongue a bit when she sewed, concentrating, risky, chancy. She hated housekeeping and shoved the vac as though using it to stab the furniture legs to death. There was murder in her look.

"No complaint with the choir," she'd say when I sang a long pop tune, "Only the soloist."

I stuck out my tongue. She never *crushed* Chel and me into shape like Fundamentalist parents. Chel and I curled like question marks on the floor and she let us swoon to the old dance tunes. My friend Tomo writes me that my early life was rich. He lost his mother twice in one year; once to adoption with an aunt, the second time final, to cancer. He feels unparented. His gaze closely focused inwards, or down into silent caves of dreamy thought. There are dangers in this, the black jaws of the wolf—depression.

Tomo says he might not have *loved* but would have loved to know Marcelle. So how did I learn the redemption and self-acceptance requisite for poetry thru this mother of mine? Maybe we were all playing a form of Murder Ball?

"It hurts to see too much," said our father. Yet we all three did, each in her own fashion. I read about Murder Ball, and look at album photos of the three of us. The article refers to a game known by names such as murder ball, death ball, blood ball, murder-the-man-with-the ball, mugby, kill-the-carrier, and kill-the-man (also accented as *killa* man), or objectionably, smear-the-queer.

"Where's the struggle in your life?" Marcelle asked me when I turned fifty. "Get a job. You're a fifty-year-old vegetable."

"Rough it. Get over it," is Chel's take on losing my legs. "It happened a long time ago."

So did World War II with its crater-shells on Warner Pathe Newsreels. So did the South, whose bomb ridden terrain still haunts my dreams and burns them open like a slow dance, a sweet song, a magnolia blossom.

Yesterday a truck ran over a child in our town—a six year old, fighting for his life. The truck was making a right turn. The rear tires of the semi pinned the boy.

It triggered memories of Marcelle saying to me, "I hope the first truck you meet runs you over!"

What could she have been thinking? I saw the truck that had crushed a child's limbs on a newsreel. Marc would have recoiled. Yet I left for school many mornings with those words ringing in my ear. *Marc* was the name she signed her paintings with. *Elle* the French for she, the name of a woman's magazine. She was seductive, flirtatious, yet I was in her hands in my moment of deepest need.

"Call the doctor!" I cried the night I came down with polio.

"I'll wait till morning," she said, "You'll wake the neighbors with your raving."

She banged the wooden bedroom window down cutting off our air supply. I looked out the window that July 1, 1951 and knew I was alone forever. The poor have no voice, the child has no voice. I knew it like Father knowing about the radios. Fast heart, slow life— it wasn't a good fit. Hope was no easy ticket.

Rapture music ran thru my mind, on my tongue.

"I had allowed my anger toward you to get out of hand," Marcelle said later that summer.

Another clip I pull out of the film case was the silver nitrate a physician poured into Chel's wound when a dog in our elevator bit Rachel's hand and the physician in the building had to flood it with silver nitrate cauterizing the open wound. The dog was tested for rabies and put down despite the fact the test came back negative. To celebrate childhood despite all this was the challenge.

"This kid just got bitten by a dog," Mother said bringing Rachel in with her bandaged bloody hand. She looked like a Civil War casualty. "The mutt drove his teeth right in, the bitch!"

They'd stepped into the elevator at 320 West End and this had happened. Would Chel ever play the fiddle again? She was thirteen.

I put the magnifying glass over a black and white after one of our battles, Mother Marcelle's and mine. What could have led a child and woman to push a dining room table up against the kitchen door? I did it to block it, then shimmied across the table on my belly, or scuttled under the table. We were two children engaged in battle to the death.

"Who do you think you are?" she'd shout. Our shouting matches seemed to last for hours although in reality they must have taken about five or six minutes.

"Diagheliv? Choreographing a ballet?"

I went over the top for her. I loved her wildly. I bought her *The Ladies Home Journal* when she was sick in bed. At all times and in grave weather, for her I did my personal best.

Mr. Radio had static most of the time but Mr. Tunes had the last word, we adored him.

A loud minority, I thought of the small maps the silver nitrate scored in my sister's hand, the polio which burned out the messages exiting my spine to my limbs.

Once our mother slapped our father in the face. He'd scolded the baby Chel when he came home to discover she had soiled her crib. He walked round and round the block to avoid hitting her back. Revelation wheel. Music, I just loved it body and soul.


*Body Memory*

Flipside *Elle* and do you find her diametric opposite? The seducer becomes the slayer? The other day I saw the butcher's wife, Dale, sitting on the bus holding a single, tired carnation which bobbed up and down. Carnations always make me think of funerals and Mother's Day.

"Your birthday?" I asked.

"No. It's banker-appreciation day," she sniffed, "this puny thing."

It was soiled-looking like those carnations we made of toilet paper in first grade.

"It's an insult. They should give us a bouquet for all the banking."

Life speaks in these strange, subliminal conjunctions— butcher's wife and carnation, made me think of the birthday when Marcelle promised me a lapis lazuli ring and threw bras at my head instead of blue stone.

When I isolate one afternoon walking, it is not a sunny day, light illuminating everything like perfectly exposed film, blue clarity, the kind when one thinks one's gone to heaven and died. It is the Irish hour, twilight again.

Fast backward fifty-five years.

I have just finished modern dance class in an old church in Pelham with its scarred, butterscotch chalk-marked stage floor. I study with the Steffi Nassen dance group. I have made the widest leap of all the girls across the chalk marked floor. It's a matter of putting the most weight on my right foot and springing. Here I come, soaring! That night exquisitely in tune with my eleven-year-old body, I dream I go to my first ball. It is *un ballo* in *maschera*. I am harlequin in diamonds and ear-high, ruffed collar, cross-gartered stockings. We are all dancing, girls and lads of in our early teens with Elizabethan grace, sophisticated though just departing childhood, the age of Juliet. All of a sudden there is a loud sound, as of an explosion. The masked ball is turning into murder ball for there are cries outside and when we go out there is a body of a young girl slain and me? I lift her in my arms. I wake up wet, covered with feathers.

Outside the dance class clusters a gaggle of pre-teen suburbia groupies (like nerves and ganglia.) I understand that what you've lost forever can come to have a life of its own. Flying red foxes in the new moon, my foxfire red hair brushed back, green eyes burning.

One has a body-memory. My four-year-old body was trained in World War II. It was subliminal. At that time, 1944, children on the battlefront at home learned a body-discipline as great for their size as that men mustered at the European front. Girls too chose as their favorite game making hankie-parachutes for little rubber soldiers. They crash-landed in our yard all the time.

I no longer say 'honeychile' like in the South. I remember the word with yearning. Yes, all one has lost has a life of its own. Marcelle reared me to hear music that "shakes that thing," to raise the rafters. Yet Rachel and I were born with an inherent melancholy strain. We sang our *niggun* more often than belting out spirituals to stepping high to a brass band— that sad, bad mood I'm in, that angel who lodges like a splinter beneath the skin, pole-to-pole, lightning charges. We need an electrical storm.

Picture fire's come and gone. Radio music is silent. They're not in the pews but they're not in the aisles either, dancing.

I left that suburban dance class and saw fiery winter trees graphed upon skyline like nerves branching in a spine. Are good relationships not built on sacrifice and innocence? A combination of the two? Mother's psychologist kept a white barn owl, screened off, the waiting room. It scared me, the owl. The love of the past, the lifelong burden of unrequited love weighs Marcelle down. This will never pass. One cannot apply the Biblical epithet. *This too will pass.* Everything Marcelle said was evocative, pulling at my heart with the hope of fulfillment, the meaning of home fractured, the unending pull of the past.

I wore my pinafore no longer.

Dance roared up like torch fire, like red hair.

If we'd not been so explosive inside all day, would we have caused that gasoline can (shoe polish) to explode that evening? It happened before I could say Jack Robinson. I was in the kitchen alone polishing my shoes for the seventh grade prom. We had some Esquire Shoe Polish. It was hard as a rock despite the evening through blue screens swimming with heat and humidity. Objects stood in light, airbrushed. (My friend Luella called it Humility.) *Honeychile* (I kept whispering to myself under my breath) *You can do it, you can.* It came upon me that if I heated the polish, it would soften so I scooped a few tablespoons full into the lower half of the double boiler. Iridescent blue flies were humming. Chel was at a child's house down the street.

What was driving me was inherent rebellion against Marc *elle*. I wanted to do things on my own. I looked at my shoes close up. They were the latest style moccasin. I wanted them to be mirrors I could catch my face in. Marcelle was stacking paintings in the basement below, I could hear her shuffling, organizing her small bottles of linseed oil and turpentine. Before I could say Jack Robinson there was a fountain of flame streaming toward the yellow kitchen ceiling from on the lit blue gas jet. I screamed. Mother bounded upstairs, I'm sure two steps at a time. By then flame had latched onto my shirttails, my jeans. By the time Mother arrived the pot was roaring like a torch. She cut off the gas, threw me on the floor and wrapped an area carpet around me. The scorched dress fell off in a film, and miraculously as she unwound me from the caul of the rug—I was unburned.

"What the Hell came over you? You thought you could melt shoe-polish? Can't you read—Highly Flammable? You could be scarred, for life. Let me look at your face."

She drew my chin to her face. I hated this. She looked quite a while.

"Not too bad. You'll turn into a looker one of these days and then we'll have a peck of new troubles on our hands like hounds."

She checked corners for sparks, beating them with a frayed kitchen towel. She took the old boiling pot and shoved it in the garbage, sat down, packing a cigarette hard, lighting up. She wore one of those checked 1940's bandanas round her hair which housewives wore. (We girls ate face cream in those days most likely for the lanolin.)

"Indigo," she inhaled and blew out slowly. "We're coming to a fork in the road. You're on the brink of puberty."

I knew about becoming a woman though I hadn't stained my panties yet. I couldn't wait to. Earlier that autumn, in fifth grade, we'd received a robin's-egg blue pamphlet *Very Personally Yours* with a woman's hand holding an invitation in script. It looked like an invitation to a ball. The boys had been told to go to the gym, the girls to the auditorium to be shown a twenty-minute film on how the ovaries mature and produce an egg each month which travels down the fallopian tubes. It was called menstruation. I didn't get my period until later that year, after polio, a prayer granted.

"Daddy," I phoned his office, "I'm a woman!" I said and hung up.

I thought she'd give me quite a rounding that night of the shoe-polish exploding. She spoke, instead, of the fork in the road.

"I saw the death bird in the yard last evening," I told her, "a boot-black raven. He looked polished."

"Don't use that word, Indigo!" she snapped at me.

She listened and looked out the window. This paltry plot of dirt in South New Rochelle, did she too feel it had shrunk and that we had outgrown our lives? We might as well have been back in the South, on some bayou, Spanish moss hanging like Rapunzel's hair made of gray-green dust. We might have been in a sad sinkhole of big-eyed Junkies.

"Blow smoke rings," I told her.

Into the slow, dull pewter evening, milk rings came, one after another like soap bubbles from a pipe.

"Wax is flammable," she calmed down. "Shoe-polish is wax," she paused, "Caution!" She lifted the can, "It's all written here alongside the skull and crossbones." She thrust the tin into the bin.

My head was spinning. I heard glass bottles shatter on the concrete drive at a neighbor's. I saw the tiny grey-mesh grids on the torn kitchen screen door. Blue. A fly buzzed, stumbled, I could see the hairs on its legs, it alighted a moment on a glass of water. By now, the Preservation Band, rag time, and resurrection music were all requiems playing in my head— five radio stations at once.

But our kitchen radio, the old battered Philco was cut off. My ears were ringing. I felt I was in a cart being pulled by butterflies.

"Can I have a puff?"

She handed me the cigarette. A half-smile made her look like a sinner. Chug-a-lug. My heart was thudding. I'd taken off my charred clothing and wrapped an old bath towel around me. I drew too deeply in, a wave of nausea swept over me.

The true vertigo and nausea came from knowing it was my twelfth summer and nothing was planned. I hated the parades, the clowns, the fake cheer. There was a hysteria to it all. I wanted to be called *Honeychile*.

After a window of time, Marcelle rose, one hand to her knee, her cigarette in the other.

"Tomorrow's the fair, not that I give a damn about it, but I'd best get ironing." She looked at me from the toes up as though measuring me. Our eyes locked. "You get off chores this evening. You can read in the yard or go climb trees, whatever you want this evening."

The phone rang loudly, hopped in its heavy black cradle. Chel was ready to be walked home. When Mother got her in the door, Chel said, "Lookee what I found."

She'd found a robin's egg and was smiling. Marcelle looked as if she wanted to go to the *Roxie Cinegogue*. "Some Jew!" she'd say, getting a kick out of the pun with synagogue.

There was absolutely nothing I wanted to do. I climbed the stairs, slid into my other jeans and a checked shirt. I left the tails dangling the way I liked. It wouldn't be long before the polio-bird would descend and lift us in its claws like the stork bringing a baby in Oslo, Norway. I strayed into the back yard. I saw the small typing table Marcelle had set out there for me, a pile of yellow foolscap and a freshly sharpened #1 pencil. The table slanted.

"Remember, Indigo, this is the summer." Marcelle came out, gave me her full and undivided attention, "You become a writer, *Honeychile*."

The wind might have wished to become a cart. I wished to become a boy climbing the flag pole, the crow's nest on a ship, better yet to be balancing a beam, climbing house frames whistling. Yeah! I wished to become a white paper crane folded exquisitely and let sail.

Later going into the bath, I told Mother, "I'm like Diogenes. I'm going to think in the tub."

"Watch out that you don't wind up in the drink," she laughed after me.

I could not sleep for a long time that night. The explosion that occurred in our lino'd kitchen was nothing to the explosion which occurred in my dream. It blew the three of us sky high, including a strange white stork. When we came down each of us was disintegrating, the white feathers whirled through air like a pearl floating in oil covering our bodies as we hit the ground. Before we hit the ground I woke. Tomo, I was falling into your deep cave of dream.

I reached for the glass of water beside my bed with the bubbles rising as if a diver were diving, but tonight I'd forgotten. Waking, I remembered Jeannine, a girl in third grade who'd been burned by dashing through a heap of autumn leaves. Whew! She had *keloid* scars all over her face where the flame bit, corduroy scars for life. I felt my smooth skin like a jacket, an envelope, as I went to bed that night, felt the budding knobs on my chest like little pulls to a child's dresser.

Earlier tonight, all thoughts of murder-ball ceased when no wind blew. Picture fired come and gone. Nobody would boss me or toss me around.

I keep losing and finding what I want to say about being let out of that dance class outside New Rochelle. Mother had given Chel a beach ball at dance class while all the other little girls got flowers. The butcher's wife rode the bus. One thinks, butchers' wife and carving knife. Those hands that thousands of times sliced meat now holding a flower, a single carnation, making me remember funerals and Mother's Day, bobbing up and down as the bus rolls. Tatty, it resembles the toilet paper cars we made in first grade for our mothers on Mother's Day back when we wore white anklets and chocolate-box ribbons in our hair, back in the war-cloud slate-grey 40's, and if we were lucky brought home a gold star for a win in the spelling bee.

"Pop!" went the little explosion under the gas.

Blur, I went into sleep, but surfaced. Right now.

I longed for sleep that night the way a soldier yearns for women and cigarettes, silk stockings, chocolate.

Fire pictures blown out, I am Diaghelev choreographing his most elegant ballet, wearing a silk shirtwaist which billows like sails in the wind. I am the youth who climbs the mast and has the God's eye view of everything— maps, town streets like little grids of letters in the printer's tray, with sun, melting like hot lead in the old Morgenthaler brought over on the ship from Germany crossing from Europe to the shores of the new world on the stormy autumn Atlantic ocean.

*Even the wind wishes*

    *to become a cart*

    *pulled by butterflies.*

        (Adonis, trans. from the Arabic)

So goes Childhood's Celebration. Certificate. Northern born. Southern raised. Wished to become a cart pulled by butterflies, but was a cart of iron with horses at the head.

# Acting Ugly:
## Spin the Bottle Kiss Me

*for* Effie Medford, M.D.

*– The narrative here revolves around the Southern phobia against acting ugly. Indigo recalls the children's game Spin the Bottle Kiss Me, a taunt here as well as the stricture against pulling out hair bows in church. Indigo's first girl cousin Nyrene appears here. Nyrene's mother puts her to sleep in metal curlers, an example of how she differs from tomboy Indigo whose dance card would never be darkly penciled or inked at a ball. Alissa, the young Canadian homemaker spends more time with Indigo than her lover.*

## Acting Ugly: Spin the Bottle Kiss Me

Down South when a girl pulled a big hair bow out of her hair in church, she was dubbed as acting ugly.

Mother's way of managing me was by saying, "I knew a girl who. . ."

She knew dozens of girls who had come to grief by doing just what I was doing when naughty.

"I knew a girl who played with matches and burned her nose to her face so it was flattened."

She knew more girls than any other mother I'd met. When I was nine years old during the divorce, a change was *indicated*. So Mother sent me to her sister, Aunt Roper, with Tisanne, my maternal grandmother as escort.

We boarded the train in Grand Central and rode all the way to Ohio where Grandmother deposited me to spend two weeks with my aunt, learn to shoot straight, shoot fancy.

I could look a kid in the eye and say, "Spin the bottle. Kiss me."

The world would be mirrored in that blue-white glass of the Coke bottle, just perfect one second, then begin to spin. I too would begin to spin. Ohio, summer 1948, with the *Sohio* gas signs all up and down the roads, ribboning over the improbably green countryside of the Ohio River Valley.

Ohio featured Standard Oil of Ohio and the Mason-Dixon line. In red neon tubing, *Open* signs hung on the Midwest night or *Sohio*. This state covers the ground of the living South and the historic North. Only one thing rose in relief against the boredom of Aunt Roper and Uncle Lem — the Carnovan Clock Castle where they'd taken me at age seven and which perpetually lived in my imagination. I learned there're all kinds of work in this world. The work of imagination might be the hardest of all.

The problem is that the honey attracts the bee. We have complementary parts. When the bottle stopped at me, I often got a gangly boy with a mouth full of metal.

"Hell and tarnation," I thought.

Our lives were so interlocked that there was no breathing space. Interaction and elegance like a dance characterized home relations. I noted that Mother Marcelle slipped Mr. McQue, my tatty old bear, in my valise, at the last moment. My aunt and uncle were flat-footed pragmatic, money-saving Republicans. They might as well not be Jewish. They had in fact become Unitarians.

They acted *picayune* and were often *chagrined* with me, although they wouldn't know these southernisms. My aunt put her daughter's shoulder-length, blond sausage-curls in wire curlers at night and dressed her mainly in party pink even when there was no party.

"I won't wear clothes the color of a cupcake," I told Mother.

"You don't have to but you must listen to the voice of reason," she admonished. This was a phrase which I thought belonged primarily to our father, the Army psychologist-major.

"You're too much for me to handle right now. That's why you're taking a train ride with Grandmother Tisanne."

I could feel that I'd been all wound up like a clock. Nyrene was a towhead, a platinum.

"What color would you call my hair?" I asked Mother. "You're a typical dirty blond."

I'd tow the line but— "I won't like it," I turned on my heel and warned her.

At age nine, I felt like an illness in the blood of a nuclear post-war family comprised of paper dolls wearing paper clothing.

"Mind your P's and Q's, Indigo," she said knowing I'd neither be a bed of roses nor a thorn bush.

It was generally thought, when Nyrene and I were paired, that she was a little lady and I was a hoyden. The patch had recently come off my right eye so I looked less hostile than when my crossed-eyes were being corrected. I'd begun to ride the city bus to school in New Rochelle and could look into picture windows and perceive that they neither looked out nor in on any picture. I was registering in my backbone the horror of the post-war boy and girl, husband and wife family. Ours was off-kilter, outside the pale— Marcelle, Chel and me, the three graces or disgraces. We were enmeshed, at times, a dyad, at other times, a triad.

"Don't waste a moment of your life," Marcelle had taught me.

"Roper will be long on girl things, and I'll be short."

I wore a cardigan for the whole trip because I'd skinned my right elbow on a bike fall the day before and gravel was ground into the wound. Besides, my knees and elbows were always bruised and scarring, the first thing Aunt Roper would notice.

I sat and spoke laconically enough on the train ride out, Grandmother having given me the window. She bore a basket of white, oven-browned sweet rolls and butter pats on her lap, plump as a partridge. Me? Thin as a rail with my Coke-bottle green eyes. I was the whirlwind in a lull. I'd start up again. We saw farm-after-farm, church-after-church with their white steeples of varying heights and ribbons of roads, sunsets of copper bullets shot into the sky and dispersed through layers of oceanic clouds.

I was determined not to besmirch my father's name. I made believe I was Heidi riding up the Alps to Alms Uncle as we crossed flatlands with barns and silos, those the thousand-some miles which ended at the homestead of my cousins, and my aunt and uncle. Halfway thru I recalled I'd left my trading cards behind. Under an umbrella elm, shaded, sat a white Colonial house with mock Grecian columns and blue shutters not unlike ours back at home in New Rochelle which differed in detail, our shutters being green.

Nyrene and I had look-alike twin beds, the window had organdy curtains, tied back with a sash. The windows panes were blue crystal clean. I plunged into a depression at once and put out Mr. McQue as soon as I was alone in the room. Auntie Roper (named after the Rope pearls she swung round her neck after one or two martinis) had sewn us, with her black and gold post-war Singer, look-alike pajamas.

"Girls, look!" she said her flappers' high kick accompanying her voice. She looked like a leftover from the swing era. "Twin jammies." Marcelle would never ever in her wildest dreams do such a thing. Aunt turned back in the doorway and frowned, "I hope you've outgrown grass stains on your sheets, Indigo."

I had felt lump-in-the throat, pain-in-the-rib alone from the time Uncle Lem had met us at the Baltimore and Ohio railway station in Toledo and drove us in his blue Oldsmobile onto a suburban street with elms cut out of spinach-green, a Crayola shade, construction paper and a lawn a bit lighter but the same cardboard. Smack dab in the middle of alone.

"You sleep with *him?*" Nyrene had said as though holding her nose the first night, lifting Mr. McQue by the foot as though he had a bad smell.

"I sleep with *her,*" she sing-songed lifting the Madame Alexander doll flounced in hoops of rose tulle.

"It won't be long before I have a real boy in my arms. I've already chosen my dress for the prom."

"What prom?"

"Don't know yet but there'll be one."

She was the sort who, in a former age, would be fully booked at a cotillion, the dance-card at her wrist darkened in, gaily swinging. She was the spitting image of her mother.

I hadn't spoken a great deal to my Romanian grandmother, was observing rolling hills as Pennsylvania crossed over into Ohio, looking out the train window at blue fog and haze, those watery miles crossing into the mid-West, but we were companionable. The lonesomeness set in when Grandmother flew home.

My first morning in Ohio, maybe I woke on the wrong side of the bed for when I saw Auntie Roper in her rope pearls set to go to the gym, then bridge, I felt my stomach flip flop. It didn't help that the Baltimore & Ohio had threaded my entire night with its hollow echoes that made me homesick, far from ideal as things were at home. She'd made us pancakes this first morning when heat waves shimmered across the kitchen and there wasn't even school to look forward to. Dad time. No man's land.

It was June recess, nothing to redeem life with my aunt and uncle from the burn of tedium. She'd cooked these flapjacks (I figured) to make a hit with me but she blew it. They were from a mix. I'd lived down South due to the divorce. This Aunt Jemima stuff wasn't the real McCoy. I hated the picture on the cover. She made the mistake of asking me how I liked them.

I said, "Hmmm. . ." and set my index finger to my chin.

Mother made hotcakes on a black hot iron skillet: they bubbled, and flowed like a miniature volcano erupting in our kitchen. That sealed that Saturday. My lightweight body felt heavy climbing the gold carpeted stairs of Aunt Roper and Uncle Lem's snug suburban home. Even my shadow didn't belong to me. (Reenie was already into her favorite occupation, dress-up.)

There he was, old one eye dangling as though he'd been mortared in a shell operation. The tatty bear was a gift to me from my Russian Grandpapa Louis. On my cousin's pillow, a Madame Alexander doll reposed, hoop skirt spread out, layers of pink tulle, snappy glossy patent leather Mary Janes to match. I'd already told Reenie that I would not wear Mary Janes, not ever on your life, not in a million years. My cousin let her jaw jump open so wide a bird could hop in.

In addition to Mr. McQue, I brought an ancient set of jacks with the little bouncing ball that could trip someone and break their neck. We were in such a slight margin from the South you could measure it between two fingers, palpate it between forefinger and thumb like a bolt of cloth. The sky in Ohio was picture postcard blue like shiny cards people send you saying, *Wish you were here*. They did *not*. They never did.

I flopped on the bed, my look-alike *jammies* balled under my pillow, my cousin's neatly folded. I wore overalls. Aunt Roper frowned and said *Tomboy!* in the tone she said such things as, *Nice girls don't touch*, and *Legs are best friends*. Girls should keep their legs together. I sat cross-legged on the white boucle coverlet with bunched white string roses, and unfolded with great care several brittle, yellowed magazine pages. *LIFE* magazine, 1944.

"Teddy, the Enduring Bear: Aged and worn but faithful to the end."

A photograph looked at me of one-eyed Connolly, age 30. I studied these photographs and splayed out my jacks on the floor, all ten tough metal silvers that had come thru war. Here was Sinnamon above

Shadrack, age 31 and Sami, 37. I wrinkled my nose until the freckles met across the bridge.

"You're the last word, all of you" I whispered.

Besides being an arcturist, or bear-lover, another thing was clear to me. I'd determined to be a writer from the age of five so I'd concentrated upon text: *The most illustrious teddy bear of all resides in the Smithsonian Institution. He sits before a portrait of his namesake Theodore Roosevelt.*

My parents were F.D.R. aficionados, devotees. Mother wept with Florence the night he died, March 1945. Marcelle saw Eleanor Roosevelt once at the dentist in Manhattan.

"What was she like?"

"Tall, slim and shy like in the newsreels."

I felt I'd been informally introduced to Mrs. Roosevelt. . . .My bear was fashioned out of brown plush in 1902 by Morris Michton, a Brooklyn candy store owner. . .I knew him too, Mr. Michton.

"To the extent of not having a teddy bear, my early childhood might be described as disadvantaged," said one statesman. Mine had certain disadvantages but was not an overall deprived girlhood. I had Rachel. I had books.

Totally out of it in my Aunt Roper's home, I let my eyes linger over the text of Emma Roger's bear who fell into a lake and turned green, so that he now wore clothes to hide scars. I came to the conclusion my overalls covered the scar of being a girl which kept me—on the face of it—from roughhousing.

A retired railroad clerk, Mrs. Rogers said, "He knows me, and loves me."

I pulled Mr. McQue close and asked, "Do you love me?"

Emma Roger's final text read, "I'll keep Teddy until God calls me, and after that they can do what they want with him."

"Indigo," Aunt Roper stood in her favorite spot, the doorway to our room. I jumped from my reverie. "Time for you girls to have mid morning orange juice."

I slid the article back under my pillow, leapt off the bed, wiggled my feet into my Keds, and thought of Mary Hadley, another bear-owner who not long ago rolled over in bed accidentally detaching his nose. I followed Aunt Roper, drank my juice thru a straw and blew bubbles.

She scoffed. "Not a lady yet."

It was June. Warm weather was coming on. Black flies buzzed in thru the triangular rip in the screen door. How could Aunt Roper stand there in the heat ironing, leaving the little triangle scorch burns where the iron stood too long, when she gazed into space of that blue Ohio backyard.

"Time," she began, lighting up a cigarette, "It's high time you girls wore pinafores." She stubbed out her cigarette fiercely in the glass ashtray, "and time for me to make more ice with this goddamned refrigerator your Uncle Lem got."

My uncle was a balding, gentle man thoroughly hen-pecked. He ran a barber shop.

"That's when I determined my daughter would have no bowl cut. She shot a glance at me, a smart shot, it struck, "Nyrene goes to the beauty parlor and I'm thinking of treating you," she wound up.

There was nothing to be done about my rule straight hair, dirty blond, it flourished with Marcelle's bowl cut and that was the only way I liked it. Amen! I'd left pinafores behind when Rachel was born. I elbowed Nyrene at lunch.

"The clock castle," I whispered. "Let's try this very afternoon."

"Mother, will you take us to the Clock Castle this afternoon?" Nyrene asked while Sami was stuffing whipped maraschino cherries into his circular face. My cousin's blond rag curls shone like butter in the sun.

"I have bridge, dear, remember, Thursdays?"

"Tomorrow then?"

"Tomorrow I play golf with the ladies. You crave a treat? I'll tell you what," she leant forward, cigarette in left hand, right hand on knee, "I'm getting out of the godforsaken home and this housedress, but you girls can run under the sprinkler for ten minutes at four p.m.

There's a water shortage in this town." This was the first I'd heard of the water shortage.

"Indigo," she added, "you must realize that I'm not a martyr to my children, like some mothers."

Could she mean Marcelle? Marcelle was a martyr to melancholy but not to our whims.

Once our father had said of our mother, "One wants to tell her, Move over Christ, someone else is coming."

The sadness created an ambience, an aura, gossamer, tendrils of fog, always blue or brown, in the home which forged our chains. Sometimes borders would dissolve like milk mist over towns and we'd step into a rare bliss radiating contentment.

I felt like telling my Aunt that many children have a fleeting devotion to a bear but then move on. Those of us who are bear-lovers hold onto the passion lifelong."

"Aunt Roper, do you know what arctophile means?"

"No, but it sounds like something nasty, Indigo." I wanted to tell her she was probably thinking of pedophiles.

"That's the name for bear lovers. I'm one. I was champion of the third-grade spelling bee and had that very word."

"You never know," she said crumbing the table.

I realized it was a lost cause because there were no books in my cousin's room. I had, by the age of seven, two bookcases Marcelle had painted, stuffed to overflowing. Nyrene had her precious knickknack shelf with glass horses, only pink dressed dolls, mannequins. I felt like knocking one of the brittle dolls off the shelf accidentally on purpose and in fact I did the very next afternoon.

Aunt Roper didn't have the backbone to give me a solid rounding.

"Arctophile!" she called me.

She might as well have called me masturbator. It was a compliment of course. So I stared at my old photo-print bears, wore overalls, washed my own hair and ran in the yard to let it dry, and never ever during those rainless two weeks wore an iron curler nor outright acted ugly.

Two nights before packing my Aunt said, "You can run under the sprinkler with Nyrene. But remember to cut off the tap in the bathroom, it leaves an ugly rust line."

When I dowsed off, she came back in, set her hands on her hips and said, "I'll be obliged to tell your mother you still get grass stains on your bed and you've added another mischief— now there are ink stains too."

"I want to be a writer when I grow up," I made the mistake of telling her.

She looked me from top to bottom, buster-brown cut—she paused her eyes on my scabbed right elbow—to my Indian Walk shoes, as though she'd not registered that. She added, "And I'll tell her you wouldn't once let me prettify you by putting curlers in your hair."

"She knows," I sighed.

We never did get to the Clock Castle. "I'll take you to Cloth Pavilion which is way better, Indigo, I promise that the very next time and we'll learn all about textiles for sewing." Must there be a next time?

The night before the last night I stared at my cousin's gussied-up doll. Back home, I had a *real* doll. Susie Doll, Kapok, with a round sound box in the center of her thread belly that cried "Mama!" as woefully as any child during the Blitz. I nightmared often over Susie after Mother and I had had one of our yelling matches which always wound up in godforsaken scenes. I envisioned glass shards strewn all about my doll with the caved-in head from a *Warner Pathe Newsreel* running in my dreams. She'd had her head bashed in and was taken to the doll hospital more often than I could count on the heels of some knockdown drag-out. We'd circled the dates on the kitchen calendar when Susie went in and when she was due to come home.

"Today, Indigo," Mother would say, "I'll get Susie from the doll hospital. It's not for nothing that the Lord gave you broad shoulders."

Elderly bears are thought placid, serene, radiating contentment. But all are steadfast, loyal. If there were a fire, I'd run for Mr. McQue not Susie Doll or the silver jacks. The phrase *radiating contentment* buzzed in my head as I walked back in the screen door sipping my orange juice thru a straw. Upstairs, my scant things packed, I spoke to him.

"We've been through so much together, divorce, war. I'm having an awful day. I'm not distinguished like you, but I've lived through a lot for a kid. You'll always sleep with me, even when I'm a grandmother, even when I'm married. Maybe I won't marry. You won't end up in the corner, you can be assured of that," I concluded.

I was closing the fourteen days like a steamer trunk. Roper had put a big hair bow in back of Nyrene's yellow curls that reminded me of a bust bedspring.

"No way I can fit a bow into that cut your mother's given you, Indigo-Hannah," she commented, formal suddenly the last morning.

Now cross the long ocean of miles and memory home. Old Roper would never brag on me. Nyrene and Sami, I would not miss. They were non-events. I realized that while I'd mostly felt ugly on that visit, I never acted it. The most Roper could report back to my mother was that I'd dared contradict her.

"I hate a lip child," one day Roper told me. That, however, could ride.

"Indigo," my tall, thin Aunt stood in the bedroom doorway, swaying slightly, martini glass with olive in her right hand, twisting her pearls with the nail polished index finger of her left hand, wiggling her toes in her red shiny sandals. She always had a musical lilt to her voice with a slightly southern inflection. This tone managed to be both demanding and cajoling at the same time. "How would you like a supper out your last night?" She paused a moment for effect, "at Howard Johnson's."

Should I have bitten the bullet? I knew that they couldn't afford often to eat out. I saw that ugly orange and blue decor I'd shunned on all our cross country drives which had been miserable in the main. I decided to tell the truth since I was going home sooner'n you could say Jack Robinson.

No more voice calling out after me, "Who left the tap dripping with the ugly rust line?"

"No thanks." My willowy aunt appeared surprised, then insulted, she started to turn away.

I was determined not to act ugly. I wanted to have been made manageable, smoothed by these two weeks away in the beating heat of Toledo its roads dotted and scarred with its Ohio signs.

Nobody ever forgets where they bury the hatchet. I suppose my first night with them leapt up like a bloodhound and nipped Roper in the cheek. My aunt then glared down upon Mr. McQue faithfully mirroring her daughter's gesture and roughly lifted Mr. McQue by the torn ear.

With a glance which betokened more character than I thought Aunt possessed, she said "Aren't we," (I remembered the we) "aren't we way too old to sleep with bears?" She dropped him on his nose as if he had a bad smell.

As quick as you can say Jack Robinson, I came back, "Not this bear. You see, I'm an arctophile, Aunt Roper.

Fast balls were slammed back down the pitcher's throat. I thought for a moment I might be sick to my stomach. I rarely threw up. She told me since I didn't want to join them for Tommy Tucker dinner with its grey mashed potatoes that looked like something someone had thrown up, I'd best get packing. She shot an approving smile toward my right elbow: it was glassy and dark red, its scar was calming down, sealing over.

"I've packed your jammies," Aunt winked at me. "I can see that once again I have been unsuccessful in making a lady out of you even with Nyrene's sterling example." She paused, "Flapjacks tomorrow morning?"

I made no comment this time.

It wouldn't be an interminably long train ride, long as a week in bed, long as the war had been, staring out a sad glass window at endless miles of rain. I was taking the plane home from Toledo to La Guardia. I was in the hands of the flight attendant. Peril it had been, dancing on a razor living that close to the South again. I'd soon be pointed true north, trained back toward New England. I'd mind my P's and Q's.

But now I had a new problem. I was worrying. What would happen to Mr. McQue once I was no longer alive? I thought about it next morning as I boarded the plane, wearing my Buster Browns. I held my head high as I was bidden. I squared back my shoulders—it wasn't for naught the Lord gave me broad shoulders. *"Mama!" cried the Kapok doll with voice box.* I flashed a smile back at my kin. Despite war, the divorce, the dull-as-ditchwater two weeks, I'd be able to make a go of it. I knew that if I were able to look in a mirror at just that second I boarded the plane, I'd be *radiating contentment* as I braved the better than one thousand miles home on my own.

# Alissa's Baby

*– Indigo witnesses the pregnancy of a young woman, Alissa, who works for her. They develop a deep friendship based on shared, though different, threads of adversity – two people helping each other become a small diamond.*

*Alissa's Baby*

Maybe only in the South there are names like Alissa. It's late August. Children are sounding like going back to school while the days are still what I call celluloid, cellophane, vinyl. In the South I knew girls of eleven, who in the last hot days of summer, in desperation aborted themselves with hangers. Some got infections and died. Some just lived.

And all Alissa wants is for her baby to come out fine. She no longer expects to deliver it since the doctors have decided to deliver it by Cesarean. She wants a girl. Desperately. She's already *done the boy thing*. This has not been a normal pregnancy.

There were troubles early on which she has kept quiet, but by her seventh month she has been hospitalized twice over it, once for four days. She goes for a weekly blood test, biweekly ultrasound, plus which the Public Health Nurse (who is smarmy, she says, and nothing like me) comes to her apartment every two weeks. Next week, they are having a conference on the baby who has stopped growing, though the movement and heartbeat tests are ok. They don't want to know the sex.

Allisa worked for me when she was sixteen, the youngest person ever to be bonded by Upjohn because she was so responsible. She was just turning seventeen that July. I met her one rainy night when my partner was in Vancouver, it was pouring cats and dogs. I had just come up from the U.S. and we lived in a hardwood floored railroad apartment where we hung a tablecloth in the window for a drapery. Mother said it was darling but depressed her.

Alissa came, fresh as rose, wearing a pink blouse, a bit late because she'd been shopping at Eaton's and had phoned. Her cheeks matched her blouse. She sautéed chicken which was delicious.

Once before she'd been engaged, but that didn't work out although they'd gone as far as planning the wedding in St. David's By the Sea. She didn't meet Dale till she was thirty-seven and had become floor manager at Immigrations.

"We've both faced adversity," she smiled with her large front teeth, when she came to tell me. She flashed the diamond, "I quite like the ring, better than the first time. And Parker, it's a last name that goes with everything."

I hadn't asked if they were planning a family, until last Christmas when I did, and she smiled with a twinkle, "We'll see what happens."

Back in those early winter days in my adopted land, I saw more of Allisa then I did of Simone.

We built a sort of life together— She'd come at five each evening, we'd each have a glass of wine, smoke a cigarette and talk about our day. I retired early, she watched late night movies.

Alissa has had a few fast balls thrown at her. Her sister turned out to be mildly schizophrenic—the pregnancy she went through—after a hasty marriage to a military person living in Permanent Military Quarters—the pregnancy and childbirth brought out latent schizophrenia. The only place she could fit in was a group home. Alissa became 'mother' to Edward, taking him at first weekends, then building her life around the boy fostering his schooling. He was now fourteen. He came, a handsome ring boy of eleven, to Alissa's wedding three years ago.

Then there was the fire.

Allisa was alone in the house when it caught fire. She barely escaped with her life and the garnet beads I'd given her. Her father wept when he told me. She was his favorite, the youngest child.

"Just think, little Allisa, barely escaped with her life," he told me.

Two years later he suffered premature death at the hands of cancer. Her mother made a hasty re-marriage. By now the boy was back in his father's care.

"My life," she laughed, "it reads like a case history." She laughed. Bitter laughter. Laughter thru tears.

She was the one who took me into emergency in my pajamas one early spring evening when I'd reached the depths of despair over having come to this country to be with the one I loved who was now gone. Planning a life around walks around the block at eleven, a trek for a television guide or pack of cigarettes at five—these were falling through. I needed more.

I got sick. Caught a slow virus.

Unable to diagnose it, the doctors thought it was a slow virus. Mono was ruled out. So~? My mother and sister came to visit. Those were the days when Alissa was closest to me.

# One Dark Valentine:
## For the Children Of the Blitz

*for* Anam Cara, Pegeen

*– This crucial story in Albino Peacock revisits the Irish woman Pegeen. "The Fatal Morning" is the one when Pegeen's brother, 11-year-old Anton is killed by careless preparation for surgery from, ironically, not shrapnel or a bomb but a slingshot some boy shot into his eye while the kids were playing among bomb ruins. Pegeen, like Indigo, lives close to deep feeling all the time. Here characters weave projected onto one another the way pieces of everyone we have ever loved embedded themselves in every new relationship. Elsa is an old friend, Seth, the husband of Indigo until she realized she would be happier in a lesbian relationship.*

## Fatal Morning

For the children of the Blitz, it had started out to be a beautiful day, that February thirteenth when Anton was unexpectedly killed. Not only in the American South does one receive dark Valentines. It was during the war, but ironically not because of the war. It was not yet spring although winter was almost over. Like this St. Valentine's, a flawlessly blue sky cut by white puffs clouds, in Kensington, daffy-down-dillys in bloom.

St. Valentine's, that fatal morning so many years ago when eleven-year-old Anton, Pegeen's brown-eyed, dark-skinned older brother was killed, was a beautiful dawn. Taken in for routine surgery, left alone while the anesthetic took, he choked to his death. When the doctor and nurse came back, he was gone. How southern it all sounded to my ears, Gothic southern, Dixie Gothic ruling all worlds.

"Just think," Pegeen said at our Valentine's sushi, "during the Blitz, we would wait until the remote-controlled rockets, the bombs, flew overhead. We children held our breath waiting for the explosion. We knew when they stopped directly above us, it was curtains. And to think," she wound up, "there are people to whom nothing happens."

We agreed. They go through life without major illness or misfortune, reversals or setbacks. They never receive a death-dealing blow, loss of child, sibling, bosom companion. If they are tragically incomplete, they know nothing of it.

There are those who are the opposite, who live close to deep feeling all the time, open to every ordinary and extraordinary hope, committing failures of the human heart, surviving terrors, enduring ambivalence and insecurities.

Elsa says she and I lead lives which mirror each other's. Remorse over bad temper prompts a husband, he brings a box of chocolates home. I imagine water shimmering in golden autumn, in winter frozen, the ironies at the bottom gleaming as though they were colored stones.

In my dream, I can walk, then let go earth, and trailing my feet behind me like those of a doll, fly to her windowsill, and ask, "May I enter?"

She answers, "Indeed!" and at last I am able to see the view from her window of a slice of the blue bay, the one that is slate some days under a sky which is navy; the bay that is dotted some mornings with butterfly sails.

At last, I am able to hold her cherished books in my hands, smell the vanilla or raspberry of old pages made of yellowed vellum, run my fingers along their spines. She may not want Simone in her space—but thru the corner window, the one that creaks when you push it up, I have come in.

I haven't seen anybody's face transformed by a smile like Pegeen's. Her talc white skin takes on color, glows. Her brown-green eyes change from dark quartz, to luminous. She turns about thirty years younger.

As to you, my husband, you were a Jewish Puritan. Like me, unable to walk. Your craggy, Yankee features proclaimed you to be from New England, your nose hawk-like, like Abraham Lincoln's. You epitomized that independence which marked—perhaps scarred and flawed—the fathers of American literature whom you adored. Your mother decreed it a fate worse than death, the marriage of two disabled people. I have dragged your sack of letters with me—war letters in a sense and love letters to be sure—from country to country, province to province, thru nearly four decades, and now I have turned them over to Pegeen.

She says we live in a village-mentality in this town: not the way of thinking which governs in a metropolis like London. She says when there's good gossip, it's fine; but when there's bad, it's back-biting. Her poverty, her pain gnarls in me like a knot, or a rock.

Suddenly, my fall begins! Down one, two, three, four stories like Alice in Wonderland—but I feel no pain, only air pushing me up as I fall down. Apple trees are in gnarled bud, some in bloom so it must be Spring. The sky is blue as though lit by an acetylene torch.

Seth, you gain the lectern—since you refused to teach from your wheelchair—wearing your steel back-brace, two long-leg braces, and at the end a gauntlet on your hand to relieve the pain, the agony of gout. In the early days you joked it was a falconer's mitt, but you never tethered your falcon.

Ironically, you went to the grave a virgin. You had lifted your tall, almost six-foot frame on your slender hands too many times. You stowed your tall crutches behind you, leaning against the blackboard. You never would have your students see you teaching from a wheelchair, although after you died, one wrote you an elegy on how bravely you hoisted the steel frame chair in and out of the back of your car, old soldier who never got to war. Winter-locked whether it was summer or no.

Pegeen saw the same war from the other side of the ocean. Evacuated to the country south of London, she and her brothers and sister, they were so brutally treated when their father came to see them that, appalled, he took them back to London for the duration of the war. The Blitz was less terrifying than being abused. Her older brother, Anton, spoke for the three of them until he was killed. Then Pegeen was saleswoman for Proctor-Silex in South Carolina, hence her southern accent. Pegeen was the speaker—her younger sister, Laurie's, eyes followed every expression of Pegeen's face. Laurie never spoke a word but lived at fever pitch.

Back in London, when the American G.I.'s came the sun shone. They gave children of the Blitz at Kensington club small toys, pencils with erasers. The children were charmed. Peg gave everything away except the pencils. You, Seth, would have been one of these smiling young men—except that you lay in a hospital bed, mute, blind, unconscious, and dead from the waist down in a military hospital run by nuns in Oregon.

Seth, you would have worn an old-fashioned frock coat by now, I'm certain, and had melancholy hands, had you lived to a ripe age, instead of dying at sixty-seven.

I am finally learning about your last years, after you married— that shadow land I have been afraid to cross. Pain will not stop me, nor the scare of contacting your widow. Only death can.

How could I have imagined a meeting between Simone and Pegeen would work on the eve of St. Valentine's? How could I have been so blind? As well imagine a southern Lesbian when I was nine or ten, yet I was becoming one?

We are no longer young, difficult evenings take longer to go down. The fact is, Pegeen, you inhabit this heart by this time, third branch from the top where sky touches evening, the color of bruised plum.

"I am black and white," you say, "Kera is many shades of grey."

I do not want the wonders worked by guilt—only by love. Elsa is the same.

Pegeen had to carve a whole afternoon out of research for me on my common-law husband in order to mail her granddaughter, Rosheen, a winter coat the eighteen-year-old child left behind. "Gran," she wrote an email, "I left it at Jenny's, at Castle Rock. I'm freezing!"

"One has no choice in such matters," says Pegeen in her voice both richly modulated and matter-of-fact. It is a voice, which has seen many loves, comes and goes. Anton, that dark-eyed, brown-skinned child who was her older brother, who wanted only to play cricket for his school in London, went in for minor surgery and lost his life.

Evacuation to the country was Hell. The children endured the entire Blitz with their parents, under the sky of fire, in London.

We meet at a teashop to discuss research, Peg and I, and she runs into all of London having fled to this small island.

"You're the same as twenty years ago, only your hair's silver," calls out a lady of eighty, waving to Pegeen. "It's lovely."

"I have mixed feelin's over it," says Pegeen.

"I knew you by the voice. I recognized it at once—"

"Everybody does," Pegeen shot back.

"Sorry about this," she whispered to me. Then in full voice, 'Last time I saw you I probably had a little carrot-headed girl in tow."

"Precisely. How are they?"

"All gone. Fled and gone to England. It's for the best," said Pegeen lifting her right hand to motion movement.

I felt no motion sickness. It was a brilliant, brutally blue bright sky outside the tearoom. I saw Elsa's mirror in silver of last night's rain running down a small hill.

"You're a sweetheart," Peg brushed my cheek, leaving, as though saying, we'll get over this one.

## Valentine Meeting

After the initial greetings, I'd felt sick slowly on Valentine's Eve when Simone and Pegeen met the second time. All the topics I'd rehearsed mentally as neutral, or stimulating fell flat.

"In England," said Pegeen very nearly as an opener, "We don't celebrate St. Valentine's. I was listenin' to a radio program this afternoon that talked about Platonic love as the best kind."

"Indeed," I smiled offering her a glass of warm merlot.

"Those years you worked on the big rigs, Pegeen, up North—what was the name of the town?"

"Fort McMurry. It was the Arctic. Freezin'."

"You taught the men procedures?"

"Yes, safety procedures."

"Kera studied welding and wrote up a procedures manual for welding."

"Really?"

Both women turned formal. Speeches quickly took the place of communication. I might as well have been absent.

"The ministry of finance," said Pegeen.

"The end of the fiscal year," said Kera.

"Shall we have sushi?" I tried.

Soon, we were into real estate. Pegeen said, "I've a friend who told me if I were set down in the Sahara I'd find a job."

All of a sudden, we were on the subject of pumps.

"Many of the houses in this area have a *sump pump*," Peg announced.

"On which streets?" Simone shot up her eyebrows.

"There's a sump pump on St. Michael's, for one," Pegeen said.

"Is there?"

I thought, one of the seven deadly sins must be boredom.

The candles were slow to light—but not as slow as the talk to ignite. It wasn't long before Pegeen brought in Lord and Lady Luxton to replace real people in our lives, and informed us of an address right around the corner from One Downing Street.

"When I worked for Lord and Lady Luxton . . ." Why then did I stand, during those tense moments, back in magnolia land, the South, with its profound song and stain?

"What was it like when you sold real estate?"

"Hard work, dawn 'til dusk. Sold two million overnight when I sold the Park Hilton. But this and that drained it, mainly illness in the family."

Finally, late in the supper, Pegeen felt the need to break thru words as a blockade and began using them as language. She spoke of true things, terrible things, the evacuation of London. Simone was stilled, listened, chin cupped in hands.

"We were so abused in the evacuation, we bore black and blue bruises over our body. It stopped short of sexual abuse, thank God."

Afterward Simone asked me, "What does one say when people tell you terrible things?"

"Nothing," I said. "Just listen sympathetically."

"Is everything all right?" Peg phoned to ask in morning.

I do not receive my Valentine till late in the day— a handmade card with dozens of tiny valentines spilled in the shape of a crocus, and glued on. Simone leaves it out on the kitchen table at my place.

Two nights later, Simone says, "I have an issue, actually it's an apology, not to you but to Pegeen. I reacted by nearly attacking her over that issue of being victim. I strongly feel we do not choose our circumstances."

"So does she."

"Yes, but I think I came down a bit too strong."

Elsa writes, "Why didn't you throw your gloves in the ring earlier? You should have sent them to bed. Keep them apart."

"Pru," Pegeen said at lunch, "has offered me a facial in return for my drivin' her to the airport.'"

"Take it," I said.

She laughed, "Don't want one. Pru says she's restless, thinkin' of buyin' a second property, thinkin' of takin' a trip, asked if I want to come along."

"Have I competition?" She probably has the most musical speech.

Soon the red hearts will come down that have been all over town. Soon I must turn the picture of my dead common-law husband about-face so that I can carry on. (He looked thinner, more bird-like and wounded with time.) If we are tragically incomplete, still we carry on. At least he lived close to deep feeling. Exactly so, most of the time, foisting his intensity off on others to the point of judging their non-response as blame.

"There will be the pain, too, you realize," I say to Pegeen, "re-reading his love letters."

A robin settled on the surreal green lawn out the window.

"Not an English robin, cheeky fella," smiled Pegeen. "I know. English robins are far smaller, more gentle."

"My father," she mused, "was a most gentle man."

"You take after him," I commented.

"So people said back in Ireland."

## Ichabod Crane

He was an Americanologist. The black ink writing down immortal words—Emerson, Thoreau, Lincoln shone in his eyes. Born the fourth of July. A Jewish soldier who never even made it out of maneuver into the rank of Private; exemplifying that bravery he taught in the great American writers, of prose, of poetry, of statesmanship.

"An *Amawcanologist*," he joked, "a soldier who never got to war."

He fought his battle here on the home front when a flaming tree crashed down on his spine.

Why now does Anton flash upon my eye again? Lit up, a child by torchlight at night in the moment when the car rounds the bend, stopping with a screech of brakes just short of killing him.

Alone when no child or human ought to have been left alone.

Because, for Seth, back in 1943, it was curtains.

Seth, you know the legends of Washington Irving: *The Legend of Sleepy Hollow* (or *The Headless Horseman*); and Ichabod Crane, that Hoosier schoolmaster with the long dancing legs, spaghetti twisted.

Too, you and I know how dark a ward becomes in winter after midnight. Indeed, that became your metaphor for earth, *this nasty little planet*, after not very long. Even when snow fell in our New England, which was for most of us a peace, a benison, you cursed it as *the wretched white stuff*. But after all, at a time when others were in full swing—twenty-one—in *medias res*, you lay with oxygen over your face, intravenous needles in your arms, unconscious on a hospital bed in Oregon, dead from the waist down.

It is 1943. Your little sister cannot take her eyes from you, Pegeen. Her ink-blue eyes are riveted, you can feel them physically like small bullets cutting holes, like miniature flames burning your cheek and your eyeball. The rural family who took you children in as evacuees did it for the money alone. South of London. They never even learned your names. They withheld sweets but fed you treacle which Anton knew enough to turn down, and for some reason Laurie didn't want. You took it.

Treacle caused you an accident, you soiled the floor, scrubbed the rug all night saying, "Blessed virgin, mother of God, help me remove these stains," you were still a practicing Catholic.

But you couldn't get them out by morning and were hit in the face by the father, five times.

Seth, when you finally awoke from your coma after five weeks, the Sisters who were nurses leant forward, cupping their ears for each precious word you might utter, then covered their mouths—when they heard—in shame.

"I'd imagine he said somethin' like fuck—" commented Pegeen.

"Worse. Mother f—"

"Of course."

And to think, there are people to whom nothing happens.

Elsa's life unrolls on the frozen prairie, mirroring in so many ways mine.

Then, surprisingly, what blooms on my inner eye are those long halcyon summer days on horsy, snooty Long Island, the Island of Jay Gatsby, where Seth and I went—as it were, hand-in-hand. People always thought we were together due to our injuries, but not a bit of it. In those days, people thought me a junkie, I was so thin. I'd had polio—one of the last—and he'd been injured in maneuver, one of the last soldiers.

We had no interest in talking of our disability.

My very dear man, as you grew older, you grew to look more like a windblown sparrow. Your body could not keep up with your mind. You struggled to gain the lectern. You lectured on Ichabad Crane, you loved Walt Whitman, Ralph Waldo Emerson, Henry David Thoreau, Mark Twain, with whom of course, Tom Sawyer and Huck Finn came along. I couldn't take care of you—not I alone.

"Football shoulders!" you joshed me.

"They ache," I said.

What interested him was friends, the Old Boys of the Harvard club, those elite in a club which allowed no women in their library or to join; and then, that great gang of semi-Bohemian Jewish professors at Long Island University, to whom we drove out Sundays—always arguing because I couldn't read a map, and he scolded, "Any old soldier can read a map!"

"But I'm not a soldier," I said.

"Oh, Punch," he'd tousle my hair, letting go of the steering wheel a moment, driving with his left hand by the hand controls. We each had a hand control set installed in our car.

When we got out, there'd be a view of the Sound, old porches to drink on in lazy afternoons, gin. Both of us erect in our wheelchairs, I'd slip my hand under the table into his. This was allowed as we decorously sipped Port wine.

"You sly Fox!" Dan, his old buddy said to Seth after he'd introduced me.

## Home-Run

You have to learn to beat the boys at their own game, to slam their fast balls down their throat," said Seth.

"No," I said, "I hate that language."

"Gotta learn it, Punch. It's do or die."

"You've struck another home-run, Peg," I beamed at coffee.

Tell me once again about the time you worked at Fort McMurry, writing procedures manuals for the men, climbing those big rigs, twice as large as a football field, four stories high. They could squash ten men and never notice. Women were called in to write safety-rules. Women had to tell the men they wouldn't climb the rigs without hard-toed boots, hard-hats, the whole thing. (Tell me more, for you're my hero, haven't you gleaned?)

Suddenly, I see her as a radiant middle aged woman, and think, "My very dear girl, you cannot imagine how much better life gets as you get along."

By the next morning, she has tried so hard to download the photograph of Seth teaching that nothing is in focus.

The day of the winged God who's blind stands like a bad dream. Only at the end of our evening, Simone's, Pegeen's and mine, did a dark agenda seem to show. Pegeen and Simone seemed to be robbing the evening of even the possibility of communication by their blocking true feeling, until Pegeen broke thru with those terribly moving images of themselves as children of the Blitz near the end.

Of course it would.

"I've given myself a stiff neck sittin' at the computer too long."

"Shall I send Simone in?"

"Please do have her phone, although I don't think I want her in my space, as I've been sayin'."

Once we were all the world to each other, Seth and I.

Once Seth was his mother's golden boy, although red-haired, a carrot-top, or more like spun copper in the sun. His hair threw off the sun. When we were married, he went to the same barber he had as a boy in mid-town Manhattan. His hair was always boyish, a Harvard grad to the nines. He always wore bow ties, no other kind.

My heart is a crowded place but better that than vacant and shining with a light which is blind.

There is Seth, and Simone and Pegeen. Rarely are they in dialogue, any one with the other two, or even with one.

"I feel anesthetized," says Pegeen, "Like I'm hung over—not that I've ever been."

Each bad evening hurts more than the ones before, 'til there are a pile of them. But look! Just at the end of the long weekend, a bonfire looms. Anton is looking at Pegeen, ripping open her dream, putting both child-hands upon her sore shoulders. Simone is looking toward me with trust again.

And Elsa is smiling—the ironic, silent smile of the wise worldly woman.

"Our lives mirror each other perfectly, Myra," she says using my name for the first time since she's left. "Keep on shining. We are all the apple of your eye, perhaps."

My spine bends, her shoulders un-stiffen. Simone does a high kick.

Seth walks across the water, is he moving toward me? His heavy wooden crutches are caught miraculously in reflection. In this very late photograph which Pegeen has unearthed, he does not look like a solid man—but almost like a negative. He could be an apparition.

So here is a dark Valentine.

Nobody brought one dozen crimson sweetheart roses.

But I can fly backward until— it is the early times. I have a back-ache, am sitting propped up in bed on a board Kera has improvised. I am tap, tap, tapping on my portable manual typewriter propped on my knees and happier than ever, we are all the world to each other. Kera in the next room. These are her domestic years. She's got a chicken simmering on back of the stove. She's even done some bread baking. She's rolled newspapers and brown bags into tight rolls as her father, the Colonel, taught her long ago.

Like that day so many years ago, that February in England, it started out picture perfect, puff clouds in the sky, gently rolling green hills out of an English storybook. Then gradually, it began to come to life—a stage-set, a pop-up book, objects stood forth so clearly it caused pain.

Then Simone said, "Be careful around her, you don't want to end up as another one of her stories."

However, afterward, that cloud came over her face and she did the surprising thing.

"I have an issue. It's an apology," she held both hands forward, she had the unblemished cheek of a child pageboy, had rosy lips without makeup as though kissed by raspberry. She was irresistible for yet another time.

A dark shadow fell, as the anesthetic of love lifted leaving me in pure daylight, not harsh, but uncompromising, projecting onto the wood floor a translucent valentine. First it trembled like a candle flame, then began steadying like an eternal flame. I watched it mesmerized. I did not cry or swoon under its power but became slowly anchored in the moment, more and more strong, certain of who I was and where I stood, and of how it is possible to love more than one.

Pegeen's voice is raised in *hallelujah*, but her applause is the sound of one hand clapping. This is the hardest work in the world.

I see her at her Catholic Convent in England during World War II, child of the Blitz. Jewish girls went there, taken somehow out of Germany. One gave Peg a Jewish star, which she wore under her uniform to her Catholic convent, because the nuns didn't allow jewelry. She hated her school shoes and used to hide them behind a flowerpot when her picture was taken. The nuns did what they could do at the Convent to help save the Jews but they couldn't do enough. They were not rabid Catholics. Rather, they gave an education in humanity when life was at fever pitch. The Jewish girls came out of sister convents out of Europe. It was a desperate time for children. For the world. On VE Day people were so exuberant they climbed up lampposts.

And to think there are those to whom little happens. Life is like a summer's day, uninterrupted blue, flowing as molten metal from a cauldron, benign, without effort or effect. There are clouds in the sky, simple cumulous ones, white and puffy as puffs of steam blown from a train in a child's storybook, or as though crayoned by a child's hand. Hard work. Ongoing.

There are those to whom nothing happens. Not in the South. Magnolia land is rife with song and stain. Not in the North either. Both lands gave birth to my imagination, truck, leaves and flowers if there were to be some.

February 19, 2000

# The Sad Little Abyss in Every Home

– *This story flashes back upon 1944 and the kitchen sink in which Indigo was bathed during the war. It also involved Beth, the ironmonger's child. Marcelle's harshness, call it that or cruelty, is again evident in this vignette of early life in Plattsburgh, New York. Rachel was an infant. Indigo is forging links like those of the chain-gang she saw in Dixie. The links glow. This is post-Chernobyl but the time makes her feel like a Southern Jewish girl-child once again. She sees the home of the 1940's as a sad little abyss. She was a heroine to her Russian Papa Louis during the war in 1944. She sees her mother, smoking "fumipogs" extending the undertaker an invitation. She thinks the devil, already rich, need not be paid more dues.*

## The Sad Little Abyss In Every Home

Some people think of the South as a back drain water of sad-eyed Jewish Junkies. I learned the abyss first down South. Pariah, a Jewish girl child in a world dominated by church pews and girls whose legs must touch or they were "not nice," like girls who touched themselves. These girls wore hair ribbons big as a country church. During the depression, the sink was advertised as "the sad little abyss in everybody's home."

Sinks were for such things as cutting a child's hair. The kid would lean forward and the mother cut a perfect bowl cut.

When I met Beth, the ironmonger's child, I looked back on my own childhood. I was bathed in a sink. My mother, when a boy first courted me, held up a dress she'd sewn me. It had a stain from liquid on it.

"Couldn't you wait?" she asked.

She was wrong about what it was. I had in fact spilled some tea.

Partly, I grew up on a ward where things are generic. It too was a sad little abyss. We kids, however, were each living our own bitter honey in our cell. There was a painting before my mind's eye then. It was a luminous and haunting last look at my childhood schoolroom: inky-green air behind it like a green window shade, with a little circle at the end of string draw pulled down. There set before it were my favorite things: a new pencil box, a round blood-red canister, a teal oblong metal box with just an edge of rust bitten in.

Edgy that's what it was; this too was a little abyss, the schoolroom. For I now saw, at age twelve, that the two grades I'd been jumped ahead by our psychologist father had shoved me back some. There was another small abyss on the playground: the roundabout dropping beads of white gray icicles. The more I looked at it, full clothed, I stood stark naked before the flailing that occurs in little gaping holes in creation everywhere. *Stricken. Abysmal,* are words which now come to mind.

That was down South: I live up North now. Ours is the sort of small town where the police lost-and-found collects garden gnomes, the kind mother culled from her dead daddy's estate about which she said she'd kill a man with if one every broke in.

"No gnome address" is the gaff the newscaster makes on this one. Once the police even had a wooden leg. (Now who would give up a wooden leg? You'd think they'd have noticed.) This could have occurred down South as well.

A link which haunts me is that between the South and Ireland: eloquent, illiterate, poor, verbal, tragic-comic. Are those correct links? It's the sort of small town where shopkeepers blush when they see the dummy's undressed, bare plastic buttocks facing them. God knows what the street saw, but there wouldn't have been anything to see, so it wouldn't have been the real thing.

Somebody here has nominated me for poet laureate. I know a writer who culls laureates like so many stones in a bag, index cards in a shoebox for a project. He has one for New Orleans and one for Petaluma, California, where the prune orchards thrive.

"Don't live on your laurels, Indigo," Mother said driving me home from my first piano recital.

My hair was an aureole of blond since she'd permed it the summer before and now, although we were into autumn, it was still blond, an afro on a skinny Jewish white girl chick. It frizzed because my father and his new wife, our stepmother, Chel's and mine, drove in a convertible cross country and it got snarled like nobody's business.

How small can a town get? Here are some of the advertisements I've seen which wouldn't make it in a big or even medium-sized town:

"Who heats your home? Angel Fuels."

"Bright & Shiny window cleaning."

"Paradise Gas."

The first suggests an angel with an Ohio safety-tipped match, the second a woman buffing diamond-leaded panes (which abound in our small Victorian town,) and the third the levitation related to all ideas of paradise. We are bilingual: *Arret* homogenized milk, *lait ecreme*.

"Down to earth gardeners' is another name I marked.

A dark day. Raven trees. Ravine trees. Muscling my way past throngs buying flowers at the market. Sinewy, a meditative morning, a novel of early old age on the cusp of the new. I live, have lived for twenty-seven years, in a late Victorian world which contains turning, enchanted many worlds some times, as though the old bronze-green church spires were cast by a spell-caster—our own city's.

I sat inside the edifice of the glass lobby on Cook Street for a Jacob's age, seven years, to marvel at how gin transformed the city buses, the bus shelter. Repeat visits to the bottle revealed a changed structure. I was amazed, delighted, or at the opposite spectrum as if high on helium, in a perpetual dream evidence could do nothing to change, petrified.

I am forging links like those of the changing I saw in Florida. But these glow: The camera *obscura* I saw as my childhood schoolroom—that ink green painting with pencil like burnished objects—it recurs often in my life. Or if not often, at peak moments. It brings me—like the white light I learned in the hospital on the cups of puberty—it takes me to an out-of body experience.

I now see that jumped ahead two grades, I was left forlorn, behind, at the edge of the playing field. Did I in some way want to crawl back, grateful to be saved? An angel cast a star into the water, goes a legend. The star is wormwood. Today, the disaster of Chernobyl, twenty years ago. And I received a lime green light to burn above my desk, transforming granules of darkness into light. Green as a banker's light. I was smart for my age, but sad. This pencil-thin light instructed me to be sad.

So back to the sink, the crater.

Do you know birds are starting to nest in the deteriorating sarcophagus built twenty years ago to contain further radiation leaks at Chernobyl? What *you* do I address? *You* who tell me I am in danger of spilling out all my life on paper, wildly as Molly Bloom lips her last soliloquy: *you* don't know where *you* are. There aren't transitions? Why should there be? Are there any real ones in life? Sink, where the child's head is battered and bathed at age three or four, becomes grades he or she is thrust forward at age six, turns into polio which lays level with earth, paralyzing the child, taking from her forever the right angel man is privileged to be granted to earth. Finally fallout develops, explodes one day, people begin to glow in the dark like rabbits

— these girls cannot give birth, free association takes over, radioactivity limns us all and one flashes, in a moment of lucidity, back to that sad little abyss in every home, the sink.

Who heats your home this winter? Angel Fuels? Who cools your wrath?

While my Scottish lover scrubs the potatoes and decommissions the clued key to our building for an owner moving out, I think of my Irish friend and the Maggies.

"Mind yourself," she says, and "even if I were in the whole of my health, this would be hard."

It's soft weather people like Marie and Mother who say, "Couldn't you wait?" who slander everyone—even to the point of incest.

They have never had the whole of love. I feel sorry for them, I do not want to be in their presence. Not any longer. For a while, I did. Catching the afflictive darts, perhaps deflecting them, perhaps buying into the masochism which is women's. But as we know, all masochism, red as a maraschino cherry and as cruel in the end, has two sides, is sado-masochism. It doesn't help that this rain bogged weekend, Simone is up island where a brute murder has just occurred of an old woman working a hospital gift shop in one of the many towns up coast named after a river. Let us call it Carn's River. I feel like a southern Jewish girl-child once again.

I woke thinking of that gift shop, reverting again to the sad little abyss.

# Undertaker Bird

– An image reminiscent of Flaubert's parrot, the Russian Firebird or the Phoenix, the Undertaker Bird reveals the magnetic power of despression in a family where mother and daughter cannot flly from reality, responsibility, divorce, and the weight of polio, so enormous a change, one cannot help looking for the reason of it. In a rational universe should there not be a reason?

So this flamboyant bird is both harbinger of grief, and also something of a joke at the grim reaper's expense.

# Keeping the Undertaker Bird Away

Rustling in his *noir* and bronze feathers, very southern, very jazzed up, like a Texas sunset, like crepe glowing like taffeta, his copper sheen and eerie profile straight out of Hieronymus Bosch, here comes the Undertaken Bird as though a curtain of heavy drapery velvet were being raised on the great rollers of the sky and he dramatically took the stage, who's in his crepes and crinolines. He moves, foot after long bony foot, cartilage livid, the incredibly grotesque the African animal. Today Monday began, and woke with that rattle in my throat which brought the undertaker bird to my mind. He smells death and struts along like in fancy dress shoes as if he could be wearing a glossy top hat and he has a head nearly bald of feathers, all skull and a few poke ups.

I'm the opposite, all dressed up and no place to go. Fancy is as fancy does.

Reminds me of when I ran home from first grade saying, "It's an insult to a child," the books, *Look Puff, Jane, and Dick* I was talking about.

My mood was all brown. I saw early that school was a rip off for a child just as later I saw some flea markets were grand but others were no bargains and all money maws. It left me no mystery to solve, school. Then one day the *National Geographic* series on twins came into my hands. I ran home and announced to Marcelle, our mother, "Finally, I've found a book that is not an insult to a kid."

I was strong, able to take care of myself, had a knowledge of my boundaries and wholeness. In an age which made little girls emulate Shirley Temple, I was a forecast of the times when there would arise from the pages of American literature, Atticus, the lawyer, and his daughter, Scout Finch.

If I was a little devil, I was the heroine to someone but to whom? Even old fishermen get lonely, a truth I sensed pounding the dirt roads with my Russian papa Louis during war, 1944, Plattsburgh, New York.

Up in a cloud, extremely sorrowful, the world had become cold. When I came down, the bathroom soap was yellow and hard. Lye soap it was called. My Catholic neighbor went to confession, but for me there was no such thing. I dressed, put my shoulder bag over my shoulder, and had no place to go. Could I *make* up one? There were plenty of graves in the graveyard and No *dogs* signs, No *trespassing,* plus a cat with one blue glassy eye. It was like a story by Poe but the dead there were not distinguished doctors and lawyers, they were mainly stock market mavens, owners of wheat and grain and American Telephone & Telegraph.

I looked at the little girl in the poster for the March of Dimes. I had an addiction to her. I was mesmerized. What was it like to wear steel and leather thongs on your legs, to go on crutches like stilts? I should bridle my eagerness. By age twelve I was to learn.

I slept very hard some nights and woke with creases in my cheek. On others, I had nightmares. I became that afflicted child, was lifted limp as a dead white bird, in somebody's arms. But then I was carried across a green body to water to where the kind schoolhouse weathered seasons waited. In it, children turn pages of books which interest them. Recess wasn't a time to taunt and bully, arm-wrestle and come down with blustering threats.

The clock was the enemy. Mother would often look up from ironing and say, "Let's see what the enemy says."

Sometimes, she'd say 'Let's *guess* what the enemy says," and Chel and I would ferret out times.

That was Marcelle making us strengthen the muscle of our imagination. Now was forever. That was a clear thing. I was in a lot in those days—1944 to 45—minding the baby.

Mother would say "You'd better remember what you forget," she'd add "And don't look glum in front of the baby. I don't want her depressed too."

"I never heard of a depressed baby."

"Humph," she said.

I knew that variety was the spice of life and imagined that was why our lives felt flat as the grey terrain of Poland. I hadn't realized that she perceived the depression in her and me. She was registering things, I was registering things. When I wanted something badly I reverted to the southernism: *Pretty please with sugar on top.* In the South a kiss goodnight was called *some sugar.*

Another thing I'd learned was that only by going *out* would I have stories to tell and bring home, real or imagined, I'd polish them like stones in the pocket of my mind, I'd do this on the way home. Later when I read John Keats' words, *In the end, truth doesn't matter,* I thought, *just so*. It was what you made up in your mind and bore verisimilitude to truth.

"Indigo, you're such a listener. I can just see your ears grow," Mother would say.

Our home wasn't whimsical on the whole, but there were two creatures who animated the kitchen and the bath. Piney Pig was our cutting board Mother cut with a jigsaw in the shape of a pig. One day I came home to find her mutilating him: deliberately, calmly, accurately she cut off Piney's corkscrew tail. She did the same with his little triangles of ear, then his belly she slit right down the middle. Heartless she is, I thought like the language she used for herself when cancer was removed from a lobe of a lung.

"They slit me open like a side of beef."

Piney Pig was kissing cousin to Teddy Towel, a towel I coveted embroidered with two bears. I'd made the rhyme *Teddy Towel likes cheddar cheese* because I also longed for cheese, which felt like a block of clay in your hands.

I wasn't born to sidestep chores, and I *was* inured to severity. Still, there were limits— how much severe was too severe? I noted the resemblance to the word *sever*, which I'd been given once as a finalist in a spelling bee. I decided then and there, on the spot, that if Marcelle became too severe she'd alienate me, her child, thus severing the connection.

Mother took to scolding like a duck to water. My eyes were green *emmies*. The South sure could use some cheering, but then the North could too. Our whole country could portray the outcome: one was ante-bellum, the other Puritan backbone. Where was there escape for a daredevil like me?

"I'm updating this bacon," Marcelle had a habit of saying when something had gone bad in the refrigerator.

It always rained for the Chinatown parade but the Chinese kids cheered up the occasion by painting the pavement, gray as glass, with red dragons. Brass bands and the South went hand-in-hand. Parades were big time in the small towns. Floats featured big in the South, and did anything but make my mood ebullient.

"Born old, you were," Mother told me. "Sit down and be quiet."

I didn't. Not ever totally.

"Only the gravel subdues you."

Well, I'd got a handle on what made people sad and the reverse. I'd discovered wherever we were, in whatever rundown type of a hotel room down South or up North, frying up an onion could stir in us the sense of home.

In one liver-colored southern hotel room, she said, "Kids, now we must boil all water. I don't like the color, taste or smell of this water."

I thought it was due to the natural bacteria. We wanted a fan.

There was no phone down to the desk so Marcelle said, "Indigo, you go on ahead. Ask the night clerk could we have a fan. You could charm the birds from the trees."

"The partition's not working," she announced one night folding the thing up. She pushed the typewriter to the side of an improvised desk and took out her pastels.

"What's that?" Chel asking.

"Rambutans."

"What's that?" I asked.

"An oriental fruit."

Mother could be the queen of scoldings or she could be great fun.

"Girls, let's turn the furniture upside down" was fun time.

So was baking cupcakes in a hotel room predominantly musty and brown.

"Don't eat too many, Indigo," she'd mourn as I shoved fistfuls into my mouth.

"Why?"

"'Cuz we don't want the undertaker bird to come."

That was when I saw the grotesque creature I'd seen in an African bestiary, bald with just a few feathers leftover from the dead, slowly, steadily coming.

## Extending the Undertaker Bird an Invitation

Then there were the solemn nights when Marcelle would tap out her stories on an old typewriter. I'd peer over her shoulder, "Curiosity killed the cat," she'd snap at me.

"But satisfaction," I answered, "brought him back."

No satisfaction here, she rose lighting a cigarette.

I pushed the smoke away from my face. "*Fumipog*," I said. I flushed the butts down the toilet thinking of her flushing her life.

"Low expectations, Indigo," she'd say, sitting down, stubbing out, lighting up again, "make for a charmed life."

If that failed to impress me—low expectations creating a content frame of mind in life—she said, "I knew a girl. . ." This girl she knew got into multiple troubles and incurred a fate worse than death.

She knew a girl for everything; a girl who leaned too close to the boiling fudge and got scarred so bad in the face she'd never allow her picture to be taken again. She knew a girl who sassed her mother and got the end of her tongue attacked by some nameless virus which lopped it off. She went through life with an amputated tongue. Mother in these moods scared me. Bent above the typewriter, as I later was to be, manic, smoking. Was she telling the truth, the whole truth, and nothing but the truth as the *Bible* and courtrooms command? Sometimes the undertaker bird reminded me of the typewriter, becoming an eerie animal at night eating up the fiction of my dreams.

"I'm putting in a screen, Indigo, so don't rile me," she said one night.

I'd said, "What's that, Mother?"

"It's an old thing I bought at a flea sale," she smiled. "I'm improvising a screen so we can each have our own space, our privacy, Indigo."

"Let's keep Death away," one night Marcelle boldly, bluntly announced, "not extend an invitation to him."

She was talking about me having crossed a road midway, not at the traffic light. I blinked long into that endless night. I dreamt of a courtroom in which a child pled for innocence in her longing for something, some books to read, which would dignify the child in the classroom.

I'd make up stories in the bathtub. "Eureka!" I'd shout, like Diogenes when I got the conclusion and would emerge from the steamy bath, towel wrapped round my hips, widely grinning.

Once Mother said, "Don't stare so long at the girl in the infantile paralysis poster." She halted at the edge of, "You'll catch it."

Maybe she said those horrible things to keep the devil away because this one came, in full, fevered form, true — stiff neck, burning spine, paralysis. It was the one disaster for which she knew no girl.

"Sick kid's a monkey wrench, Indigo," she said for sore throats.

"Then why do they say I'm the little girl worth her weight in gold?" I queried.

"Because you're good at chores, when you mind your P's and Q's."

We did battle with traffic but not on the fourth of July. We shunned national holidays. A past master at discipline, Mother was not a tyrant. She had her charisma, but also was unassuming, forthright. The magic happened when a child was lowest. After polio, we invented Mr. Nimble Thimble who sewed me clothes because nothing fit right.

One night when I thought the worst was over and I was home from the hospital where I'd lived half a year, I woke not with the blue meanies but the shivers. I wheeled up to Marcelle's bed, tapping her awake.

"What? Indigo," she asked."

I swallowed hard. I raised my fourteen-year old head high. I had become a woman that winter. Just before my fourteenth birthday my period had come.

"It's—it's the undertaker bird I think coming."

She sat bolt upright, threw on her silky man tailored dressing gown and said, "Follow me. It was her March walk."

I followed in my wooden wheelchair whose reflection I caught, grotesque, long exaggerated wheels, in the China cab's reflecting ancient doors, wood and glass.

Behind us in the doorway Rachel shadowed, "Sleepy," she said.

"I'll take you back to bed, child," said Mother, which she did.

"Now, Indigo, you and I are going to have a private midnight party and we'll chase the shadow of that old bird away."

She lit up and packed down a Camels cigarette. She switched, for what reason I never knew, her brand of cigarettes after I had infantile paralysis. The Phillip Morris which accompanied her everywhere, in her hip or breast pocket, became Camels. She'd buy them by the carton and stash them up in the hall closet with the cloches hats with feathers. I could see she was racking her brains how to handle me now. This was in our second Manhattan apartment. The kitchen overlooked fire escapes and water towers. Our first apartment had been prettier and had more character but Mrs. Friender, the manager, had run the vacuum at two in the morning. We were renting the first floor apartment at a professional rate, a thing our father had arranged and we weren't professionals. We were three women trying to survive.

Mother seldom was bankrupt. This, however, was the three a.m. of our year. I set my chin in my hands. "When are you gonna quit? You did everything you could to get me up and walking again."

She rose and ran the water, probably to cover tears which she never showed before me. I was sorry I said it. I was trying to square with myself.

"We've installed parallel bars, we've turned the bedroom Chel and I share into a gym. We have the black medicine ball, we have Mrs. B three times a week. When will you ever knock off?"

"The morning," she turned around facing me square on answering, "that the cow jumps over the moon."

I shuddered. It was the mention of an animal. I still felt the hideous bird approaching.

"Look," she said, "if you didn't die then, you won't die now."

My blood sugar must have been low. There was no response adequate to what I felt. I closed my eyes a second. Those girls who never were shot through my mind, those who had suffered setbacks, falls, betrayals, the worst burns. Once naphthalene had exploded in my face when I heated Esquire shoe polish on the stove. These disasters horrified me. Thank heaven Rachel didn't have to be in on this scene. We were both grim. Mother turned out the light plunging us into the nocturnal twilight of the kitchen where, in total silence, she blew milk-blue smoke rings. I looked at her face, then down to the pack of Camels.

She knew what was coming, "Want one?" she asked.

I smiled, she lit mine. After all, I was fourteen.

In Europe children smoke. Auschwitz, Treblinka, Bergen, Belsen—the barbed wire birds of our time. Those horrifying words, "Arbeit Macht Frieden."

Work makes free at the black wrought iron gate to Auschwitz in Poland. It might have been Europe during the war where I imagined us two smoking in the kitchen, beyond hope, beyond despair even. Just floating.

Then, measuring each word, she said, "Indigo, you might have thought it was him."

"I did."

"But one cannot be sure. Describe what you felt."

I hiked my shoulder, he cast a long shadow. He had leggy spindly silhouette, a nearly bald head the color of wax or flesh with a few feathers."

"Did you see him or just the shadow of him?"

"Shadow but becoming form."

"Did he make any sound?"

I thought, pondered. "Yes," I said.

"What kind of sound?"

"A kind of brittle, dry sound."

"Was it a rattling?"

"You could call it a rattling," I sighed blowing out smoke rings, ragged, imperfect ones. Ours mingled, hers and mine, the rings. I saw the shadow of my childhood passing.

I thought of Rachel's incredible presence on stage playing Lalo's *Symphonie Espanol* in Hartford, Connecticut at age ten. I flashed back to my audition for the elementary school choir.

"What voice do you sing?"

"Any," I said.

But when she heard me she said, "Hopeless."

I could carry a tune perfectly but had no projection. "That's what I told you," I said, "low hopeless," that's what I sing.

I felt low-hopeless now. I did have an alto voice. In the ward I sang duets with Karenina, her high to my low, my crush on her overwhelming. The nervous little mongrel pup next door in a large wooden box now began barking. Weary, I put my hands to my ears.

I thought of my first recital. I wore a blue dress with black trim. My hair was streaked with blond from the sun. I played a Mozart sonata and felt the terror of Mozart even then. I missed exuberance during this time in my life and the Mozart made me half smile. If you stared long enough at Marcelle she'd rise and rinse out an ashtray. If you stared long enough at Rachel, she'd give in and smile. These were the two people in my life.

Marcelle was hard to flummox, yet now she said to me, "Indigo, at times you mystify me." She flicked the old Philco radio on which we kept in the kitchen. Late at night WQXR played jazz.

"Please don't," I said. It made me feel at the brink. She understood.

The milk boiled. She made us each a cup of cocoa pouring the thin stream of blue-white milk from the old chipped enamel pot, white except where little maps of Africa, of India were carved black into it.

The South was always heavy on our mind. Like methyl mercury poisoning. Marcelle was at such times as this a cross between the dispossessed southern belle and the Jewish mother. Her voice was lilting, musical. Her eyes were mournful. The South was big on parades and floats. An analogy from music suddenly came to me. When you're on a bridge it goes on forever and ever. I thought of the twenty-six letters of the Alphabet, which inspired me to write. Also, there came to me a need to laugh. It began with a little giggle. I started to hear, *It's only a paper moon, a Barnum & Bailey moon,* until it was all a wild whirl in my mind. Soot and soil, clay sands of Coney Island, sand between my toes, never again.

"I'll never get sand between my toes again," I said to Marcelle.

"*Paper Moon,*" I loved it. It was one of the *Songs that Won the War* by Harold Arlen, recorded by Ella Fitzgerald.

"Marcelle?"

She came up to me and put her hands on my shoulders.

"Indigo," she said, "That wasn't the undertaker bird you heard."

"Prove it."

"Ok," she came away and faced me again. Her touch never lasted long. "Did he go like this? Rat-at-at-at-at? Or was it all a jumble?"

"It wasn't all a jumble."

"So that proves it."

"Proves what?"

"That it wasn't the undertaker bird."

"What was it then?"

"That, my dear girl, was the typewriter bird. He was hitting his black ribbon."

She knew so many girls who had come to such dramatic grief. The long mournful trail rose like a wraith of smoke now. She knew a girl with big green eyes. But she never knew a girl who stared so long at the polio poster that she caught infantile paralysis.

Marcelle leant in close to me. "He *will* come one day, Indigo, when we least expect him. There's no turning him back. But don't let's extend him an invitation."

I shook my head. Then began nodding, "Thanks," I told her.

"For what?"

"The cigarette."

I saw Marcelle do what she rarely did. She doused the evening with a little Scotch in a tumbler. So much of me she loved was undersea.

"The map of Ireland in your face," she smiled ironically when I left that night.

Once or twice, when she was piqued with me she'd call me *Shiksa*. "How can you be Jewish? I can see the map of Ireland written on your face."

The cocoa has been warming. There was the macaroni and cheese casserole from our dinner. The spigot dripped and left little runnels down our enamel kitchen sink overlooking the water towers and fire escapes.

I wheeled back down the hall to my twin bed alongside Rachel's. She was fast asleep. I couldn't, like Diogenes, get into a tub and shout "Eureka!"

But I lay awake a full hour after, composing with those twenty-six letters of the alphabet, in love with the **"M" "O" "P"** each its own shape, the **"H"** like a little Quaker chair. My hands were itchy, my mind restless too, a windmill turning. After a while, my eyes closed and I pictured the quaint circular keys of Marcelle's old Underwood typewriter. I put the paper in the platen.

In those days we didn't speak of re-inventing the past or of melt downs. The past unscrolled as it was. Giving in wasn't melting but melding with the reality of our lives. Tonight we'd rounded a bend, I'd just about gone through the wall. I recalled reading that the oldest example of a parchment book is a copy of Homer made in the third or fourth century after Christ. I wanted to listen to Vaughan William's *London Symphony* but I couldn't do that either.

A *friend* told me when I was in my early twenties, "If I were you, Indigo, I'd have committed suicide long ago."

Now, while the enemy ticked, now, the bird with the almost bald wax flesh-colored head rustled and horrified me in his coppers, his dress feathers for the grave, his scavenging. The sound may have been that of the typewriter bird but the shadow cast upon my eggshell white bedroom wall that night was the shadow of the undertaker bird, his noirs rustling. I could almost see the phosphorescence in his feathers —and it took all my willpower to transmute from this Gothic, this

177

Hieronymus Bosch mystical death figure, stalking in his rustle and glowing crepes and taffetas, with ashen complexion who stalked our ward— into the snappy the swanky typewriter bird my mother wished to guide to my hand. I'd seen the undertaker bird scavenge children in the ward. The southern Jewish girl-child in me was then most alive.

"We might as well be burning in Bergen-Belsen as be here," Mother had once said in Florida.

One night we were dancing, my thin hand in his claw, the tip of his feathered wing. First daybreak was here. I saw the elegantly smooth surface taking the words like ice taking steel blades of ice skates. Mother first taught me printing, then school taught me script. The twenty six letters. My hand was moving now, taking down the words, very slowly in dictation from the tall formal winged creature in black high shoes and top hat, but not the graveyard denizen. I was transcribing, in a mystical transport, for the typewriter bird who quietly as winter's last snow had come.

May 22, 2006

# *Cry Me a River:*
## *A Story in Five Sections*

I never understood what quality it was that made an actress until a recent night in Hartford, Connecticut.

It was New Year's Eve, 1952. Heavy snow was falling. I joined some two thousand frostbitten New Englanders in the barn-like New Parsons Theater to witness the opening of a play, Midsummer. One of the on stage participants was to be my daughter Jenny, then nine years old.

I had kept away from the play's rehearsals and had never heard Jenny do any of her lines at home . . . as I sat this snowy night in the theater . . . there was about Jenny at nine a curious pride and fearlessness that would keep her back straight anywhere she walked. After Geraldine Page, another character appeared.

I could have sworn it rose out of the stage for it seemed so much a part of it. The character was Jenny. She moved toward Geraldine with feet that seemed not to touch the boards, and with one arm floating lyrically in the air. And around her was such an aura of happiness that no sooner had she spoken her first lines than the audience let loose a thunder of applause. Jenny, who had never faced an audience before, paused, considered briefly what was the correct thing to do and decided on a small, friendly bow. Straightening, she returned to her work.

Jenny's performance was excellent. But it was not her performance I watched as much as her happiness.

>Ben Hecht, A Child of the Century,
>(dedicated to Jenny 1954, N.Y. Simone & Schuster)

Note: My sister, Chel went to *Professional Children's School*, in New York City, with Jenny Hecht, who died of a drug overdose in her twenties thus proving herself, tragically, to be indeed a child of the century.

– Life is a river. The story begins with a flashback to Jenny Hecht, wunderkind, who went to the school for gifted children Rachel attended as a child. But its focus is the East River which is powerful, like the Mississippi, but which ran outside Indigo's hospital room. Isolation which may be the deepest pain of any illness is evoked in this corner in which Indigo sees the iron lung gleaming in the corner of her room when she was in the acute phase of polio. That time is over fifty years away but she still smells the brine and tells the story now nearing her sixtieth year. North and South are once again polarities here.

## Prologue

Britta, woman from northern Europe, together we have done translations of the Jewish poet who transformed the Holocaust dust into birds that sing: you from Bavaria, me from Eastern Europe, we both have known rivers—there was one, you tell me, that flowed beside the Camp. We inherit a tradition of restraint, but underneath are real tears. We used to live in the same town. Now, you write to me every day about the changing Mud River, you who have moved away to the Canadian prairies while I remain on the coast, the western ocean. You communicate to me how the Mud River looks when roiled, blown; or on the other hand, when it is a tabletop, when it's a glass mirror for skies and trees you too are calm.

## Largo

Let me tell you about a river. The East. Unlike the Mississippi, my other river, it was not in the South. In the South we skipped first on our right foot then the left, the little white girls with hair bows bigger than a country church, spelling out in great glee "Miss-iss-ippi" always giggling with I pee-pee sounds at the end. These Dixie girls knew the meaning of *acting ugly*, just as they knew *Legs are best friends, they stay together, a nice girl didn't touch and didn't let a pit of underpants show.*

No the eastern river occurred the summer I lost my legs and like all Jewish eastern girls knew, book learning was the thing. This river, it ran outside the window of my hospital room the summer I was twelve, carrying mainly barges loaded with lumber, and some bright rotund tugs. It was my consolation. In the corner stood a silvery cylindrical object; I didn't know it was an iron lung.

I did not know it then, but my disillusionment as a child must have been deep as snow, my sense of earth turning pale must have been as wan as ashes.

Even though that time is now fifty years ago, the smell of brine in the sea this evening, plus the green Annabelle eye shadow Sweetpea brought me along with a pencil sharpener, brings that river back.

If wars make adults of children, after that summer, when I could no longer walk, the second part of my life began.

Simone, (Sweetpea) searches the Internet. She who can be *Deirdre of the Sorrows*, with the sweetest smile, telling me she's found a photograph of my old flame Marie, now sixty, an aging diva with silver curls where she once was blonde. What is she doing in the deep South, Athens, Georgia with its classical name?

*Zydeco*, she improvises on her cello to B'hai poetry. *Chedida* I call her, softly in Spanish who would be at home in Spanish Harlem, having thought herself a "dog of the streets" when young.

There, the earth is red.

There, the air is scented with honeysuckle but menace lurks in the old manses, the Spanish moss so shroud-like and deceivingly lacy.

We used to improvise music. Now, I have hung a stuffed toy camel, by a thin bridle of fine leather, on the door to my writing room: Be Patient!

I'm pretty Catholic in my tastes. Majored in the history of English painting. When I came here, I brought my oils with me. I joined a pastel class but not enough people enrolled. This afternoon, I've been pottering; I face South and all. At two o'clock I went out, read, did a bit of knitting. It's been going on a couple of years. I don't get on with a lot but it's a hip-length jacket of knitting.

"Who for?" the voice inside me asks.

"Me!" the other voice answers, it's green-turquoise.

"What'm I reading?"

"A spy story."

Rochelle too became an adult in a child's skin.

Rochelle down the block, Rochelle who says all over her, made in

Ireland, whose grin's as wide as the ocean. I've not told her the details of the child in crisis in our family, my brother's daughter, Lily who had the breakdown.

Rochelle's many deeds of kindness have been repaid—Rochelle with contralto voice, which is silky and casts her in a cone of mystery, like a stage light, wherever she goes. If her bread has been cast upon the waters, it's come back buttered—but she didn't do it for that reason. Wined and dined at a posh restaurant overlooking the water, what did she order? Liver and onions! With *crème* caramel for dessert. My one weakness.

Rochelle for whom I had one of my indigo blue caftans altered—a slit cut down the front for a zipper.

"It's so comfortable like an easy chair."

She lays her right hand upon the table at lunch—the hand she can move. I look at it and think, that hand began long ago in Ireland. That hand has dressed sleepy children at night during the Blitz, their overcoats on top of their pajamas. That body, as a child, has gone outside at five in a winter morning to see earth still smoldering red from the bombs.

She looks twenty years younger than when we met, and turned up today with the music to *Porgy & Bess*, was wearing white Adidas, and a white Sweatshirt that said, "Bourbon Street."

Which brings me back round to my old love, Marie.

She still does it to me.

"Get me a wet cloth," I told Simone when she brought me the photograph.

"I'm not insecure," Sweetpea smiles, "I know if you wanted to be with her you'd be with her—you want to be with me."

"Yes."

Only, Simone trips over her own long sentences the way an adolescent boy does over his shoelaces. Rochelle calls her goodbye the "long operatic farewell."

I could have sworn it is the ghost of Rochelle that rises from the dark, her right hand extended . . . child of the Blitz, stepping out into a morning in which a pile of smoldering bricks, small red fires against the dawn, world in which a hole exists where there was a house last night with mother and child. And making his way, stepping cautiously across the rubble, wearing his white coat, carrying his glass bottles, one hand extended to keep his balance—the milkman is coming. Like an odd, long legged seabird, perhaps a sand crane. A frigate bird.

What else ruptures the surface of memory's glass-calm?

My brother Josh's fourteen-year old child, a prodigy with the Bolshoi Ballet from age eleven to fourteen had had what she calls a sort of breakdown.

At the school she was adored, she might have been God's messenger.

Josh is an archeologist, teaching at the University of Southern California, in Los Angeles. In desperation, her parents rented an apartment for ten months in northern Spain.

Lily, too, is a child of war. So we form three—Rochelle, child of the actual Blitz in London, a war whose depression was in the air everywhere around, me child-soldier in a war that was never officially declared, that I never enlisted in, my legs taken away from me one summer morning, now Lily, battling the obsession of perfection, ballet so pain-oriented. And of course, you, Britta are in the background, born in a Displaced Person's Camp in Bavaria translating the language of the enemy into a human tongue when you translate the German-Jewish poet for me.

Lily took the breath away.

At nine, at ten, at eleven: on stage as dancer, defining a new form of the ballet, her arm movements, her slender exceptionally long neck made her move as though liquid.

She did well her first half-year away from Los Angeles, with her mother, and younger sister, Jesse, who is a dancer too, but more a gymnast, who lives in a wheelchair, as though a tree-climber. Born nine weeks too soon, she was given an overdose of oxygen. Brain and bone scans revealed it would only affect her lower limbs.

Lily threw away her cigarettes, and let her bleached red hair go back to its natural honey-dark blonde.

But now, Lily has had a relapse: she has cut herself again. This is the first blood in Spain. And she has shoplifted. Her father tells me.

Stolen under things! I picture the filmy substance—how could she even have wanted them? My sister-in-law, Lotte, still tapes her daughter Lily's phone calls. She began this in Los Angeles. She heard the theft planned with a friend.

The confrontation—terrifying.

Afterward, the tall, lean woman-child of fourteen, with freckles across the bridge of her nose, and magnolia-pale skin, depression deep as snow, sin pale as ashes, slipped into the bathroom down there in southern Spain to make use of her daddy's razor one more time.

I flash forward to Rochelle, that hand born long ago in Ireland—her boy and girl fifteen months apart, an old Catholic nun who'd been kind to the family visiting them. Her daughter at three wore a blue dotted Swiss eyelet. It was July. With bow in back and quite short.

"Lovely child," said the old nun, "but cover her."

"Yes, sister, of course."

She knew the Sisters bathed with their undies on.

This there can be no covering.

Filmy, I picture the river Ouse in England, that river Virginia Woolf drowned herself in that day when the war was thick upon the land of England—but viewing the total picture—the war had barely begun.

I close my eyes, have a nap, a daydream and start awake. The body of the slender girl, Lily, washes up on the shore of early evening.

So it's not that beauty is an obsession with the copiously talented Lily. It's that she wants to be in the limelight again, as when she was the darling of the Borzoi, dancing, whirling and whirling until she dropped, her cheeks red with fever, exhaustion and elation. It's that she adores taking risks. But this? She will break like the flower of her name, slender tall neck so perishable.

I daren't tell Simone, who will side naturally with the adolescent.

I will not tell Rochelle, whom I do not know intimately. Nor Marie, either, whom I haven't seen in decades, not since our farewell kiss in Manhattan.

Whom can I tell? You, Britta! With whom I did the translations.

Another chance to communicate with you—first about the river which matched my mood in all seasons, whose thick elms along the East shore turned ancient and dusty grey-green in summer, then a flat antique gold in earliest autumn . . .

You, who are far away, write me of the river's mood, morning, noon, and evening. I can tell you of the river when I was twelve, rolling outside my hospital window, the summer I was paralyzed, its sluggish mud grey, drab-brown waters nonetheless towing the barges, the stout tugs along. Some evenings, the very sky seemed to have died. It was white, ancient like a body of river fixed in the sky. Or the sky could be an eerie, gaseous yellow thru the brick stacks of chimneys, and the dusty old elms. And I can lie down inside my closed eyes and throat.

I began by telling you about the river that rolled outside my hospital window, keeping me company, where the silvery, cylindrical object stood in the corner, which I never knew, was a lung. Now I will tell you darker things, Britta, that may remind you of a river in Bavaria where you were born.

*Allegretto*

Jesse, too, knows that a river can canter like a horse, run like a mustang.

Jesse wakes each morning as if it were a day the Lord had made.

In the same rooms, her rebellious sister wakes; the halls are sun-flooded, or winter-darkened, the apartment in the North of Spain. Jesse slips out of bed into her narrow silver wheelchair and goes to the sink to lather face and hands. Then she rolls down the hall to the kitchen, where she turns the gas ring on.

As for Lily-Amiel I want to shake her by the wide-slung bony shoulders, "Kid, you had everything."

Her eyes moved without her turning her head—from early childhood on, they flickered like snakes, they darted, those dark lamps. She was born to dance.

I will go down tonight and cry my fill in the river, thus rinsing off Lily-Amiel's twenty-two cuts.

*Gentleman-John*, you, the lily, smiled, bowing to the asters, after doing a pirouette, then an extension that left people gasping: *Lady Elizabeth Lonesome*. Miss Lily-Amiel, you wanted the eyelet, the white lace like the alyssum. You craved being a star again.

Like the song-boy, finch, out my window, I learned to be utterly alone that winter with the East River, my soul, rolling outside the window.

Jessica-Rachel, too, has learned to be utterly alone. Everything about her is jazzy, sporty—from the neon-pink ball-point pen she carries in her bomber jacket embroidered with flowers, to the way she smiles, a gap-toothed grin in her wheelchair, when that jacket darkens so that, she claims "The flowers spring in the rain."

When people tell her to carry an umbrella, she buttons her lip, she shrugs.

You, Lily, have slit yourself before—but this is the first time you've stolen.

"There's no ecstasy left in my life, Mom."

"Lily, you give me grief. Sometimes I think you have nothing from the neck up," says Lotte, indicating a scissors snipping the neck after she discovers the new blouses, pants, jewelry in your bedroom drawer.

It turns out you've stolen all these things and there, where the laws of juvenile court are tougher than in America, there in northern Spain. She could be deported!

Your mother bolts the door, makes you sit beside her on the sofa, and says, "Lily, write a list of what you've taken."

Your eyes of a doe fill with tears.

"Why?" your mother asked, "can't you work at being content, like your younger sister, Jesse? She's only eleven."

"I'm not Jesse, Mom."

This, you realize, Lily, is a crime. "Write me a list the things."

"Bracelets" you wrote, hesitantly, with pencil.

"And where did the pants come from?" your mother said, casting her eyes toward your bedroom.

You shrug.

"Lily–" your mother reproves.

"Ok, yes, I took those also, Mom."

"And the blouse?"

You write it down. Sunlight strikes your mother's face. Her cheek is lit, you can see the pores, as though they sparkled diamond. She looks graphite-drawn and grayish some of the time, but now, with the sun setting . . .

Your mother rose, slowly, feeling like a figure in a Greek tragedy. She laid each of the stolen goods in a brown paper bag. When she came to the blue-striped tailored blouse you'd pointed at in the window of the boutique in town—she saw blood.

"There's blood on this blouse, Lilian!"

"You know what I do to myself when I'm trapped, Mother."

She had you hitch up your midriff.

"I thought you'd never, ever do this thing again."

There were the more than two dozen red razor slits.

You've been wearing only short tops—above the belly button, the thing this summer in Europe. You've pierced your belly button.

You suddenly realize something and strike your hand to your forehead. You suck your breath in, "Now what will I wear?"

"I have no idea, Lily. Darling, I took you to the ends of the earth, we went to the holy land Israel, we were in Palestine just weeks ago for Passover, we touched that holiest place on the planet, the Wailing Wall. You bathed in the Dead Sea, you climbed Mount Carmel."

*Now you say you love me.*

Your mother began to sing that old pop tune you always sang to each other when things went terribly wrong

*Cry me a river. For I've cried a river over you.*

Your mother sits back beside you on the sagging couch, and hangs her head in her hands.

When she has done sobbing, she says, "I'm giving you more St. John's Wort. It's an anti-depressant. In Europe it's used a lot."

"But what will I wear? Everything I own now is for my belly button showing."

"Lily, what you've done's a wrong thing. I don't know. I need to think a long while. So do you."

You, too, Lily have been crying, but silent sobbing, shaking, holding yourself with your arms akimbo, rocking on the sofa.

"We could go shopping," you say.

The black phone rings—but the cell phone in your lap is silent. You look at the silent phone and moan, "Daddy."

The sun sets upon the rented suite of two simple rooms in northern Spain. But first, in this Basque region, the rooms, like small caves fill with reddish sun, the basins of rooms scooping sun up to drain the last light and color—corners of cracked old pain appearing like mossy maps, which then fully crumble, and disappear with darkness.

Where I am, the river this morning looks brackish, flows south, golden-green. The reflections are olive brown. It's almost tortoise-colored.

Slow-as-a-tortoise life moves.

On the roped-in, white-hot high school playground, the Monday noon, after your Sunday self-mutilation, you are crying. Carlos-Felippe, your boyfriend of five weeks, flings his arm about you who crumple like paper. He can feel your bones through the cloth jacket you are wearing. This is a strange time, the *sirocco* season.

"Why do you cry, Amielito?" he asks with a touch of tenderness in his tone, his macho manner for a moment relaxing. (He uses the Spanish derivative of your middle name, which is close to the word for honey.) "See, Amiel, look about you! The sun shines!"

"A while ago, I had my heart broken, when I had just turned fourteen." You tell your Spanish boyfriend the story about the ballet.

He is frightened. "You are sad? Why? I do not like sad persons."

"Then what are you worth? A hill of beans! Listen! I've had a lot of problems. Two years ago, when I was twelve, at the Bolshoi Ballet School, well, I used to be a star—my mom still wants me to be a dancer but when I was fourteen I had this breakdown. Don't scowl at me so. I hate it when you frown. If you cannot understand, you can at least sit on a bench with me, you can sympathize."

"No, I hate unhappy persons!"

"Then you're shallow! Carlos," you finally nail him, pushing him away roughly, the way the girls at recess in Spain have taught you to do. They don't tamp their anger down.

"Oy!" he raises his eyes to the sky, "You make me wish for the monsoon. If you have problems," he backs down and softens, "the thing to do is—you should cover them up, Amielito, the way I do. Nobody will know a thing. Look," he rolls up his sleeve, and flexes the biceps on his right arm.

You look away bored, heavy-lidded.

"Look here," he says pulling up his shirt, "real hair! Come on, be brave, you can hide your feelings."

"No, Carlos-Felippe, that's what I used to do, that's bad for me."

"I would have liked you better then."

"You look!" you say, and raise your tee-shirt showing him the scars from the twenty-two slashes you've made.

His jaw drops open.

"That's what I do to myself when I feel trapped," you say in a low voice that is, however, free of shame.

The shock value of it is great, but when it lessens, the fright of having told sinks in, ending in depression.

Daddy is thousands of miles away teaching. But he can sympathize by phone. You want to murder your mother who, you suspect, still wants you to dance again. The phone rings off the hook this time.

Neither one of you, mother nor daughter can rise to answer the phone.

Maybe these devastations are like the *simooms*, those dust-laden winds blowing at intervals in the Arabian desert—*Simoom*, whose name derives from the Arabic *to poison*. The *sirocco*, whose name is also derived from Arabic, is a Saharan *simoom* reaching the northern shores of the Mediterranean, or a warm sultry rainy wind in southern Europe—this wind blows over the grass of northern Spain.

You cried so hard this afternoon at recess that the kids brought you to the nurse. She was the one who noticed the blood coming through from your fresh slices to stain your pale green tee shirt. She phoned your mother who took a taxi all the way out to the school—past the winery which she thought would make you feel so good to be alive, which you passed daily in your walk to the bus, out finally to the international school, which is beyond the pale of the city bus, to bring you home. By tomorrow morning, everyone in the high school will know what you've done.

## Sarabande

Charlotte woke in acute anxiety at four that morning. She could hear Jesse's even breathing, Lily's troubled breathing as Lily turned in her sleep. Lotte reached for the green pill to her right side in the dish. The walls of the small room in northern Spain began to wash with light—paler, more horrifying than any full light of day can be. It is like a deathblow, waking.

A candle burns in a milk glass dish, casting a shadow, like a rose butterfly, between mother and child.

"Cry me one, Lily," thinks Charlotte, sitting by her daughter's bed where the glass of warm tea turns stale. "I've cried one over you."

A murder of crows is noisy overhead.

Then the air falls silent.

It is Pentecost, White Sunday, a festival celebrating the descent of the Holy Spirit. Flies buzz in the room in the descending light.

"But it is also," thinks Lotte, "the Jewish harvest festival, on the fiftieth day after the second day of Passover. "We're not there yet," she consoles herself, drawing the curtains the next morning to a blazing sun.

What is Pentecostal? What characterizes Christians and people emphasizing the gifts of the Holy Spirit, who express religious feelings by clapping.

The child, Lily, was too fragile not to succumb to pressures, those within herself, more than out there in Spain.

Her older daughter is still asleep, her younger girl moves about by the stove in the kitchen, turning the gas ring on, as she does each morning, smiling, lighting the coffee pot.

Later that morning, Lotte phones her mother-in-law in Fairfax. She asks her how the weather is back home, what she's had for her dinner, how the cat is.

Not because she wants to know but because her heart is broken.

"How do you shop there, Lotte, without a car?"

"I do what everyone in Spain does, in the little villages at least. I take a string bag and shop each day. Today I bought oranges, next week perhaps green beans."

Her mother-in-law asks, not because she wants to know but because she hears what's going on behind her daughter-in-law's words. She misses Jewish Fairfax. The bagel and lox delis. In the morning sunlight in California, Miriam closes her eyes.

"Hurt me where I live and I'll cry," she thinks, intoning the old Yiddish song.

The day after Pentecost, it pours with rain.

Lotte finds Lily at the end of the garden, crouched near the stone boy who is nude, his penis spouting water into the stone basin.

"Lily," she puts her arm on her daughter's shoulder, "I think we must leave Spain."

Her daughter faces her, her face wet to match the sky.

Lily throws up her arms and puts them around her mother's neck.

"I'm sorry, Mom."

"About?"

"About the theft, the lying, the cutting. Sorry about what I said to you and Dad, how I hurt Jesse."

Charlotte, for a moment, feels earth open—she begins a descent down a black hole, but then, there is that one twig sticking out which she clutches when almost at the bottom. Her throat is thick with tears, but she reaches out her hand—as she did in her dream last night.

"Darling," she whispers, "Lily-Amiel. This is tough. This seems to go on and on. But you will find your way out."

"But all the kids at school, Carlos-Felippe—I've lost him, I've lost all of them."

"No, Lily. You've lost some—those who are frightened by what you've done. But not daddy, not me, not Jesse-Rachel."

"I am so alone."

"No, Lily."

"I'm cried out, Mom," Lily said.

Then she stood up, stretched, reached her fingertips as if to tickle the ceiling and began to smile. "Remember when you and Jesse and I took that trip to San Francisco without Dad, that long weekend and found a guest house with only the bridal suite left?"

"Sure do. That was in Castine, Maine."

"There was a four-poster bed with a canopy."

"And Jesse transferred from her wheelchair and said 'I'm the bride, who's the groom?'"

"You said you'd be the groom—but I said, 'No fair, kids, I'm not sleeping on the couch!'"

"Yes, remember that fancy little couch in the corner all decked out with ruffles? A baby couldn't have slept on that thing."

"Certainly not a baby!"

Lotte—as she closed her eyes, could visualize the house she'd grown up in, in New England. The wind in spring had blown the hornet's nest clear from the laburnum into the holly. The nest blew as though it was a disembodied spirit. She saw her young Jesse this way now. She saw the three of them packing up to leave Spain, to cross the ocean back to Daddy again. She saw the whole nightmare rinsing out of her mind. She pictured Lily back at her practice bar at home, how radiant and whole life had been before she gave up dancing, when she worked out like a fanatic, a maniac, those long hours. And, there was Jesse, a computer whiz, at her computer desk at eight, so precocious, even before that, seven . . .

## Coda

After a night of bombing, the seven-year old Rochelle used to step out to see disembodied buildings, houses disemboweled, leveled buildings, holes where an apartment house stood, only small piles of bricks smoldering, as the eerie light of dawn came.

Where there had been a family, a mummy and daddy and three children, there was a hole against the sky and within.

That terror struck her that comes just before the light returns to earth. All wars made adults of little children. At every step pulling back from the sentimental, she knew there is no consolation but life itself.

Simone has refreshed the Annabelle green eye shadow, its pencil sharpener had left it going blunt near the bottom.

Lotte, believing herself to be at the end of her resources, sees her child, her disabled daughter, now down by the stone fountain. She recalls what her husband taught her: depths always have new depths.

They exchange places. Lil had helped roll Jesse down, and has climbed back up to where her mother stands.

Lotte looks Lily in the eyes.

"You're crying." Face-to-face, they stand. Lotte puts both hands on her tall young daughter's shoulders.

"Nope. Remember, my new contacts, Mom."

Lotte breaks into a wide grin. Her freckles show. Her skin can glow golden to match what's left of gold in her salt-and-pepper bob and bangs.

"You're only supposed to keep them in how many hours a day?"

"Two and a half for the first week. This is the second."

"They make your eyes appear as though you're crying."

"Yes. It's neat. The large-eyed look."

Lily, who had long dark brown eyelashes, batted them like Bambi.

"Run and get your camera, Lil!" Lotte said, "Look, the sun's setting the tips of the mountain are on fire."

"Remember, Biggles took a bite out of my camera, Mother."

Lil bent her blonde head forward like a mustang about to charge. In her shingle haircut, the perfectly straight bob caught the light and glistened like a curried mane. Lotte was always struck by the dramatic contrast in coloring between her two daughters. Lil with her blonde hair, hazel-brown eyes, had dark golden skin. Jesse was magnolia-white with her ink-blue eyes—her dad called her *Periwinkle*—and her jet blue-black hair. But they had this in common. They could both be battering rams.

"My memory's a sieve these days," her mother says, laughing.

"Mom, there's no quick fix," her older daughter lays her hand on her mother's shoulder.

Lotte casts a glance toward Jesse. For this one, things would always be twice as difficult as for other kids. But she'd get things done with panache, with elan, and a grin. When she broke her right hand at age five showing off, wheeling herself over a bump, she had a fall, her good hand was casted. It came out purple-blue as a bruised flower. But Jesse, she taught herself mouth-brush paintings, and would spend hours at a time, in winter back in Castine, Maine painting on the child-size easel her mother got her. She set up in the attic, simply a gabled room up a few steps from the main part of the saltbox house. But the house was so tall and thin back there on the seacoast, they called this mysterious top-room the *garret*.

Jesse had to be carried by her dad, her legs dangling, like a limp pecker, or in the heavy steel and leather braces she wore in her first four or five years of her life. Josh carried her gently.

He'd set her down, "Now there, Jesse-Monet," he'd stand back, hold his hands forth and smile.

She loved doing tiny dots like Monet in his garden.

Josh even bought her a periwinkle-blue crush-beret, velvet. She wore it at the easel to look like Titus, Rembrandt's son. She'd grin back, her eyes slightly crossed. She wore thick lenses in wire-rim frames in those days before her squint was corrected. She shrugged her bony shoulders and giggled at the name, Monet. She was born with astigmatism.

Castine, Maine.

Lotte liked to remember her way back to Castine, Maine, her ancestral home. Hers was a life of sea wind blowing the hair, a rugged coast, granite which sparkled like diamonds in the sun. Not the glaring merciless sun of Los Angeles, not the cruel Mediterranean sun of the Basque country, in the Pyrenees, Spain—this was to have been their eyrie, but all their cover had been blown.

I fell into a deep sleep.

Rochelle, during the war, going to Saint Christopher's, two years older than her next sister, came home from school and two chocolate biscuits were laid out for her. Mavor and Maureen giggled, younger by a year each. Mummie had credit at the store and had gotten hold of some chocolate biscuits while the war was still on. She gave each child two. Mavor and Maureen ate Rochelle's two, in addition to their own. Then they panicked. They searched everywhere for where Mummie had hid the tin. Finally, they pulled out a chair, one giving the other child a boost and found the tin! It was in the back of the very highest cupboard. The girls tried to arrange things as they had been. They laid out two more so when Mummie came in, there they were on the plate.

Rochelle pulled and pushed the sleepy body of her younger brother, Justin, her baby sister, Maureen, into heavy winter outer clothing. The bombs have not stopped above—so it's not curtains.

But Mavor was always a clumsy child, Maureen, a sleepy one. Elbows and knees felt like bumps and sticks, circles and long lines of bone in the dark. She struggled to shove the limbs into the clothing—a coat pulled on, Mavor's onto Maureen, a scarf wound round Maureen's neck that belonged to Duncan.

Out into the night the cluster of children, and Mummy and Daddy go. It is nighttime London, the raids go on and on.

"It's a long haul, there's no quick fix, and I never believed in Jesus, Mom," the tall fourteen year old girl is saying.

She has a dream of the albino falcon. In it, she is dancing, at the barre, breasts lifted like young pears to catch the light. Moving is as easy as breathing. She looses a small white falcon from her wrist, for, miraculously inside the ballet studio this falcon has flown. She looses him, then blanks out a moment. When she wakes she is sitting on a bed, here in Spain, holding sheer underclothing in her hands. She draws her breath in 'til it stings her lungs. She wakes.

It has become a subject much talked about. Lotte is afraid to have them returned since her daughters are illegally in France. They got a visa for half a year, which the family then extended, to a whole year. If Lilly were to incur a record she could be deported, she could be put behind bars. One thing's clear: the stolen clothing will never be enjoyed. When Lotte puts on chamber music in evening, Jesse listens closely. Her father plays cello in a quartet of archaeologists every other Thursday night. She listens long hours to recordings of the chamber music, the Mozart quartets they rehearse.

Josh says he's receiving more comments about his playing than ever which reminds him he hasn't forgot how to play.

"That's because your heart has been broken open," I say.

"It's Lotte I worry most about," he tells me in a phone conversation about Spain. "I can help Lil some ways, but Lotte, I heard about this latest episode of stealing and cutting—she saw it all. I'm thinking of flying over to Spain to help them pack up the apartment once term's done."

"Good idea, Josh."

It's June, month for wedding bells. In the local florist stands a mannequin with bridal dress. There's only one hitch: she has no head. The headless bride I call her who floats at the end of our Main Street at nightfall. The brick buildings which seem so rich with promise, which sell sensible clothes, stout walking shoes, suddenly flatten as though made of cardboard. The brick turns poor now, all promise, hope, a flattened dream.

The headless bride sings in my dream. She holds roses, long-stemmed, wine-roses in her hands, before delivering a long operatic farewell. She, who has no head, thus presents an enigma.

That's what Rochelle said Simone delivered to her. When Roch offered to drive Sweetpea to the airport, "The hour doesn't matter, no mater how inconvenient, I'll come," Simone phoned back last thing in the evening.

"I knew I was comin' down with somethin' said Rochelle, "because her long operatic farewell irritated me so."

Josh, however, is the opposite. It is an alternate Thursday evening. There, in Jewish Los Angeles, Fairfax, he meets with three colleagues from the university, two men, and one young woman and digs his bow into the music.

Daddy, the archaeologist, first discovered this part of Spain on a dig.

A stone box, a root cellar, a shaft of light—they'd all four dreamed of it for years, and here it was, the suite of rooms in Spain.

Lily-Amiel goes into the Mediterranean bathroom, stone sink, turns the ancient rusty tap on, a line of brownish water trickles into the basin. She's taking her contact lenses out, delicately, cautiously laying them into their round blue containers.

Jesse-Rachel bends forward in her child-size Everest & Jennings wheelchair, with its shiny chrome frame bouncing sun off it. This is the wheelchair the Haddasah in Fairfax helped her buy: she looks hell-bent for glory. She begins the long—for her—push up the hill from the stone statue boy to the small vegetable garden outside their kitchen in the dirt yard. Not much will grow here, but a few things do.

I'm weird, Lil had thought to herself the other evening. I dreamt she was laid in a stone casket for a little king. Small, but royal.

Here we are, the dysfunctional American Jewish family, exiled in Spain—Lotte, shoving back her sunglasses, taking with them her bangs, putting her hand to her forehead to wipe the sweat— gardening. The South often looked bomb-ridden. So did our rooms.

The stolen, the bloodied things have been washed.

The sun does not try to come out in this region of northern Spain. It floods out, blinding everything.

Britta, do you dream of that trickle of water that ran outside the camp in Bavaria? Until I told you about the river outside my sickbed window the summer I was twelve, I hardly dreamed of it.

I think I never understood what it took to be a dancer until I saw Lily dance. Then it was the light of it, her happiness which was luminous and fell like stone dust, marble dust from the hand of the sculptor as he released the form in the stone.

Her spirit was freed by dance.

"I think of Jesse as trapped, not disabled," said a friend to Lotte.

"That's the way I have always seen Jesse."

Her ironic speed was one that transcends the loss of lower limbs. Bent forward for glory, it is a thing she achieves although she captures no gold ring, like the woman Rochelle who has lost the use of one arm. Her goggles, sunglasses are all she needs at nearly seventy, shoved back, she is sporty, jaunty at the market, swinging the dead weight of her arm.

At last, Britta, I see you and I see my city, New York City, tarnished in evening.

It wasn't what you looked like—although it was that, too—but when I met you I knew you were someone from my former life, the life back in the metropolis, New York City, where figures and shadows moved by night and by day. Where memory was its own movement, where the buildings were old stone, what my mother called *European*.

There was a sepia, antique cast to your face when you turned it away from the light toward, let us call it, the river.

You sold art, that's true and that would have been enough for you to magnetize me.

But you moved with energy, purpose—separating the wheat from the chaff, the deep emotions from the appearance, the surface behavior toward people and things. You told me once you were born old. Like Rochelle.

"I feel old as Methuselah," she once told me. "All war children are little people in an old skin. When Churchill said to pull our belts in—I panicked. I thought what more can we do than we have done? I felt depression in the air in London all around. I was always the eldest, trying to make things right for my younger brothers and sisters, to fix things."

An old hand, born a very long time ago in Ireland, turns the blind to let morning in.

"The rich people in this town—they are such a tight-arsed bundle of bein's."

Is it because I am an old child myself, or because I never had a child, that I buy a disc of lullabies? Or because I feel un-daughtered by Simone's no longer needing me.

"My *dawtah*," says the wise old voice from Ireland, "until her final year in high school, was perfect. Then she turned into Florence Nightingale for all the class drugees would phone at four a.m., and I havin' to be up for work at six in the *mawning*."

The *mawning*.

What is there so terrifying, because so unrelenting, about the return of the ancient sun faking a new earth for the millionth time?

Britta, we have done translations together. When at last, we are all translated from now to Eternity, will it be a place, like a town we have known, with railroad tracks and yards, a city we have walked through? Will the streets bear similar markers so that we know how to walk them? Where to turn left? Where right?

You say I help keep you connected to where your heart is—yet you became angry with me, once, recently. Only yesterday. Rochelle, whom I had given a tiny photograph of me at age twenty-one in New

York City, enlarged it, antiqued it and made several cards, addressing them for me. I gave her your husband's name.

You said, "I gave up my last name—but not my first when I married him."

How could I? But how could I not? You see, it is once again the historical uncertainty, the historical tragedy, encapsulated in us like a cancer surrounded by healthy tissue. She is Irish; she survived the Blitz in London. Even though you were born in a displaced person's camp in Bavaria, even though you paid the full blood price as well as the guilt—nothing can change the blow to her ears of your native tongue. Translate as we might—how can we change this?

So you received it without your strong birth name. You received it with the softened Scottish name you have, in fact, not taken from your husband. Forgive me, Britta.

But where all waters run back to their source, where your peaceful, pleasant birth town in the Bavarian mountains still stands beside that body of water which was merely a trickle—so a good place to locate a D P Camp—where energies are at their font, are we not all bound, fated, to forgive each other. Are not all rivers one?

A murder of crows.
A Basque wind.

A song sung by a voice in Bavaria, a voice of a child of wars also, an adult in a little child's skin. A song that can be translated into another tongue.

It rains.

"Rain, rain go away," sings the woman from Bavaria, who, despite all the dislocation in her young life, thrives on life going as it ought to go. Down South was long ago. We hopped first on one foot, then the other, giggling at each other, we girls.

A morning. Long ago. London. The bricks are lit red by the rising sun; small fires are here and there burning. A child blinks open her eyes to the morning. Lo and behold! Over the rubble, in his white coat and his tie on, one hand extended to balance himself as he steps around fires and over glass, all six bottles blue glass shining, the milkman's coming!

    Victoria, B.C. June 16, 2000–September 2004

# Music To Get You Out Of the Pews, Dancing

— We arrive at November when a chalk-white sky hangs over the world. Keva, a woman whose marriage is dissolving, makes her appearance. Indigo recalls that her mother brings her borsht when she is ill. It is Indigo's sixty-fourth winter. She compares and contrasts Catholics with Jews, using Keva as a model Catholic. Indigo speaks again of "Mr. Scar" (mentioned early in "Polio: A Girlhood Noviate.") This scar of paralysis is to cover her the rest of her life. She recalls the night she caught polio. She is given a dream instructor: "write your own tale, storyteller, listen to the narrator-hurricane." Mrs. Olivia returns here too and Grit-Soul. Polio, she says, was the sculptor whose hands were to shape the rest of my life. My twelfth summer contained scene, action, detail and color, which were to be background for my existence. She is one step nearer November in Music To Get You Out Of the Pews Dancing. November is symbolic of age and ultimately death.

## One Step Nearer November

The sky was chalk-white when I hugged Keva over the loss of her marriage. Holding Keva was like one photograph, translucent, imposed on top of another. Our divorce was what my mother wanted. Losing my legs at age twelve was something altogether different. For the divorce, I was nine, each day taking a step deeper into symbolic November and the calendar's eleventh month. There is something magical about my childhood because I could walk then.

"Marie has died," Mother had told me the summer before. She had spinal meningitis and went overnight. "She is," Mother said mysteriously, "one step nearer November." After that, one step nearer November meant closer to "the fellow in the bright nightgown."

Our hallways at home had several Daumier prints, lawyers, sharply caricatured. Later when I saw a film strip of the *Water Tribunal* which meet every week in Barcelona, Spain, to weigh water cases brought to this open air-court, I compared them to Daumier's *Avocats*.

Whenever I was sick, Mother brought me borscht, which always stained my nightgown. Scarlet on white. *Foxfire*, she nicknamed me, whose real name was Indigo. When we drove down to the dock in Manhattan, occasionally the fog would be so thick that we saw ghost ships. Fascinated, I'd trace their outlines.

This afternoon, my sixty-fourth winter, when I held Keva in my arms, as she sobbed, she smelled clean as a chapel. There was the smell of talc in her hair. It was as though I were developing one film upon another, in a superimposing, since Mother too lost her marriage, but when her marriage went on the rocks, my own mother never let me near. She had jet black hair, with curls reminiscent of the gypsy child she was, touring in Romania, at age five. Even the night I felt the viral fire of polio burning in my spine, Mother kept me at a distance.

Keva is a Catholic, for whom marriage is life. We are Jews, not observant ones. She is from Wales. She wanted a chapel as a child, replete with altar and pews.

Before I was paralyzed, I wanted a small forest. I had not been in a temple or church for worship. I would kneel at the shrine; I would make rows for worshippers. Although I couldn't see them, I would assign a name to each: Mrs. Olivia would be the wind, and air; Mr. Scar would be fire; Weightless, teal, cyan water; and Grit-Soul the earth. I got lots of Grit-Soul crumbled in my shoes my last year walking, lots of Mrs. Olivia washing over my limbs and always in my hair, I became Weightless over and over again. Mrs. Olivia exchanged roles with Mr. Scar.

Androgynous, they slipped swiftly into each other's skin though I thought little about gender then despite the pears ripening on my chest to replace the raisins, the small knobs which opened the little doors of betrayal and love. I was twelve years and four months. It felt as though my future was behind me. My past, strangely, ahead. I was folding away like bright linens, my dozen years and several months walking.

I tried to tell myself stories that day. I was the family storyteller, recalling the storyteller always got the best place by the fire in ancient days. But that day, dizzy, I was standing at the helm of my uncle's boat, which had docked, in our small Westchester Suburb. I could dress *in a flash* because I learned during the war for air raid rehearsals. I'd gone to bed earlier that day feeling ill. I whipped off my jeans, shifted in a flash out of my white nightgown into frayed jeans. I had never been in a boat. I felt like a torch of fire riding, riding the waves which were first teal, then darker, cyan and at last the hard hooker-green of Keva's eyes. I was perched on a wilderness wider, wilder than wheat.

Although there was no flame, I was to be covered for the rest of my life by Mr. Scar. I was to walk on stilts like a stork. In my restless dreams before that final walking waking, I saw cupboards, the pantry in which my cousin, Nyrene, was born. I saw little pigeon-holes above the jam cupboard, with wooden knobs, all painted white, or natural blond. I pulled open each and found a postbox letter for me. The first said, *Read this, then write it all down.* The second, *Read this, then toss it to the winds.* The third and last, *Write your own, storyteller, listen to the narrator-hurricane.* My backbone burned, each vertebra, a fiery knob lit with the small letter in it lit too, my legs were turning to water, my body melting to wax.

*Paralysis*

Climbing down my last five stairs, I reached out my arms to Mrs. Olivia but she had died in my arms. There was no more mirroring wind. She was a shadow a heavy one. I looked up to the sky. She too was heavy, leaden who had been so light, in betrayal, in my arms. Grit-Soul under my feet had betrayed me too, turning into quicksilver: I did not hold her/him, but he/she sucked me in as though I was being sucked back into the birth canal, becoming smaller and smaller 'til I fit again into the womb of she who brought me to earth.

My parents' marriage had dissolved, become air-brushed, evaporated like a wave dashed upon a sharp pinnacle. My four worshippers were dissolving. Perhaps it was like Keva feeling about her marriage, becoming the child who died in her arms.

Where is the *Water Tribunal?* There are grave matters of love, of mortality to be weighed, souls like grains of sand. Juror and jury are mute as sea stone. Judgment is needed, the scales to be weighed.

Polio was the sculptor whose hands were to shape the rest of my life. My twelfth summer contained scene, action, detail and color, which were to be background for my existence.

The fog I wake to this morning is like a coffin floating up to the window, but also a boat I could step in if I could step over the rail, but I cannot. I smile at the four worshipers in it as they bump the old brick building.

I am one step nearer November, I see *The fellow in the bright nightgown* skirt past in the fog. Mother will bring me borscht and it will stain my white nightgown. Here is Mrs. Olivia, Weightless, Mr. Scar, and Grit-Soul. They have no expression but then they gain one—cherubic, granules of stone, smiling. I abhor the glassy sunny days of Summer and wait all year for Autumn as one would wait for birth if one knew it were coming. There is buoyancy in carrying your legs around rather than their carrying you.

Paralysis remains mysterious, first a stunning electric shot which torches one's body becomes a constant fixed desire – so strong. October, albino world, alabaster and foggy dawns, mist at night, finally snow. There are ghost ships on my horizon. We are one step nearer arrival and November. But not more shy of the South, those hauntings, those rich guilts. I will cross my legs in plaid skirt with suspenders and my underpants won't show. But not because I'm a good southern girl afraid of acting ugly. The storyteller will get the best seat in the fire ring when December comes.


*Fancy Plugging Your Ears*

The thing I hate about summer is it's so in your face. And I caught polio then. As a child I was taught not to be insistent. It was a naughty trait. Your nose in shine. And I got sick over the fourth of July. I think of burst mattress buttons down South and having to smile when you want to cry. Fancy is not my name. Don't forget to keep cool. It's a grotesque inversion of Brueghel's "Children's Games," in scorching Hellish heat.

On the bright side, my little Waterford Crystal clock from Mother twirls as though wearing crystal pinafores and reflects in the bureau, as though the cabinet a tree was killed for was a mirror.

Fancy, if anyone calls you colorless I'll clobber them. We have lots of lonesome prairie songs like that written by Hank Snow. I've gone and bought you a red and white sweater with Canada's colors on it for Canada day, but it has a lighthouse.

"Florida," I thought, "You want to turn yourself around. The dreams keep coming."

"Substance abuse," you cried, "That's what this year was all about."

Now I am in my ebon old age and what infuriates me is that when we cross the little theme park you seem to want to control me. Control never works. Yet last night, before bed you had pink lemonade, you told me, and a peanut butter sandwich, proving you ineradicably a child.

I dance on, whirling, until it becomes the fourth of July which I observed from my hospital bed. Only a swatch of blue sky. Now I do the Foxtrot. I dance in my Waterford like a translucent jellyfish. Next comes fireworks. I plug both ears while Fancy stands out on the terrace in ecstasy. I want to tell Fancy about needing to dress up to please one's love after thirty years but she just stands out there in her undershirt listening to firecrackers. The wheels, the fizzles, the waterfalls. I'm the eternal feminine. Gloves, pale lip gloss, shadow on my green eyes. I can't complain. Think of the trans-gendered child. I begin to slice a potato into my morning cereal thinking it a banana. Just think, one day we will not be here. Other souls will be breathing in other frames. I look out on a flawless morning. These are the precious morning hours which soon flatten, wane into afternoon, then rise again in evening. They're like Christ that way.

Our daddy drank himself silly when I got paralyzed, then realized I had a sensitivity and dimension he had not imagined when he remade my acquaintance at age twenty-one. Now I am unstoppable, at the edge of storm, riding a rollercoaster, both arms wide as a phantom jet, a wild bird, Fancy here I come!

# Ebon: Old Age

*The edge is what I have.*
 Theodore Roethke

– *Now the indigos of youth have become molten and are flowing into the metals of age. Indigo sits in a room up north, the South still alive in her. She is now two years shy of seventy, but shy of nothing else. She reminisces on her last love, last loss. She remembers the man she loved before her marriage to Jake who has died. Gordon, the first love's phone is broken. Ebon old age is around the bend.*

*Edge*

The little boys are not here. They dream, eat, sleep the four bases of a baseball diamond. They come skidding into dawn toting the home base after them, skinning their elbows, debriding their knees of dirt until they bleed into the dust they have won in a spectacular otherworldly home-run. They are growing baseball wings. Diaphanous, wings droop behind young males as they ascend the stairs. Wings make for that extra infinitesimal weight when the boys put themselves under the covers at night. Once they dream, and then alone can each wing begin slowly to stretch, unpleat like a fan, and fully open.

The indigos of youth have become molten, flowing into the metals of age. The cyclamens of mid-life are no longer copper-tipped, rather silver.

"The edge is what I have."

Beware the brown. I remember Mother's brown satin wedding dress. I live like the people of Canada live—like land mirrored in water, the people reflective, reflecting. Life came to me in one body of experience when young. I rode the rail. I took the day in my hands.

"Look," a woman said this morning, "they must be twins. Their legs are the same length."

Whereas I found days of different lengths in youth and mid age. In the burnished years I find them long, of the same length like twins. As though I were twinned, the windows are lit, but low-lit. I miss Indigo and Cyclamen. It reminds of moving form Iowa City to Des Moines, singing peripheral psalms. Only 150 miles apart but a world between; a marriage, a job changed.

I sit here in the room, a woman two years shy of seventy, but shy of nothing else. A bud vase holds one long-stemmed rose which has lasted so long its petals are outlined with iron.

Ebony flow the street lamps, the cabinet tops, all and everything illumination. All blackness alive and shining. We are foundlings. In a foundry. It hurts to lose what one has once had, walking, youth, beauty. In a flash, it is gone. While we were not looking, great age has come and the boys are not here. They are coming into home plate dragging the base after them in the dust, the air rising before them an oblique, cathedral slant of diamond.

## Last Love, Last Loss

Once one has lost it all, what is there to fear? Just weeks ago, he wrote me a belated birthday card, "You're a masterpiece."

It was the first time he ever forgot my birthday. Then he phoned after a week in the hospital which began at Sunday morning church when he fainted and the Minister accompanied him to New York's public hospital. Today he phoned and left a message, "You nearly lost me and so did everyone else."

He was my first love. I was twenty-three, registered for my last term at Hunter College and buying books in the cellar bookstore. He was behind me. "Can I carry your books?" he said, right out of *Our Town*. He was thirty-three. He helped me to my car, a Chrysler Imperial classic model jewel green which my father had bought for eight hundred dollars U.S.

"May I have your phone number?"

I gave it to him. "But when you meet my mother, don't call her ma'am. We Jews don't like ma'am."

"Mother," I said when I got home and closed the door to our West End Avenue apartment behind me, "I've just met a Harvard man."

"Humph," she scoffed.

He called the following Sunday flowers in hand, "Pleased to meet you." He shook Marcelle's hand vigorously. I held my breath.

"Very pleased, Ma'am."

"Where did you find him?" Rachel snorted.

"He followed me. He carried my books."

Our first date was at the Cloisters. He lifted me out of my wheelchair and carried me down the stone steps into Medieval France. We looked at the Unicorn Tapestries. He soon became my escort everywhere. I wrote him a poem  *My Pilgrim, St. Francis came knocked at my gate.*

I was a virgin the weekend we went up to Harvard and a virgin when we came back. But he was the one for whom I was to get my first pessary. He had wanted to be a medical student and taught me to use the one vinegar to fit in my *pocket book* then the two then the three so there would be no pain upon entry. Still there was pain. I bit my lip.

Some blood ran on the sheet and he said, "Indy, I've come!"

Now, just like that, he may have slipped over the edge.

We made love that summer, the twin beds tied together by a dishcloth. Grandmother had offered us her Fifth Avenue apartment but Mother Marcelle wanted that, thank you very much, so offered us her West End Avenue apartment.

It's nearly solstice. The intensities build: can't find Gordon, e-mail is broken. Ebon old age. I am the only girl to whom he ever proposed marriage. Simone wears the twin ring I was to wear. I was a southern Jewish girl-child and budding lesbian the winter I was nine. I saw Ingrid Bergman three times in *Saint Joan,* and never came home but I looked in the mirror and swooned. I was her real daughter, who would never bear one. A freedom fighter, I have never left the south truly, neither by underground railway nor by flight. He has kept his ring. Now the partner may have flown forever over the rim of earth. My mother sang all night the night I was born. The bottle spinned and stopped at me. Ebon age is next to touch us, north and south, east and west. Old age is not that despot, death. I came of age both in the Deep South where Mardi Grad exists and Nuits Blanches from dusk to dawn and in New England where Puritans stand above acorns in Autumn turning into Winter and preach the word of the Lord.

No old age is ebon itself, neither white nor black, Jewish nor Christian and knows no radial points on the compass,  will deposit some of its crematory ash upon our wing, where it will  shine.

# Cuffing the Boy's Shirt

– This story deals with the Conti-crayon drawings Marcelle did and the child moving, learning sex during story-hour. It is a story centers on Rachel rather than Indigo. Rachel was eight when Indigo had polio. Indigo still is narrator but focuses on the meeting outside her hospital window when Chel is first brought there by Marcelle, a daring act since kids weren't allowed in the ward and the girls hadn't seen each other in months. "Indigo sat up in the pool!" Chel had one day breathlessly run into Grandmother Tisanne's bedroom declaring the blood tie between the two sisters despite all odds of separation. The tale goes on to describe Rachel's gifted daughter, Lily-Amiel, who is Rachel's second self. It also concerns Rachel's wish for Indigo to visit their now-dying mother Marcelle. Indigo resists, and finally declines. It mentions the Nickel and Diamond store, the longing Indigo had for dregs, Lily for the dance. Both gave up her heart's desire. Indigo remembers Chattanooga, Tennessee but not the day she was born. The old Dutch elms of New Rochelle frame the sisters again. Life is perhaps nearing its end, coming full arc.

# Conti-Crayon Drawings

The child moved her hands toward her sex, then remembered it was story-hour. She had spent winter in the South where her mother got the divorce. There, she'd learned to be what the nurse who nursed her thru a broken leg at the hip taught her: to be *taciturn*. Not to *chagrin* people over things that were *picayune*.

Nothing was *picayune*. She rolled the southern sound of these three words under her tongue.

Her older sister had had polio and was paralyzed from the waist down. Her older sister had earned the title at age nine, *Local Spelling Bee Champion*.

She herself, Rachel, known as "Chel" by her friends, was eight years old. Sitting on the wooden library floor, in the cold New York winter, this act alone—which she had just discovered—brought her comfort. She was with, but did not belong with, the other third-graders in Riverside School where they had moved when her older sister, Indigo, caught polio. Cross-legged in her school-girl neatly pressed, pleated blue skirt, she experienced the white light. It gave her a marbly, silky feeling.

She had mild scoliosis of the spine which hadn't been diagnosed yet.

Sheets of ice blew outside the schoolroom window, rippling like corrugated roofs but made of glass, then settled in a skin over the pond.

I, Indigo, her sister was in a hospital upstate. Chel and I hadn't seen each other for half a year. Kindergarten, the old Philco 'fridge, the Chevy pickup—these icons of our childhood were fading. I, too, had found the white light, the same year. We were ages eight and twelve. I had curvature of the spine and was just learning to sit up in a wheelchair.

Outside my hospital window, ice rippled, too, then sheathed over the pond. Heart armoring would not break up for a long time.

All three members of our enmeshed Jewish family were maladjusted. All three were women.

A great Dane would veer in sight and Chel's eyes would widen, "Horsey Dog!" she claimed with awe. I ransack my memory for things she said as a child and this plus one other come to mind. She cried when I played the song form Peter Pan, Who Am I?

New York. 1951. For how long now had Marcelle been cuffing back the shirtsleeve so the boy might pick up the violin? Only, the boy was a girl. It began with the pulse of dance at the gate of life. Someone had put purple flowers in her hand as she took her bow after the short solo in the ballet. In our lives, cut flowers in a glass vase, always stood in the brown room stretching back to the very beginning. First, in summer they were stiff, straw flowers but by October, they were crepe and in winter changed to black-purple silk flowers reflected in the old mahogany. At age nine, when poliomyelitis struck her sister, Chel gave up dancing.

At age eight, I had nearly annihilated myself when I had stuck my finger in the light socket, got my first electrical shock which volted thru my body from hand to heart. I withdrew my hand just in time to still see trees outside the window. My hair had not been frizzed into curls. I was not burned to a crisp. I gazed amazed at the velvet evening of New Rochelle and knew in a small way, in my small bones and skin, what it meant to leave earth and come back again.

Past the First Presbyterian Church, of old black-red firebrick, in New Rochelle, I see my legs, my last walking legs, black-stockinged, scissoring, hopping off a bus at nightfall having dropped Connie off after the Metropolitan Opera, which excited her so it made her sick to her stomach. I'd had to see her from the bus-stop to her house in a strange part of town, then come back on my own to the bus-stop, stopping at the library to phone Mother.

No cradle Catholic, Constance had been converted by her mother when Connie was nine years of age. She took communion. She adored opera music. The family was dirt-poor, literally church-mice, her father playing processionals, funerals, and weddings, plus Sunday service on the old organ at First Presbyterian. Her mother sold lingerie downtown at a glass-fronted boutique, with all its little cabinets equipped with brass or glass knobs, near the church. I looked at my past thru smoked glass, darker than this window front. I remembered drinking blue milk during the war.

Connie's dream—Connie, born in Coventry, Connecticut—was to hear the Metropolitan Opera live, a thing which our class got to do that winter. We witnessed a miracle. Connie told me it was in the realm of miracle, a small one. She saw these shocks of culture as edifying.

Outside the church, I saw tree roots, exposed and frozen.

She and I studied bell-towers in Bruges.

"I lived before," I told her on the roof outside her bedroom where we crawled to do our homework and look over the dusty elms of Westchester County.

"What were you?"

"A medieval boy age twelve. I was the bell ringer."

Her eyes widened ash-brown. She was wearing leggings and a burgundy muffler. I brushed back a lock of chestnut hair from her eye. Her bangs were always in need of cutting.

The 1950's, I see, in violet-brown New York City twilight.

I am sole witness as Chel impatiently thrusts her right hand forward so that our Mother Marcelle might neatly rim the long-sleeved white tailored shirt, "So that you can get another day's use out of it, Rachel," she says, "at least."

That done, Chel is back in our black hole of Calcutta, our den, warming up with Paganini's *Devil's Trill*. With the slight peach fuzz on her upper lip of an adolescent youth, a few years under twelve, she's maturing earlier than expected due to my illness. She broke Eucharist, body and blood of Christ, most cleanly in the pure and dark light of our daily life, separating quite young the mundane from the holy.

Looking back with the perspective of sixty years, I see that everything in my adolescent life had the Midas touch.

"May God's face shine upon you," Connie told me, "and you have peace."

She took me with her into the Catholic church, the chapel scented of sandalwood. I felt heady with the smell of incense in the church, leaving a smoke in the air like the Indian Bazaar. As a Jew, it was foreign. Yet—the magnetism! Was our father's field not abnormal psychology? Was I not an example of this? Sheets of ice blew in the air, and I knew to bear that light. To be Easter children, celebrant of the Eucharist, was my burning goal.

Whether it was first lessons in art or on the violin, the best teachers were found. It was as though the dire circumstances of our lives combined with our European heritage of exile demanded we seek out those who had truly studied, known their art and made it their lives, do or die, make a place, a home for yourself in this world.

Who first set the tea-colored lace, a perfect clock-round, under the lilac flowers in the brown room?

Who brushes back a lock of her daughter's hair as though the daughter were a lover?

"Five minutes till play time."

It was a noirish movie, black and white keys in a grainy film once Rachel had shown that she was a star rising. But in 1951, Chel still has a child's voice. When it matures it will sound like a viola. Now it is half-boy.

Lock and key to darkly-knotted human life was father's psychology.

In the aftermath of illness, things are heightened. Black mirrors capture silver, reflections become subdued. After extreme contrast, there is monotony. Those swirling blue hours of our immense struggle were pierced by the shaft of understanding. The wheelchair, rickety, its brakes locked, held the blue bedpan, Beppo, during nights it stayed between Chel's bed and mine.

Mrs. Bartenieff with her immensely expressive hands tells me a message which lips alone cannot convey. In a similar spotlight, but literally on the boards, Siobhan McKenna takes New York by storm with her portrayal of *The Maid of Orleans*, I memorized her soliloquies, was the quintessential St. Joan, her emotive hands shadowing Mrs. Bartenieff's.

And Chel saying, "I want to be a singing waiter playing the violin, a gypsy."

When Chel came to visit me, after a bout with a slow virus I was thin as a stick sitting up in bed. Nonetheless she found reason to envy me, "I always wanted blond frizzy hair like yours."

The year of my polio, comes my piano and theory teacher Ernst Oster, a German refugee, well-dressed punctual down to the small hand of the clock, ringing the bell to our West End Avenue apartment. Round the corner was tenor Leonard Warren, who died young, literally dropping dead on the Metropolitan Opera Stage, and Domenico Savino, who, in the shadows of Julliard, wrote the melodramatic movie music for *Nosferatu, Gershwiniana.* At seventeen, I became one of two women composition majors at The Manhattan School of Music, sister school to the famous Juilliard. The only disabled one, with sticks, climbing up and down stairs, up and down from desk chairs five or six times a day to put in the long Thursday. Thursday was the day when all composition classes are programmed, starting with Ear Training with Ludmilla Ulelah, moving on to Composition with Vittorio Giannini. The two women students always had their weekly exercises and compositions propped last on the old black grand piano to be played by the maestro.

It went without saying that the men came first. Rachel and I had decided that we were both boys, wanted to be great men when we grew up. Our periods stopped coming.

There was a brief brown bag lunch period during which hour Marcelle would taxi across town to help me up the huge concrete step to the only john I could manage in the Manhattan School of Music.

At times, when it was hard for her to manage, I saw Marcelle as a girl herself bringing home new hats, strapped as she was by funds, wiped out by my disease, flirtatiously trying on a chapeau with feather in front of a mirror, posing, my child-like mother frightened me for I felt more than ever I was the older one, and alone.

Afternoons at the music college were long. I waited for the light to slant promising fall of evening.

Jo Abramovitch, a Brooklyn jew, was my godsend who blew me away because he got me outside. It is the dream of every hospitalized child to fly. Books were one liberation, music another. We took so many taxis in those days, to doctors, brace-makers, concerts at the Mannes College of Music, Carnegie Hall, recitals in old West Side Brownstones—everywhere and in all weathers. The autumn I enrolled in college, we met Jo and had an idea.

If I gave him my schedule would he pick me up on West End Avenue and then again in the afternoon at the music college for a flat weekly fee? We did this for three years. Each September, I gave him my hours which he taped on the visor to his cab. Wherever he was in the city, he'd come to pick me up. It was Jo who helped me climb down those three flights when the elevator was on the fritz due to construction. Slowly, with the patience of a monk, he'd hold one crutch and go down one step backward before me. My rides home from Harlem to West End Avenue were the drama in my life. I allowed myself to dream, I composed a song about the weather in October always raining. I fantasized that I could walk into one of those small flower shops glowing on Broadway like a Monet painting, buy a fist of flowers wrapped in 'cello, a bouquet of mauves, yellows, rose. I lived for these rides home, on the mistiest New York spring evenings, the iciest winter ones.

"Never be unkind to your mother," he told me, "she is so sweet."

Hardest of all to take was spring. One might fall in love. One might walk along the river with a young man, arm-linked-in-arm, as I had dreamed from my hospital room. In the backroom, Gertrude, our maid, who lived on Audubon Avenue in Harlem, was ironing. Blue wreathes of steam billowed and floated about her in the kitchen.

Why against a backdrop of marble does this intensely lived life arise? Our foyers were granite. The two steps had a modest brass rail.

Chel's violin teacher helped me prep for music college. We played Brahms' *Hungarian Dances for Four Hands*, Ronald Murat and I, rhapsodic, naturally knowing melody of the Roumanian and Hungarian gypsies, ash from his tobacco crumbling, perpetually carving his ivories with nicotine, so they were sepia by now. The room had a swell, sweet smell. Late summer crickets and cicadas sawed in the lime green trees outside the screened-in window of the music room.

I was unconditionally admitted to all departments. I had donned the hospital anonymity and nun-like serenity. The candle of discipline was carried from one room of my spirit to another, the way Rachel snuffed out dancing, but re-lit violin playing. I'd spend hours over the wood drawing board loaned by the family printing company, and set to the left of our pre-world war II Steinway Grand. To my left, as well, was a window giving onto water-towers on roofs which shimmered at noon, and at dusk turned bullet-silver, defining the Broadway skyline.

During the war, Steinway's factory was turned into a casket manufacturer. I would emerge in late afternoon like a turtle from its shell, covered with the notes of all those great composers I'd copied during the hours. I had blue rings under my eyes, my scoliosis made my back ache, my hands were trembling. Soot-grey birds flopped like velour hats on the pavement and in the gutters in the heart of coldest wintertime.

Day came down like closing a lid to the grand piano. Night came like the banging the lid to a coffin.

Serious. Every single endeavor of the child was taken to heart, the best piccolo bought when Rachel hankered after one at age five and our father granted her wish; the finest music teachers found for each of us, Mother Marcelle filled with a furious intensity the miniature of our life, like a Dutch painter's interior or portrait, until the portrait that emerged was an oval with a girl's head, but androgynous, a young girl at the age she might have been taken for a boy, drawn in Marcelle's delicate brown conti-crayon.

Rachel, whose daughter was phenomenally gifted as a ballerina, paid the devil his due for Rowena's three years of glory in ballet between ages eleven and fourteen. Chel who had been her coach, her mother, her unfailing mentor, her second self, Rowena's best teacher, had to eat crow, got kicked in the teeth, bore the worst pain a mother could.

"And when she loses her virginity," I asked. "what then?"

"I'll die."

We, on the other hand, went along quietly from year to year plying our craft, biding our time. The razor which drew blood was anathema to us.

By the same token, the nine-to-five routine was unknown to us. No father in the home meant nobody going out to work at nine, returning at five. We lived round the clock with our passions with just that needed modicum of discipline.

Normal was a term that never occurred.


## Doll-Face

The banging lid of the coffin which ends Beethoven's *Seventh Symphony* marked the close of our Sabbath, Sundays.

Is memory history? I remember more and more, no longer wait for Godot but experience God in the rush of flowers, the knowledge I will be given the grace, the strength when I need it? The purple wisteria smell sweeter with each year.

Throwing a penny in the fountain, I watch bronze plash on cold water remembering it is not good for all one's wishes to be granted.

When I ran away from my Mother Marcelle's home to our father's for those benighted, yet rich, four months, she cut the inscription out of Frances Hodgson Burnett's *A Little Princess*.

It had read, "For Indigo, a writer of imagination and compassion."

When Rachel was a child of nine, sex, that white bird, brought her bliss. Did she look with tenderness upon her child-self at that age, when her own daughter, a bit later, at age thirteen, began cutting, getting perhaps the rush of adrenaline needed to make her feel good? Was it like orgasm? Did the white light come for her daughter as she razored her own flesh? Rachel was to spend more than one year in hell following her exquisite daughter through these self-inflicted wounds. Perhaps they released serotonin, the endorphins the brain makes to create well-being.

And how beautiful the daughter was! Almost blue-white skin. The elongated torso, neck and limbs of a dancer. One born to dance. The fine high cheekbones, wide spaced hazel eyes, ash blue-black hair, lustrous, copious, shining.

Rowena was Rachel's second self. They breathed in unison. When Row was having a bad day, her mother was having a bad one. When they spent the summer in New York for the American Ballet Theatre, they took the subway both ways together. Chel took Row back to the old neighborhood where she had grown up. She walked her past 320 West End Avenue, where she must have looked up to the eighth floor and heard echoes of herself at age thirteen and fourteen, practicing the fiddle, studying in those days with Ronald Murat. That brown trench coat. Those fights with Marcelle.

The classic gesture of cuffing back a handsome, man-tailored shirt suggests a boy. But look up, it is a long-boned girl of fifteen, her marble forehead, bent above the book in lamplight, studying Latin, studying a score by Bach or Brahms, with serious dark eyes. The blond sister? She has hoarded up all the ecstasy she can in early girlhood.

The metronome tick-tocks. Disciplined by his two girls, the father runs a current, blood memory throwing its shadow. Lose memory, you lose history. The young girl and woman are threading Manhattan's West Side. Lose memory and you can live. Indigo is threading the West side unable to walk, but can fly.

"I haven't seen Marcelle in fourteen years and do not miss her."

"But she misses you. Indy, time is not on her side."

"When we had more time, she declined to have me visit."

Wisteria curl in a green glass vase.

Hopping off the bus near New Rochelle's First Presbyterian church, old black-red firebrick, I clearly remember black stockinged legs scissoring beneath me. My last day of pure sunshine.

Rachel, you are taking your five-minute call. You check that there's no toilet paper stuck in your gown—nobody looks at the floor—you wash your hands a last time so they're not sweaty, you pack up your violin case. You who started at Curtis in Philadelphia, where the family feared you'd lost your virginity at age fifteen. Marcelle called you back to New York. Will there be good energy on stage this night?

Yehudi Menuihin hears you and is wowed.

"Do not waste your life, girl with the pearl earring."

We live right around the corner from actor Peter Lorre, who always played the monster in old black and white movies. He was squat, thick shouldered, had an expression as though he'd been burned. Yet he was the gentlest of men and would always nod when he passed us on Broadway between 75th and 76th street. Our Russian and German-Jewish neighborhood.

In my dream, I wake because he has met me and stares me down eye-to-eye. I stare back and slowly, gradually my face relaxes into a smile.

There is nothing to be afraid of the voice says to me.

In the same dream, Marcelle re-inscribes *The Little Princess* with the words "For Indigo, a poet— compassion." She has conjoined our names again.

It began with dance, the pulse, the impulse from the womb. Then polio in the home changed home into another map, another country, exposed frozen roots of trees, root-cellars, stumps of incinerators and brick chimneys. It drove Chel to abandon dancing, take up the horsehair bow and fiddle. Within days she is bowing like a trueborn Tzigane.

All the while, the still-young mother weaves an atmosphere which is brave because she is afraid. My child-like mother with the high voice, the sudden turns of mood; my own Marcelle with the delicate mouth, the interminable chains of smoking, the nervous hands, the fear of people, is plotting my healing, while she helps outline in pencil the intricate plot of Dickens' *Tale of Two Cities,* and with the pen (or less severe, conti-crayon,) drawing on reserves of her strength, drawing her last resources out of the bank, documenting it all as fervently as a child kept a record in a concentration camp like Bergen-Belsen.

How clearly, now that I am sixty-five, I see her tragedy. I superimpose upon it the catastrophe in Asia when two trains carrying fuel exploded upon hitting a dangling electrical wire. Schoolchildren were lined up to wave at a passing dignitary, thus were burned, blinded in a row, symmetrically. If the authorities had been more careful, if the country had not been so rundown, and totalitarian.

Part of all totalitarian countries is mythology. So Marcelle, if only her parents had paid more attention to her, helped her to imagine more freely and realize her talents, her psyche would not have been so borne down that anger was her last expression of individuality. Perhaps.

Or perhaps she was simply born averse to human touch and contact. Some nights, I wake seeing her spirit as a field of radiant daisies in bloom. First blown all flat by a gale force wind, then—brutally—mowed over. It is a truth that in North Korea last week, many children were blinded and burned facially, all in one direction. The theory proves correct, they had left the primary schoolroom for a special event in a drab country, drab routine. They wore white socks and shoes, boys and girls of eight and nine had lined up to salute a dignitary passing on the train. Everything within a kilometer of the massive fireball was razed.

Had Rowena succeeded in taking her life with the first razors, Rachel's life would have turned transparent and in one sense been done. Sheets of ice ripples, now sheets of blood stiffened to clear red glass.

Maybe Rowena bore this in common with Mother Marcelle. A high-strung temperament, a quick temper, an extreme passion and suicidal feelings she turned against herself, but then was able to turn outward by expressing a inexplicable wrath toward her daughters. Rowena took it out upon her very body. But there is the camera! The black box, perfect to record and unfold her secrets, her drama— an alternative, a release. They come up like black tulips this spring, row-after-row of city roofs she photographs in evening, steadying her immense will-power, flair for the histrionic, the extreme, and her mature nerve upon leveling the eye of the camera at them, upon developing—rather than her painful adolescent body fighting scoliosis—developing black and white after black and white until her world blooms quietly again in color, if somber color.

When her body left being a child—as much boy as girl in some ways—she despaired at looking in the mirror for hours at budding breasts which swelled body, from a Giacometti body, a Botticelli *Printemps*, turning it into something to fight rather than join, hand-in-hand, spirit and body—marble again, but marble pitted and scarred, no longer perfection.

She did not know my secret of becoming cup-bearer to the king, bell-ringer with his legs shot out, in his sonorous ecstasy.

The first flower of evening is light brown, lilac brown, a curl of smoke from a chimney pot on the horizon.

"Did you wish to have been born a boy?"

"No. Did you wish me to be born a boy?"

No answer.

Did I wish my voice to remain opaque forever? Yes, like a choir-singer in the loft, my feelings transparent, translucent my body.

January, 1952. Tomorrow is a school day. Beside the silver violin stand opened for early morning practice, Marcelle has laid out the white tailored shirt for Rachel. Mother Marcelle will cuff the sleeves in morning. The body, I remind myself, is a house with four windows but no door.

In the story-telling circle, the eight-year old child, Rachel, sat cross-legged, her hands folded over her blue-pleated lap. She had memories of what not to do.

Connie, no cradle-Catholic all the more embraced the faith, was an Easter-child, a person who saw the Eucharist when she was too young to pronounce the name.

Another out of body experience, like sticking my finger in the light bulb and nearly leaving earth and coming back again, or the white light, running through fields of high blue-green grass in the poor part of our suburbs, where Connie from Coventry lived with her father, the church-organist at First Presbyterian which turned to fiery brick at sunset I dream of being bell-ringer, a medieval boy, who rang a bell by leaping from stone, ledge-to-ledge, feet flung out. I am certain I was a Medieval boy in my former life. Carts with wood wheels got stuck in mire in spring, wheel-ruts rocking them. Lark Festival was come to town. Jack the wheel-boy and the wheel-girl Jill shouted their names to the hills.

The white light.

Chel and I turned into women, but didn't leave the dream of being a boy behind. This light, both of us felt it, whether copious or severe, it could come and limn an entire day, or an entire season, gradually a year, a decade.

Why did we not catch the tragedy of Rowena sooner? The child under incredible pressure, twisting one leg behind the other at the supper table, saying "I'm a dancer," her face taut, blue-white, declining dessert.

How could we not see that Row was, at age twelve eerily thin, like a child from Belsen, with pipe-stem neck and arms? The light could have shone thru her making her translucent, like me after my severe illness, at the age when Christ wandered into the wilderness. Twelve, when we are most vulnerable, androgynous, bearing the gifts of both sexes, on the edge of puberty which will forever lock us in to one gender or the other. We are most malleable, permeable, imbued with translucency which makes us—like glass, like porcelain—capable of fracturing, and of transmitting spirit most clearly, without shadow or confusion. Eucharist, bread and wine, body of Christ, thankfulness, are all broken, taken. No crib-Catholic, but a Jew.

Sheets of ice blow across the window, like corrugated tin, but are glass. Soon a skin of frost seals the pond. One hectic, red autumn leaf is iced within. The two of us, the pair, the brace of daughters, thirsted for intensity and quenched our thirst at the fountain of music.

I wrote a Memoir subconsciously those days. I was too young to know of Memento Mori, but had many evidences of children leaving objects once cherished behind as they went into the white light.

When Rachel was no longer a child who said "Horsey Dog!" or who forced me to stop playing "Who Am I?" she went through a period of silence—a few years after Rowena's cutting.

"You don't tell me much about your life any more."

"I know it."

Whether in the free form conti-crayon drawings of Mother's young womanhood which haunt my days, or the flat doll-face of the Japanese Mona Lisa, I see us, Rachel and me, captured, memorialized, with long shirts and silk cuffs when the *five minute call* comes. We are not miniaturized although the interior has the luster, the perfection of a Seventeenth Century Dutch Interior: I see tree-roots exposed, frozen. I see a reduction of two serious girls, then, who could still smile, shouldering the burden, yet turning it into a freezing silvery thrill, lifelong blessing.

## The Angel In Question Is Rosario

Trying on the third outfit for the wedding I know I won't attend, I shimmy skinny hips into silk.

Perfect.

It is Nicole's wedding.

Yesterday I got a Hindu taxi driver who told me his name means "No Enemies."

He had none but one.

Who?

Himself.

In my few months at The New Lincoln School, trying to break out of homebound education, I made one friend: the woman who slung hash in the kitchen. When I had to leave "due to health reasons," she gave me Gogol's *Dead Souls* to read. I remember stretching out my hand to receive it and wondering how it could possibly cheer me.

# North and South:
## Nickel and Diamond Store

– Nickle and diming it down South Indigo, her mother and sister, live a borrowed life in a place on loan as the rich dialect of place inform their humor and the business of daily life, a life on hold as the three wait for the divorce to finalize.

Picayune, taciturn, chagrined, Catholicl, protestant, northern, southern – this time Rachael has a broken leg and Indigo isn't sure it's not her fault.

Back home up North, she hides a beautiful glass door nob in the back of a drawer.

*Before the Loan Expired*

In the Northeast, I was born. But in the South I was re-born when I nearly short-circuited out of existence by driving an electrical current through my heart. I inserted my finger in a socket without light bulb. For a few seconds, I thought I'd gone to heaven and died but I got out before my hair frizzed and my toes curled, before my mouth froze and burned in the same instant as though I'd had an Epiphany, seen the Eucharist, when really it was a rictus of agony.

We nickel-and-dimed it down South that winter of the divorce, 1947, four years before I caught polio. I had my special vision of things. I was the family entertainer. I called the corner store filled with all sorts of amazing junk the *Nickel and Diamond Store*. Only I skated on thin ice, I played with fire. I told it to my delayed friend Carrie, who blinked, then whose eyes opened and opened in that sad town on the Gulf of Mexico where the Barnum & Bailey Circus had their winter headquarters, instructing me quite young that circuses are just about the saddest place on earth.

Down South everything was suddenly black flies buzzing and snap beans in the metal pan, a metallic water bending in corrugated waves over them. We satisfied ourselves with these rations despite the scent of oranges so heavy and heavenly in the air when we crossed the Florida line.

"I do believe Eucharist has come," I said dramatically to myself having learned the term from my Roman Catholic friend in New Rochelle, Bethy whom I adored.

Everything in life is a barter, a trade-off. And for every one you pay some interest. You borrow time and return it but it and you are changed. The interest is high too, many times.

Whenever I sense a poverty to my days, I evoke the richness of memory. By the rusted orange gas pump general store was the old five and dime store we called the *Nickle and Diamond*. Mainly local color was local drab. Even then, perhaps mainly then, I thirsted for intensity.

Like now at age sixty-five, my eye slides open before first birdcall. For what am I so eager? Hungry?

At nine, I was legs.

The southern flowers were blowsy.

Even though the air smelled of blossom, the predominant tinge was poverty. The *Nickel and Diamond* store had everything: nails, screws, pink *Eberhard Faber* rubber erasers for back to school in autumn. Many items were back to school: the pencil cases of mock leather which smelled of graphite, the yellow #1 and #2 pencils, the small boxes of *Crayola* crayons and the giant ones with four layers ascending vertically up hill, the terraced crayons for the rich bitches which we coveted. But in Sarasota there weren't many of those. Even though it carried so many things, however, the sense was of futility when I entered that small dark space smelling of raisins, the screen door never succeeding in keeping out flies, banging behind me. I'd catch it by sticking out my fanny but not always in time.

In the North, our lives were heartbroken, but felt rich. In the South we felt poor and there was a finality to the heartbreak, which had been like an arch thru which one could work up North.

Mary Quant flowers, nineteen sixties, proliferated. The sky was the color pink-orange of cracked crab. The old chimney was a heap of brick rubble on the ground. This, of course, is an anachronism. We were deep in the heart of the forties, in the blues, the dogwood which repeated their pattern like the days which hit one over the head with hammer-blows, one's mind being the nail.

"Get your face out of my food!" said Suellen.

I wasn't a crier but I wasn't used to being addressed that way and knew better than to be *Goodie Two Shoes* and say, "I beg your pardon."

It happened to me over and over, this hammer blow action which resulted in numb feelings. It happened Christmas day 1947, when I wore shorts and bounced my pink spading saying, *One two three O'larey* in that merciless southern sun. The North had mercy. Although there was terror in both regions, it won out in the South. Why?

Iron board flowers I called them. The ironing board was always out. Everything in fact looked flattened yet there were moments, especially when the children's choir sang, when I was lifted out of that region. William Bird was a Catholic who wrote music for secret, and religious services. The Anglican church featured him.

But the corrugated cardboard days of flattening, pummeling rain—days too warm to be real winter, then was when I most longed to go to the five and dime.

The rosebush out my window, like my mother's life, clings fairly in its pale pink to its thorn stem. Mother lives on lettuce. The rose on little sun.

Five miles as the crow flies the diamond store sparkled down the road.

I looked up to see geese fly South in winter, forgetting I was there.

I loved to yank my tee shirt over my head and feel the new sun on my midriff.

Thru the shadowy afternoon I was on my own, after school, the screens blowing, letting a buzz snap bee thump against them. The sky was the color of tea. The house had a habit of becoming too lonely when I'd go out to the puny yard. I gulped down a tall orange juice forgetting to blot my lip with my napkin after. I never had the house to myself up North. It was too big, there were the stables behind. Besides, I was too young. I had the house to my self too often down South.

*Picayune, taciturn, chagrined* — It became a haunting. Of course, it wasn't a proper house with attic and basement and like our big home in New Rochelle (my last shell) with many rooms. It was a bungalow a half mile from the beach, one of a number of bungalows we rented from a kind Jewish couple, the Gersteins. I remember her name was Rose. It felt as though my lanky child body was a ghost haunting those shallow rooms with screen windows, no protective glass. The yard was stubble and scrub. It went with the emotional, spiritual landscape of the South. We were too poor even to rent a piano now, with the divorce proceedings, and Rachel's broken leg and all. I felt we were living on starvation rations.

Down the dirt road in another bungalow, a boy was learning the B-flat trumpet. The notes would crack breaking across the white afternoon. I was happier back in the kitchen snapping beans, watching them, like silver eels drop into the shallow tin pan. They seemed to have a life of their own, to slither and slide thru the shallow water making a pleasant plash sound and bouncing off sun in their pale green.

"Indigo?" Mother would come in and see me looking melancholy. "One person," she'd say in her own defense, setting a hand to her hips, summing up our situation, "One woman, Indigo, cannot do everything."

It was a non sequitur. Of course, I mean I knew where it came from but was like a diving board propped up on sheer air. We hadn't been talking about the difficulties of our life but there it was. Chel in a body cast from a broken leg I didn't give her, but couldn't prove I hadn't, Christmas eve horsing around on the cot in that shack where we were holed up to establish legal residence. The fact was that Grandmother, our hope, our line to the money, was still up North, although coming for a visit in her furs and perfumes quite soon. Rachel's live-in nurse spent hours on the phone to Decatur, Illinois. The fact was that we were a daddy-less family.

We didn't need to enumerate all these things as we sometimes did, Marcelle counting them off like, "One two three four five I can feel your ribs you're so skinny! The knobs on your spine." My personal rosary. But it was behind her saying this.

"And this laundry," she'd wind up, snapping open the ironing board with an explosion of a gun—its leg always stuck, rusted as it had become—"When will I catch up with your socks and your white shirts for Fridays, Indigo?"

"It's that school you choose for me," I winced. "It's all gentile. The kids all wear white and neigh like horses and have long blond hair they thrown back, whinnying." Three years later when my legs became paralyzed by polio she wished she had back my dirty socks she said.

"Jewish children wear white shirts and your hair is fair too."

"Dirty blond," I corrected her.

"Yes. It's one of the better shades of dirty blond."

"I'm only one person," she said again and lit up a cigarette perching the little glass ash tray on the side of the ironing board.

I felt unloved. I wasn't anything like pre-puberty but my knees and elbows were bony. It's true, whatever my appetite in those days, I was rail thin, put no weight on, and my hair was thin stringy dark blond.

There was no way to burn off energy except counting cars with Carrie down the road. Back North there was the carriage house, the stables Rach and I would play for hours in. Down in Sarasota I could walk the thin line of road being especially careful not to get hit, up the road and round its elbow to where Carrie's father counted cars for the State after twilight. In the day, we did it just to fill the time. It was a frantic diversion, watching steel hoods bounce off sun.

Then I must have known profound childhood depression.

"Zip a dee doo dah," Carrie, my age, sang.

I sang it with her although I'd hated *Song of the South* and that song. We did it while she lost her balance in her spanking white anklets and her party-pink shoes and I had to pull her up from the mud by my arms. We did it swinging our arms back and forth. I never lost balance. I towed a thin line.

It was then the diamond notion hit me. Looking at how flat and colorless this whole world was I said to Carrie who was slow, "You know Mercy's, the five and dime down the road?"

"Uh huh," she nodded.

"Well its real name isn't that at all. You know what it is? It's The Nickel and Diamond. You know how come? 'Cuz often the sky here is flat like old nickel but once in a blue moon, it sparkles and turns diamond. Once in a blue moon, Carrie."

She blinked. "Blue moon," she said losing her balance another time.

## After the Loan

I stood a glass of water on the kitchen sill. It balanced precariously.

When we got back North I knew I'd miss my father a whole lot, but Marcelle wouldn't miss him. Pretty soon no one would even remember what he looked like, but I'd remember him and keep a locket with his oval portrait in my heart to bring out and burnish from time to time. We were nearing that time.

"What's wrong with it?" Mother asked sharply.

"It's dirty."

"Tap water's good enough for me," she said.

Saying naught, I watched the bubbles climb to the cup and form along the rim. I shook my head. My eyes were tired. I wanted to fold a piece of bread and slather peanut butter in between but there was no eating between meals, not that anything could spoil my appetite. I seemed to be ravenous all that winter in the South. My depression came from the fact that the pendulum of the clock ceased to swing.

Swingless, those hours between coming home and supper time. They moved a bit, but sluggishly, after supper up 'til bed time. It was southern time. Paralyzed. Marcelle lifted my plate and glass and left both on the kitchen counter when I didn't want to eat, a rare occasion.

Other times Marcelle would shake her head, I felt rejected then.

'You mystify me, Indigo."

"Mrs. Meizenheimer says I'm a mystification."

I felt guilty that winter because Rachel's leg had broken, the hard fact was whether or not I did it, I'd never know. I felt blue because we were in a world to be forever sealed fatherless. I didn't often act glum but I got so pale Mother said my skin seemed made of gauze or cornstarch. Rachel could only have mini poos because of her body cast. Mother lavished olive oil upon her dark haired daughter. I looked in the glass and stuck my tongue out at myself.

I was nine and didn't have a friend in the world but Carrie and she was only an acquaintance.

"You need friends," Mother Marcelle said one evening as I helped her dry the supper dishes.

I said. "I have a few acquaintances."

"Not enough."

"I've taken a shine to no one here."

She lit up. I walked away to the yard. The yard wasn't much to walk in, mind you, not like our one up North, spacious, lit by the green fire of large old protective elms that were like a father. There was no human on earth to whom I could tell my feelings. The house had that nasty habit of becoming too lonely, even crowded with the three of us: Mother Marcelle, Rachel and Rachel's Nurse, Mrs. Liebling and me, usually excising myself from the scene.

Rachel's nurse said one morning, "I'm tickled pink. I reached Decatur in no time flat."

I looked between this stout Midwestern woman whose face was wide as the plains, and our mother whose face was pointed like a ferret. I wondered if Marcelle would ever be happy.

I could hear Marcelle's voice in my mind. She was the original steel magnolia. The hard fact was she must have loved me some since she drove me all the way to Tampa one night to see Ingrid Bergman in *Joan of Arc*. I had decided Ingrid Bergman was my real mother. But why had she deserted me? I felt orphaned there on the brim of the Gulf of Mexico where days are so tepid, evenings so colorless and calm without being soothing, easing to the mind.

By spring our time in the South had almost expired.

"Mrs. Meizenheimer says I'm a quick learner," I told Marcelle one evening, hopping first on one foot, then the other one. I'd read my report card, as usual, on the way home.

Mother shot up one eyebrow. "Good for her."

Once or twice, Marcelle caught me by the elbow while I was leaving the supper table and swung my thin body round. "I heard you breathing on the party line." Once my dress was so thread-thin that it ripped when she turned me.

I blushed but said nothing. I was figuring in the dark of the night how to loosen that glass doorknob.

"We're giving it back," Marcelle said, lighting a cigarette, hauling cardboard valises from the shelf of our one closet, snapping valises open. "The whole damned South," she spit out the words like bitter seeds. "The divorce has come thru, Indigo. We're rid of your father, free of him," she smacked her hands as if ridding herself of some poison.

The loan was over.

This frightened me more than living on borrowed time. I knew it was her intention in bringing us South, knew it was what she wanted. My uncle who worked for the Transit Authority up North wore gun and holster and wrote me he was glad we were coming home. I wasn't. I picked up a knife and poked a hole thru my supper English Muffin. The sky was the color of tobacco, a nicotine sky.

"Don't, Indigo!" she came down on me. "Bite into it. Don't twirl it on a knife."

But I just went right on twirling.

"All I taste is dust," I told my Mother. "It's nice, good like sand."

"Spit it out."

"It keeps getting in again."

She raised her index finger. "Tell it to hush, can't stay with you." The sorrow was so thick you could spread it with a knife.

"You nibble muffins all evening long."

I turned my hand on the glass doorknob to the bedroom I shared with Rachel, the one object I loved in that house, the glass doorknob. When we went back North, I wanted to find a way to wiggle it loose and take it with me.

In the North, the train whistle sliced the winter and summer nights in half. In the South, nothing sliced time in half.

## Back Home With Interest

I woke up and hugged myself the morning of May 15th 1947. The car was back. We had made friends with a black couple with whom we'd drive home. We'd completed our barter, our trade-off. The loan was repaid and we were driving home with interest as Mother Marcelle put it in her impeccable banking terms.

"Is our state of emergency over?" I asked Marcelle.

She said, "Could be."

"Yes," I answered, "I think our state of emergency is drawing to a close.

I began folding my five shirts warm from the laundry. I looked at the shabby rundown old Bendix washer and dryer-not like our up to date model Northeast, back home. This would be the next to last laundry she had to do here, Marcelle. Rachel was healed, not entirely. There was a little white scar in her back from the body cast.

"Look at that, Indigo, and realize she'll have it for the rest of her life."

"I didn't do it," I said for the thirteenth time.

The loneliness of childhood is immense, it fills the whole universe. It is long and leggy like the scarlet runner beans in our southern yard. We're going home. I had been taught you couldn't step in the same river twice, nor could you push the river. It will be different from what I've known but the stable will still be there, our bedrooms. What I hadn't counted on was getting hives on the way home, Marcelle cutting up her silk underpants to soothe my blistered face so severe people gave me nickels and dimes thinking I'd been burned in some accident. What none of us had counted on was the fact that Melvin and Mary argued most of the time. She was fiercely jealous of her new café au lait husband.

"Melvin, he could pass," she'd grin.

"Not me. I'm High Yaller as sin."

So we drove the thousand plus miles with them spatting and me dabbing at my face with mother's silk panties and Rachel staring and staring, counting telephone poles which I had once done.

"You're lucky you don't have lockjaw," Mother Marcelle said.

"That's why I had your tetanus shots in fall.

"Furthermore," she added, "you won't get trench mouth like me in college. My teeth have never been the same." (Trench mouth, — the words haunted me.)

It wasn't my teeth which bothered me, it was my skin. I thought I'd never be in the whole of my health again.

"Your lesions will be healed by the time we get North, Indigo. Wait and see." I was waiting and itching, breaking scabs bleeding.

"All your imperfections will be gone."

I pulled a face.

"Right now, you're leggy as a scarlet runner bean," she said.

I remembered Carrie's mother saying "A sick kid's a monkey wrench."

I screwed my face to the car window filled with streaming rain. The loneliness of childhood is like no other thing. It is immense, it fills the whole universe. Our cat had died and Melvin had flung him in a shoebox out the window so that poor cat's body had flung free of the cardboard and just spun and spun in space. Driving home I thought over our time in the South.

What troubled me was something I'd overheard our last night in Sarasota.

Rose Gerstein had confided to Mother Marcelle in the screened-in front room our last night, "I have to get my bowels checked."

I'd overheard and worried did she have cancer?

"Is Mrs. Gerstein ill?" I asked Marcelle anxiously the last night.

"You're jumpy as a fly on a griddle, Indigo," she said.

"It doesn't concern you. You've been polishing your habit of eavesdropping."

"Mother, is it terminable and inoperable?"

"Terminal, Indigo. Watch yourself! You're mis-using the English language again."

The front room of our bungalow had been turned into a small hospital. Rachel's bed, the sick room supplies, the bed stand housing the fever thermometer and the tin cup always filled with water. I memorized the scene which was to be repeated in far more dramatic blacks and whites in my own twelfth summer.

I never did learn what was wrong with Mrs. Rose Gerstein's bowel. Marcelle said not to dramatize. But she had been kind to me. She rubbed me down with a bath towel the night Rachel's leg broke.

She'd come into the room and say, "It needs more than a sixty watt bulb in here, honey."

I told her, "Mother's economizing."

She shook her head and whispered, "There's economizing and economizing. A child's sprits can darken."

She knew this kid was near a hysteria of being unloved and guilt ridden that Christmas Eve.

"Will I start piano lessons again when we get back North?" I asked in my high nervous voice.

Sometimes, she'd tell me to get it an octave down. I hip hopped.

"You're like darning needles, Indigo," she said. I waited about those piano lessons.

"I imagine we'll be able to afford it." Smiling as though I'd had warm bread from the oven, I thought of the yellowing ivories and the ink black keys.

"And Rachel her ballet?"

"We'll see. After that broken leg she might not want the ballet so covetously."

"I wasn't eavesdropping."

"I heard you breathing in the next room."

"There's a difference. That's because I'm alive. There's a difference between eavesdropping and breathing."

I waited a second.

"Carrie asked will you be a spinster once you go back to being unmarried?"

"Not on your life. Indigo, I've already been married."

"I told Carrie that's what I thought."

"Look at you!" she pinched the skin on my upper arm. "You need some flesh on those bones. What will Tisanne think?"

I shrugged.

"I was strong enough to ride that horse like the wind," I reminded her for I'd astonished the woman at the stable.

"You're a lark on a horse," she declared. I'd taken one horseback ride and been so skinny I was nearly thrown, but I'd surprised them, miracle of miracles by holding my own. "And don't be so archaic and formal with your mother."

You're not my mother, I wanted to say, Ingrid Bergman is.

I carried these memories back North with me.

Down South all we could afford was a party line. Back North, we had a line of our own. That was only one example of our poorness and richness, relatively speaking. An important distinction.

After polio, three years later, I dreamed and dreamed of that one time riding, wind whipping my hair. If I could turn the reel of time backward and only have back one day, one morning, one hour. . .

Despite all the torment with the poison oak, sumac and ivy combined on the endless ride home, we endured and my skin was smooth as a newborn by the time we got back North. Marcelle put her hand to my cheek.

"Humph!" she said. "A kid glove. Softer than the day you were born."

But I couldn't remember the day I was born. I remember Chatannooga, Tennessee and Chatahooggee, Georgia. But when the sign rose before our eyes, "Westchester County," it was like the Eucharist come.

For I'd learned that one word from Carrie, a crib-Catholic: *Eucharist*.

We broke bread and light, body and wine of Christ.

The old Dutch elms of New Rochelle framed us once again.

"They've got Dutch elm disease," Mother said.

We were quit of the dry-as-dust light, the washing-day light of the South that incurably sad, but incurably haunting abode. But the frame to the portrait was now a bit warped. Melvin and Mary had escorted us back North without slaughtering each other.

I was nervous about what I had wrapped at the bottom of my valise, something I'd stolen that could turn into a prism. I wondered if it would land me in prison. A child in the can.

Yet there was a sort of slaughter which had gone on in this first borrowed, then returned, then returning time. We were all three punier than when we'd gone to Sarasota to establish residency.

*Slaughter. Laughter.* I puzzled over the way the words sounded so different and looked so the same. I puzzled over the way the three of us had got thinner but put on a kind of strength. She hadn't gone back to being a spinster, our Mother Marcelle. She was something with much more depth, dimension, shine. She stood there in the northern light ironing, quietly folding clothing and I fancied, imagined, that it was the ghost of my hard bad year, of the bad break at Rachel's thigh and the final break of our parents in the divorce which had strengthened her the way a challenge makes character.

Count the rings in a tree I'd been taught, for the age.

"Mother," I asked her one night, "Do you feel the South challenged us?"

We were home with her fancy hats in the large boxes and her high-heeled shoe collection. She was more herself as soon as we stepped inside the front door of our home.

She'd told me when you take out a loan you pay interest on it. "Such a big investment has got to have dividends," she smiled taking our father's picture out of its oval frame, blowing the dust off it, slipping it into the green velvet lined top dresser drawer in her bedroom which I knew also now housed her wedding ring.

I looked at the four of us framed and wondered if she'd remove that too like a splinter from the flesh, an offending slip of wood. No, she left that one alone. But the more I stared at it, the more it seemed our very expressions were slipping around like fog over statues.

Hammer dulcimer blows now to evenings.

I missed the Mary Quant flowers massed against pasted blue skies, but I cautiously, gingerly opened the dark mahogany lid to our upright piano again. It was a half note too low.

"Indigo, cat got your tongue? You used to speak a blue streak and you haven't spoken more than a string of short sentences since we got back home."

"I'm ok. It's quiet here."

"Good and quiet. Those last few days in the bungalow the phone was ringing like a church on Sunday. You look as if you've lost your best friend. Indigo."

"What's wrong with the Dutch elms?"

"Dutch elm disease. What's wrong with Indigo?"

"I miss the *Five and Diamond*," I told Mother.

Marcelle questioned. She shot up one eyebrow.

I was back in the stir, the lock-up.

She came over to me and counted the knobs on my spine, "One, two, three, four five, and pull back your shoulder blades." I jerked back my blades which daddy used to call my wings. "I think you have a touch of curvature of spine—just like me," she sighed.

Soon nobody would remember him. At least she hadn't discovered my stash, my treasure, the glass doorknob which I lovingly lifted out of the bottom of my valise and wrapped in a towel which I rolled up tight in my underwear drawer. When I couldn't take missing the *Five and Diamond*, and missing him, I'd hold it up to the sharp sun and watch it make rainbows— my diamond in the rough. I'd brought it off. I'd unbolted it and brought it home—*Five and Diamond*. I realized I'd used my very private term. I felt discovered, exposed, raw like when she heard me breathing in on our party line.

But we were back North. The sky was the color of a Dutch boy's breeches. Soon there would be snow, powdered snow.

"Looks like the angels have been baking," our Grandmother Tisanne would say.

I would free myself from the small Egypt which enslaved me, depression.

"Indigo, you put things in a way which could mystify some but not me. You always were a rather mystical child, but the way I'd put it is life's a challenge wherever you are. It pretty much gets around to being unbearable. There down South where we dwelled, or back here up North where our marriage with your father is over. But what I'd say," she blew out blue smoke rings which I adored seeing her do, the blue melting with the lime-green elms just maturing at first touch of spring, "what I'd say is we stepped up to that plate this year, daughter. That time spent in that particular cell—for the whole world's a jail of different kinds—that slot of time, Indigo, it put a shot of steel into our backbone."

*May 10, 2004*

# Whips:
## A Family Story

– This narrative explores the use and abuse of discipline in a family. Indigo's family found love at the least likely moments. They sat on the window ledge overlooking West End Avenue and West 75th street on summer nights of spine-melting heat and during winter midnights of snow and stars. Indigo waits for the pain in her, a stone, to explode like a bird. "Love," she observes, "always has a quality of a whip." And feels that the visionary, the incantary, was first realized down south. Writing, pen above ink, she dips in and begins with the strictures of the time line of their lives. It is a family story she has been telling and will end telling.

## Whips: A Family Story

Most families from Ireland, from Bavaria, who had whips for disciplinary measures, used them for boys. Families with boys had baseball games on Saturdays. Day was clocked around the Little League.

Tick-tock, the cat in the window, cleans her paws.

We had dancing and music lessons. We had vocal practice in New York and theatre coaching with Peg Norton. Although we never saw the whip, we felt its streamers fluttering above our back, white in the wind, threatening to land.

Our mother had cut herself off from the pleasures of life. That sadness tinged our girlhood, Rachel's and mine. Perhaps it was as inevitable as tragedy occurring in Athens at the Olympics— Greece, the birthplace of tragedy.

One found love at the least likely moment. Love was the lodestar, for the young people we saw outside our window on 75th street were awash in its madness, rapture, despair. We were that Japanese floating world, complete in ourselves. Intolerable at times when we broke the bubble, this world became complete when we yielded and remained within it.

I ran away to live with our father for four months. Rachel commuted from Manhattan to Pennsylvania to consummate her first love affair with a freshman in college, relieve herself of her virginity. I lagged behind my younger sister.

Marcelle saw a stain on the blue dress she'd sewed me herself on her second-hand *Singer* and exclaimed, "Indigo! Couldn't you wait?"

"It's like urinating, for men," she said, then flushed the john, banged the bathroom door and left the room.

I was waiting for the stone of my pain to explode into a bird.

We got free of this bitterness, Rachel and I. It took me longer.

Only many years later, in my mid-sixties, did I realize that Marcelle has passed along the whip into Rachel's hands. Chel told me to *Rough* it and come to France to spend time with them in a huge old French country house. Rachel told me to let helpers go from Upjohn, which she called upchuck, voicing that same fear of frailty. And now I'm hearing it from my nearest and dearest, the echo of the whip, the shadow of its white sharp body falls when she says, "You are not who you were seven years ago."

I shed silent tears. "Who is?"

"You're losing your strength, you move more slowly."

I want to cover both ears with my hands because I need to pull a quilt, a comforter over my head. I hear the echoes of New York that more than half a century ago.

At first I thought I would cry, then drew myself to my full height in the wheelchair. "I'm doing more, I have greater endurance, I've never felt better."

"But you're losing strength.

There was no corner to run to.

I would write a poem about it.

It stuck to me thru day like glue.

I felt the loss of who I was. Was it love and its relinquishment? It was my song and my sermon.

Oh you with your Granny D and your Deirdre, can you not see how this hurts me? Perhaps love always has a quality of the whip.

Then there were the incantatory southern nights with pulled-taffy clouds at sunset. Above the crowd, my spirit sat on a chair high as the lifesaver's chair, teetering n the Florida night breeze. Incantatory and to whom was incantation addressed?

The stone of pain would explode like a bird above Mother's Singer sewing machine. She could never dress down my disability. The stranger came to town, came and came again, yet still I did not know him.

At first I thought I would study music, musical composition. It was awesome, curious. After three years I'd had enough of counterpoint. I wanted a specific context for human action and turned to my next love, literature. I read Milton, Chaucer, Shakespeare, learned *Olde English* in graduation school, learned that one could love both music and literature, not choosing one over the other. Yet still there was that stone of pain, above the orange trees of California as above the old horse chestnuts of New York. It had yet to explode into song.

## Incantatory: Triangle Island

I look up the word: the chanting of magical words, a formula in casting a spell, any magic or sorcery.

Was it sorcery I relished down South?

All these years later, Marcelle has not had a failure of nerve. I can still see her the afternoon in January when I graduated Hunter College. Being a midyear celebration, there were only a handful of graduates. It was the sort of cold which makes air feel like ice you can see thru. And in this deep freeze, there she stood, our mother Marcelle ironing. I cannot remember what she said but if asked half a century later she would justify her choice to stand there ironing above accompanying me, Indigo, to college graduation after all the years of gymnastics, physiotherapy, logistic struggle to get cabs, drivers, doormen and elevator starters to help me in and out of two colleges, after all the trips back to hospital, this cool white linen blouse it was, I remember, with blue piping around the puff sleeves and collar, nailed her to the spot, kept her from coming with Rachel and me to sit in Hunter's auditorium and hear my name read. She might say something like:

"Indigo, if it weren't this particular blouse, which is a special linen, I'd go. These cuffs, this collar require the finest type pressing. One cannot leave the job."

During those miraculous moments when my wrath bloomed like a rash I imagined a place, *Triangle Iron*. It resembled the ironing board with its nicotine colored stains. It was all the world we three had. On this isosceles triangle our living space was designed: all the joy we had, all the friends, geology, geography, took place on this island adrift in a sea of blue smoky New York air.

Sometimes, I feel a connection with my walking body, all a blond gambol. Of course, it is mystical.

That afternoon I took Rachel by the hand and said, "Come on, Rach, we're going to celebrate. We'll pick up my degree then I'll take you to the King of The Sea for lobster."

But hard as we tried to be celebrant over that lobster there was a lump in my throat. At the last moment, I bought an Aegean blue, or what I imagined to be that color blue, pitcher from the King of the Sea. I kept it for years remembering my graduation and those words which Marcelle had used on another occasion, "I'm going to take every single happiness you have and break it."

The mercury read a steamy 90 degrees. We were stuck in town with the big fan whirring, its metal blades slicing air in our West End Avenue apartment. Everyone seemed to have left town, including Marcelle who had taken the summer in Europe, mainly France and Switzerland, with her mother whom she claimed not to love, but to accept, Tissane. Chel and I both learned to accept and love each other that summer like no other time.

She made the trips for me in the city of the stone canyons and the unreachable azure summer sky — the New York Public Library, the 52$^{nd}$ street main branch with the stone lions in front. She came home panting, 'Give me a drink, Indigo!" and I poured her lemonade or juice from the clear glass tumbler.

"No," she exclaimed, "Now that Marcelle's gone, let's use this one. She plucked the Aegean blue one off the shelf where it lived, dusted it off with her finger, ran it under cold water smiling. She took ice cubes out of the freezer and they went in with a clink.

I read voraciously.

She practiced the violin.

It would have been a totally happy summer had my great uncle Nathaniel from Romania (Tisanne's younger bachelor brother) not tried to rape me.

He had apparently done the same thing when left alone for a few hours with my older cousin Nyrene. That I wasn't more horrified has always surprised me. Chel was away overnight, Nat was staying. He'd had a few glasses of whiskey at dinner and pushed me into the bedroom in my chair after saying, "Baby, Baby," then lifted me out of the wheelchair and sat in the tub chair by the window and told me over and over how he loved me, how he'd loved me all thru my teens, how nobody else would ever love me like him. He slipped my blue dress off my shoulder. He lifted me onto the bed and began to roll my panties down when I told him to stop and leave at once.

I don't even remember trembling.

I do remember blinking in the dark, saying words which I thought were an incantation, "After great pain, a formal feeling comes." Only, they were Emily Dickinson's. In the morning he left. I told Chel what had happened and we made up our minds we'd never see him again. We never did aside from at Rachel's wedding where we sat far apart. I now understood the photos of nude girls he'd inadvertently shown me when he opened a drawer in his bachelor room hotel to give me Palgrave's *Anthology of Golden Verse*.

The sad part was that Nathaniel was a good man—suppressed, quiet, undermined by the rest of the family, but a cigar-smoking, good older uncle who accompanied me with the patience of a saint on long walks in Manhattan's West Side.

Most families, from Ireland, from Bavaria, kept whips on the sideboard, high up, to use on the boys when they misbehaved. A whip was never taken to Rachel's back or mine. Yet I felt the deep cut of chastisement from Marcelle quite often.

Always to burn, like a lamp, at my brightest was my goal. Yet I felt dull as lead, as pewter, at times. The incisive blows came from silence on happy occasions and aggression, like not attending my graduation, like shutting herself off from the bloom and heat and copious color of summertime forever in a frosty winter of the soul. Is she the original steel magnolia, I ask myself, combined with the ice queen?

Simone holds onto her childhood. Like Marcelle, she learned how to endure melancholy at a young age. She was sent to a Convent School in France where the sisters used the teaching methods of the Swiss Maria Montessori. Nonetheless, she was unhappy. This was during the sixties. A quiet child with an alto voice that came out of her like out of a fourteen-year old boy, she stunned those around with her beauty: porcelain cheek, ash brown locks and eyes. Not that different from Marcelle, now that I consider each of them. Although the episode with great uncle Nathaniel was awful, it was a onetime. Simone suffered over and over at the hands of the nuns who chastised her for reading as though it were a dark act for a girl to commit. Mother Marcelle suffering over and over not having what she desired with all her heart: toe slippers, ballet lessons.

Writing. Pen above ink—I dipped in and began with the strictures of a time line, following elementary school discipline. It was a family story I had to tell. Pulled taffy, southern dawns and sunset, incendiary North-eastern winter evenings. The touch of someone was always at my back. Was it the wind? The small voice whispering? Was it the elation of that incomparable summer of 1959 when I was twenty and Rachel sixteen? Having the West Side apartment to ourselves, free of Marcelle's melancholy figure and stern words, we did not blossom in the sense of becoming garishly loud colors and with whoops and screams of freedom. Quietly, two Jane Austen girls, we tried our profile at different angels in the mirror. We smoothed cotton tops over our small pearl-like breasts. We piled our long brown and ash blond hair respectively up in chignons. We went to the corner for a root beer. These are the daring things we did. Nothing compared to what we might have done.

Chel had quietly given up her virginity: I had held onto my own. We each held our own space by now, she having taken over the Black Den of Calcutta, the back room which was tiny, but was hers alone to occupy in the L-shaped old apartment on West End Avenue. How I envy her. I couldn't fit in with the wheelchair. It had a window with hexagonal wires set in for grids. It overlooked tar papered roofs and water towers. The sill was lined with a fur of soot morning, noon, and evening. Anytime you dipped your finger in that eggshell colored sill the finger came back grey. But it was her own. I had the big bedroom we'd shared for years. We each had our own john. One or two postcards came from Tisanne. I typed out my first drafts of poems those summer evenings, read hungrily all the Millay, Frost, and Sandburg that Chel came piled up with, back from the New York Public Library, the 52$^{nd}$ street, the main public, with the two stone lions in front.

In our quiet way, we entered maturity, and with it, modernity, majority. No longer under the shadow of our mother, we learned to limber our bodies and laugh over suppers of sardines and hard boiled eggs with seven up or cheap red wine so rough it scratched your throat going down. We ate at the card table which needed a matchbook under one foot to steady it. We jumped like a shot fox when the phone rang. It was a boy for her most of the time. After three years at the music college, I still had no friends. Mrs. Bartenieff, back when I'd just been entering my adolescence, worried about my having no social life.. Now, I was beyond it. But I did get to set scores aside—instrumentation books and theory of counterpoint and the various species of it— in summertime. Autumn was round the bend, and shades of the cellblock, but in late August we were still free.

I had a notion I might not be returning to music college in autumn. I wanted a specific human context for action and decision. The melancholy which had imbued me like a cobalt, an indigo stain turning my white dress blue, was lifting. Gradually the stone was exploding, not yet into a word, but into a shower of words which I hammered out nightly at my old Underwood while Rachel's scales went up and down the G string of the violin.

I felt a threat returning. Marcelle would be home soon. I bristled when her call came from Geneva that she and Grandmother would be touching down at Idlewilde in morning.

"We'd better shop fast," I told Chel as I wheeled up to the old wheezing fridge and throwing the door open took out a bundle of things that were going bad. Laughing, she knelt, her dark hair swinging forward over her face sniffing at carrots, cheese.

"These go, Indigo, absolutely!" she said pinching her nose.

"I need to go through here with a clothes pin on my nose, girls," I said mocking our mother Marcelle's tone. Then I pressed a five dollar bill into her hand.

"Hey, run down to discount liquors and buy us a last bottle of red wine."

"Yes," she smiled. "And a tin of sardines,"

"And two kinds of cheese," by now we were both laughing.

We laughed so hard our sides hurt. I realized I hadn't seen Chel so happy since I'd been a child of ten or eleven still able to walk.

"Rachel!" I opened my arms wide in the Madonna-gesture.

But she said, "Don't go mawkish on me, Ind," and I folded my hands across my chest, then reached out a lanky arm for the pack of cigarettes in the top drawer under the iron.

"Don't tell Marcelle about this." I said.

"Not in a million," she said. "Indigo, give me one."

I lit one Pall Mall and handed it to her, then lit my own. She pulled out the stool on which Mother sometimes sat when she ironed.

"Don't tell her a thing about Nathaniel."

"Never," I said. She held out her right hand, we shook on it.

"Don't tell her about the smoking and the red wine and . . ." The list went on and on until I realized it was an incantation, a litany of things we had done with wonder this summer free of the shadow of the whip. We stayed up all night and talked.

When the phone rang at five a.m. "I'll get it!" Chel cried.

"No, let me. I'm eldest."

Set a good example, Marcelle always said.

We were no longer smiling. Rings were under her eyes. I realized suddenly that she looked as if somebody had kept her up all night every night since Marcelle had left us on our own in early summer. All those cigarette butts flushed down the loo, those ashtrays scrubbed out, those trips up and down the elevator with trash. I thought of us as girls of eight and twelve touching ourselves in the dark in our twin beds.

"Did you get the felling yet, Chel?"

"Yes, you?"

"No," I always came slower.

The fridge was stocked with a dozen fresh brown eggs, we'd scrubbed the vegetable bins, and scrubbed down the shelves. I'd done a stack of ironing and Chel had run up and down the garbage stairs with five laundries. We'd vacuumed and put fresh flowers in the vase. But suddenly, rolling back from the grand piano, the dusted and vacuumed living room, all at once it struck me like a blow in the face—our place looked like a funeral parlor. Neat as a pin, but breathless. I thought of the endless hours I'd spent in that room writing music.

I wanted out. Period. I tried to imagine Mother coming in the door with a dozen new hats and new shoes from Switzerland. She'd wind up all the clocks tight and they'd begin ticking again. I hadn't seen Chel laugh in so long and now probably wouldn't for a time. But we were no longer Triangle Island, a Floating island, that spell had been broken.

"Sleep, Rach," I whispered to her. "Even three hours will do you good. I know I can."

Mother was taxiing in from Idlewilde airport and would announce she needed a few days of nothing but shuteye.

Incantation: the chanting of magic words, or formula to break or work a spell.

It was dawn over Manhattan as I caught my forty winks. We'd polished off a bottle of rough red and disposed of the bottle. All the evidence of our summer of libertine leisure and freedom was removed. Within a few years, Rachel herself was to take Geneva by storm winning the Prize in the Viola Competition and given a special Max Reger prize, created in her honor.

Marcelle always said, "Rachel is not for us, she is for the world," but this summer we were for each other.

I'd never again slip my bike gloves onto my hands to push the wheelchair fast down West 75th street to Broadway just to have a coke, or watch a movie at the Beeman Theatre, get a sandwich at the C & L restaurant. The wheelchair had never moved like that on wings.

Now the full weight of it sank upon my chest again, I reached out and touched the cold silver in the night. But a singing started in my bosom which I knew was the explosion of the stone into bird. I shuddered a moment as the shadow of the whip came down across my shoulder blades, but then I shrugged it off, it was just a dream. The stone lions of the 52nd street library stood guard over me. I gave myself over to the soot colored angel of late August New York city dawn.

# The Kind of Day to See an Albino Peacock

for Anne and Katy

She loved birds, and kept swans and peacocks at the place in Milledgeville–but...no more sentimental about them than . . . about any of her human characters:

"I came back from my trip with enough money to order me another pair of swans. Mr. Hood, the incumbent swan, little suspects that he is going to have to share his feed dish. He eats out of a vase, as a matter of fact, and has a private dining room"

Flannery O'Connor *The Habit of Being*

– This last story in the book occurs the day Marcelle dies. Simone and Indigo drive to see the children's zoological gardens. Zoos were always emotional peaks for Indigo's mother. It was cold as though the little ice age had returned. Frost touched the donkeys and there was no Alabama moon. Indigo remembers key figures in her life: Grandmother Tisanne who was motherly to the core, a plump partridge. She relives the hell of her withdrawal from a prescribed drug. Even then Marcelle remained the dispossessed southern belle in the sense of being the steel paw in the velvet glove.

## Peacock Weather

The day my mother died could have been southern; it was filled with omen, Christ-haunted, despite the fact we are Jews. I knew it was the kind of day to see the albino peacock. These days are always emotional peaks. It happened, nonetheless, up North. We have one or two at the small children's zoo. I woke up wanting to tell Simone stories but she wanted to sleep, mellow soul she is with the alto voice I love in women.

The little ice age had returned. Frost touched the donkeys and no Alabama moon shone overhead. No moon the color of Grandmother Tisanne's hair, piled in copper-blond braids round her head. Mother Marcelle's mother was the elegant and earthy woman whom Magritte calls Aunt Suzanne. I cannot see Tisanne as an aunt. She is motherly to the core for me, her plump partridge breast heaving in a well packed blouse like the sailor boys with their well packed pants walking the boardwalks of Atlantic City, New Jersey, in war time. I was embarrassed when I saw them and turned away. Later, down South, the women said.

"Rope your eye in on him. Scoot them sweet rolls 'cross the table."

Up north we had doorknob biscuits we call scones done in gravy, buttermilk biscuits, milk pillows with a knob of butter.

Custer La Rue sings: a street the hue of Custard, North and South are the two polarities of my life.

When I lived down South I can remember writing *Tennessee Moon* from top to bottom of the chalkboard. If I started at the bottom my hand got tired by the top but starting at the top I could relax as I reached the bottom where the wood tray held the chalks, only a few colored rose or green in those wartime days of my fifth and sixth years. This was all because I'd misspelled the word *Tennessee* first in a bee, and then in a short story. I was curious about the birds and the bees.

"A little boy holds himself," Marcelle, our mother, began politely "when he goes to the bathroom."

"All the time?" I asked.

"Most of the time," she said.

This too was down South.

"The bee is attracted to the honey. The bee is the boy, the honey the girl. We have complementary parts. He introduces himself to her when they come of age."

What was of age? What more did I need to know about introductions?

Oracular, more and more apocalyptic, life became in the South. Harrowing in the North, life expanded and then contracted like a fist or heart-muscle in the South. I pledged allegiance and my heart changed. What unites the Jewish child and the southern child could well be vivid, at times Gothic—imagination.

It rarely snowed in the South, and then it was magical, like torn confetti, but it was white. Insistently white. Hatefully white. Marmoreal white. Funeral white. Clinical White. Yet the wound always lay beneath the scar and the South was glassy with scars.

My little sister Chel broke her leg the second winter there so I see her cast from ankle to above waist. She will bear a scar for life in her midback—her cast put on, the bone was set by a drunk surgeon in Sarasota, the best orthopedic surgeon in the area, Christmas Eve. Sipsie's cast, which made misery of her fifth winter and made a mess of mine, was opaque yet at certain enchanted hours it gleamed, white as lilies, white as swans, white as the peacock who could bloom the day of Mother's death, fan against sky, defiance against depression.

There was a time, during withdrawal from a prescribed drug, when I lived between the bed and the bathroom.

"Why not sleep in the bathroom?" Mother asked.

Even though my red blood count was radically low, the white soaring, I struggled to remain a gymnast. Goodbye, bullet, hello sun. Mother became natural around animals, dropping the air of dispossessed southern belle. The steel paw in the velvet glove. She lit up before the giraffe in New York's Central Park Zoo. She told me the story of Gloomy, the Camel before the supercilious caramel colored camel, the hue of butterscotch, the creature was aloof. Gloomy was one thing I was not permitted to be.

"*Defense d'etre triste,*" Mother instructed me in her bell-like southern French.

I scuffed my Buster Brown back and forth, feeling more threatened than menacing—not even when my helium balloon floated off from me with a will of its own, like those big bloomers, hang gliders that Evelyn's aunt took off in one summer, and set sail through the moss and cypress groves till they snagged among the Spanish moss. And who among us would say, but who could resist thinking pubic hair with panties tangled. My balloon let go and I watched it go bump, bump, bump up to the top of the vast three storied zoo cafeteria ceiling. The only ceiling I knew that cathedral-high was that other modern cathedral, Grand Central Station. The final bump of my white balloon on the ceiling reminded me of the lonesome hoot of a railroad train, both senses locked hands.

"Not to cry," Mother advised, "So our soul finally leaves our body."

So there was a way we finally got free. But it had to wait for the day the hand let go the string. I collected string the way my cousin Nyrene did buttons.

"Why collect string?" Marcelle, our mother asked, one hot noon in Florida.

"For practical purposes," I answered. "It's picayune."

But my Scottish friend's mother, Finoola, had said every bit of string was handy. Save them all, from parcels, from gifts. I rose to my feet, planted hands on hips, my typical posture of defiance and said, "It ties things together."

"Which reminds me, Indigo," Mother snapped back, "it's high time you tied up those old Jack and Jills cluttering our parlor."

I threw back over my shoulders, "It could bind our lives."

The sense of our lives having unraveled after the war, and during divorce, haunted me.

I walked, or rather stalked, into the parlor. It's true that in the North we would have called this room, into which the auburn moons of autumn and winter burned, our sunroom. Here there was so much sun we needed a parlor-shade. Up northeast there were so many witch hunts and so much steely light that we captured, like fireflies in a jar, all the sun we could when it shone into our New Rochelle sunroom.

Here we rested up after various childhood illnesses which were legion: burst eardrum, mastoids, tonsillitis, a wool muffler wound round our neck, given hot tea to sip.

"Isadora Duncan was strangled on one."

"Well, you won't."

"How come?"

"'Cause I'm too smart to give you such a vainglorious thing."

Vainglorious. That was a new world. "I could choke though," I came back, "this soup is so thick."

"Down the hatch," said Mother.

I remembered this after polio when the only thing that could save me from chronic constipation was one tablespoon of cod liver oil mixed in with half a glass of milk of magnesium.

Down the hatch went so much. Our grief went down it like coal sacked thudding into the basement down the cellar chute. Brighter was our pleasure which too was shoved into darkness, like red autumn apples making a quilt color and a quieter drum roll than the chunks of anthracite and bituminous coal delivered each October by the coal man with smudged features and thick gloves. We always had our first hot chocolate of autumn turning to winter after the coal man left. It was one of our holy rituals. Oracular, I thought, turning the luscious word round on my tongue. Visionary. But was it as far extreme as apocryphal?

Strung like a hammock between North and South, I grew long, willowy, lean, loved to snap green beans into a metal wash pan in which we also bathed in summertime. North and South shared certain things, the aisle-like order, symmetry, the discipline of the ward I was later to learn. The bandages were crisper up North, longer down South, where they began from the beginning of time and stretched it seemed forever— the ninth day of forever, the tenth is an infinitesimally small yet long time. Down South our counting began, however, with the number zero pronounced *ought*.

So we chanted, "*Ought one two three four five.*"

Numerically speaking, I did better down South. One schoolhouse, one classroom. There was one anthem to speak each morning, one Lord's prayer (in whom I, a Jewish kid, did not believe) one flag rolled up the brass pole, one blinding sun.

Up North, there were multiples. A brick school with many rooms, many lessons—dance, art, piano—many houses to the towns, many rules to obey (set against the South's one: respect) and a sun that split into shards that made rainbows like oil on the road in a swirl, and shone in a metal wheel in winter.

This is how my New Zealand translator friend iconographs my name:

> The surname is also possibly of Old English and Gaelic origin, meaning: waterfall or pool, and probably would have been given to a family living near such a body of water. Sometimes used as a diminutive of Linda:
>
> Spanish: Pretty. Used especially as a middle name and as a feminine beginning or ending in many name blends:
>
> Lin: beautiful jade    Liona : light
>
> Linaeve : Tree of song    Lynna : waterfall
>
> Lynsey : Linden tree    Lyneth: beautiful one

> Lynn
>
> Tree of song
>
> Waterfall of words
>
> In your kelly green shoes
>
> You outshone Pavlova....
>
> Without your feet ever leaving the ground.

This is how she iconographs Anne-Magrittes:

(this one was for Anne)

*Anna from Hebrew Hannah : gracious*

*Aneko (Japanese) : older sister*

*Anam : Gaelic - soul mate*

*Ankareeda : light in the night*

Magritte I do not remember as a little girl but she remembers me, one of the few souls on this earth who could have seen me in Buster Browns walking. Was the child truly schizophrenic, insomnia—both southern traits and stigmas like the marks of the stigmata—I meet her again as translator, professional linguist, when she is in her seventies, I in my late sixties, we are three years apart and she does prove to be the gracious, older sister, light in the night.

But am I, Indigo, Lynn, waterfall of words, tree of songs? I taught myself the tree of songs, the liona, the waterfall of words later in hospital when orgasm swept over me, its white billows transcending the hospital gown of medications, shimmering. I know I learned the meaning of apocrypha then.

Mother did not put me in ringlets because she knew better than have metal bite my skull. *Wringlets* my New Zealand friend writes it. How perfect. I think of the reams of our words, the one long sheet Mother put through the wringer of her morals, her moods. Some days it turned out that ice cream was blue, blueberry-blue, some white. It depended also on the nights. We had a nurse lady from Decatur, Illinois who came to look after Chel, Susanne.

I called my little sister Sipsie all that hot winter in Florida probably due to the fact that I drank lots through straws. Anything sipped through a straw cooled the back of the throat more. This nurse was good, but Mother's moods were like the moody skies up North, now marble white, now blue thundershowers with the element and possibility of electrocution. I was lectured in my diction, my elocution. Electrocution was another thing.

Like Scout Finch in *To Kill a Mockingbird*, I was forthright and didn't believe in putting crosses or stars on graves. I imagined, before my opaque green-gray eyes, ocean waves and waves of confederate and federal grass, when my pets died. They all did. First the kitten, Lacrosse, then the canary, Tebaldi, and so on. There were cycles of death near sand and limestone.

*I thank you kindly.*

*You have a gentleman caller.*

Southern phrases return under an Alabama or under a Hoosier, or a Massachusetts moon.

I am sassed when I don't even hear water running. The South lost the Civil War and it is stamped all over its face like war poetry, which squares the shoulders and puts a bolt of steel into spine, like scars on a forehead and chin. I lost the war against polio. Another way, paralyzed, transfixed, I was pierced by my vision. Witnesses were called for. Yes, war calls for witness, a fact. I was hard as a nail driven in when I was nine turning ten, a veteran. Strategic, poetic my statements tended to be. My New Zealand friend wrote me a postcard from Italy which I thrilled to at age nine being in love with language from the cradle.

I write too fast and make spelling mistakes.

I remember my Grandmother saying that when I was small. I realized after I left New Zealand just how Irish an upbringing I had…even much of my vocab in English is influenced by Gaelic.

I started to teach myself Gaelic, but have reverted to Maori instead. It is more inspiring for my painting and I feel more kiwi than Irish really.

Well, in the South I was Elizabethan, Jewish, northern.

What the Black & Tans wore was so different from the Redcoats yet underneath there was the uniform always streaming, blaring forth its colors like a trumpet fanfare. I plugged my ears to it. I am a Redcoat marching up and down the attic stairs. I carry the Union Jack only to set it on fire. A high spirited, rambunctious child, I would find Sipsie's urine samples in the fridge with the little orange caps and pull them out and gaffe, *Chidden soup.*

I was in five different first grades. "And you never reverted, Indigo," Mother boasted.

"What way?"

"Reggies' kids took to wetting their beds. You never did."

We moved so often, I remember the sound. This is one of my most vivid and early auditory memories— lots of glass tape wrapping boxes when we moved, lots of cutting when we unmoved as we came to call resettling.

"We're like the early settlers, girls," Marcelle would beam.

"You mean the pioneers?" I asked. Or do you mean the Puritans, because the latter conducted some of the worst witch hunts in our nations' history.

Of course our mother meant the pioneers. The log cabins we built outback in the North, we did not here down Dixie way where the magnolia trees have their small cigarette burns. But we toured the everglades, posed for photographs, Sipsie and I, before St Augustine's Fountain of Youth, and we saw real live crocks.

The day Mother died we saw the miraculous unfolding of a white peacock, like the silk white handkerchief unfolding and unfolding from the magician's hat to save the world from drabness. For that's why she was sent. That was another way in this revelatory life we got *free with our souls*. We needed to see an albino peacock—sole bird to counter the mahogany luster of her long-awaited divorce and death, long-suffered-toward death.

So Simone and I drove out, the South full of me, stinging my bosom. The woods were dark-bright, chiaroscuro. It was May. My mother and father died exactly the same day, symmetry a woman like Jane Austen might appreciate. It was a small yet profound touch, a fine brush on ivory.

When at first Simone and I drove to Beacon Hill Park where the peacocks live, all was silent like before a big storm. The sky was strewn with mares' tale clouds sliding thru trees, a rainforest dripping from recent rain.

I felt loneliness, I told Sipsie when I was about nine, crawling up from my stomach (with the deep belly button of which I was proud) into my throat.

I recalled a friend's aunt's grave, traceable only by a depression in the soil and 1941 scratched into the headstone. She had reminded her niece of a yellow finch, which stuck in my mind.

"The name as scratched on with a nail," Sabella told me.

Nobody could explain death to me better than that cotton white balloon letting go. But now there was the death of herself, who'd told me it was the soul getting free and no peacock in sight.

I recalled a bag I tied together with string of southern wisdoms: oracular, apocryphal, one boils steel straps to get the scent off, overlap palmetto roofing so rain slides down, soak deerskin two days and it comes out with two days softness. I could understand these things.

Her death. No lien-to affording us shelter, Mother. Simone and I unscrewed the thermos she herself had given me, Gadabout.

Coffee steam rushed forth, fogging our glasses, causing us to smile.

"Gadabout," I smiled, "that's what she wasn't."

She had loved the zoo. I saw through trees like through windows pocked, chipped from years of our gazing out. Everything was going smoothly as greased lightning. Like lightning, however it struck outlined us, her two children, daughters, and sweetheart in blue.

The linen canvas of sky was bare and then we heard a blood-curdling shriek such as one hears form the bolted window of an insane asylum. Is there any asylum for the insane?"

"There he is!" Simone said in a stage whisper.

It was a heart stopper. A pain struck beneath my left ribs. Whiter than snow, whiter than the South, stiff as starched dress for first communion saying his vowel over and over, "Veeyowl," the one white peacock strutted under the trees of green flame, under the remembered chalkboards of the South, beneath the arched and chill vaulted sky of our mother's death.

I woke, even before she died, with the knowledge hot in me that it would be a day to see the Albino peacock. The bird disappeared like a Diamond Safety Match struck on the foot of Daddy's shoe and, like him at the final hour, gone.

## Nectar Drops for Nerves

Simone and I had a bit of a hack up last night. She made whipped cream (wicked cream) for pumpkin pie. I helped myself to seconds.

She said, "Hey! Leave some," but it was a bit late. A war child, I am a goner for cream.

Today, Sunday, we drove down Maud Street and saw a sign, "Character for Sale."

They'd left out the word house. I thought of Sipsie's first child, daughter Raissa, on nectar drops for nerves by age three. I thought of the buttocks boils I'd had in my adolescence from scraping along the pavement to the pool which they said was good for post polios. I hated that term and kept thinking of ballroom dancing in my wheelchair. I could spin on a dime.

"It's the kind of day one could see an albino peacock," I told her, packing brie and cheddar sandwiches, with lettuce and sliced green onion and putting it all with Mother's Gadabout thermos in a blue jean bag I hung on our front brass doorknob.

"What's that?" I asked.

"What do you see?" (I always needed to have a child, a daughter preferably.)

"A picnic," she laughed.

So we piled in my fifteen-year-old Buick Vita which I no longer drive but which really belongs to Simone now and drove to the top of Beacon Hill where we looked out.

"That's my land," I said,

"No?"

"Eh?" she said.

"Oh yes."

This was the hill from which ships were signaled and beacons set, flares. *Warning* said everything about my arrival north twenty-seven years ago, yet I not only came but stayed — where rubber-banded mail stood unceremoniously in a wicker secondhand basket, bought at the Sally Anne, rather than being hand-delivered in brushed metal slots, as back in my homeland, the States.

When you have been a child in a hospital, when you have had boils on your buttocks and age twelve, and seen children take the drip—nothing as benign as nectar drops for nerves—before you turned a teen, you turn toward anyone who takes you in with Kind— Kindness. The southern kind? No, the human kind. Where is your *heart*, we could not say to the nurses but longed to.

Maud Street with its "Character for Sale" receded in the rearview mirror.

There are other kinds of days on which to look for an albino peacock, its feathers like curled cream but not many. They don't have to be birth and death days. You might have won the spelling bee as I did at age nine. Your mother might have died. The red letter day you had expected at the music academy might have turned pewter, dulled to steel, then blown to crematory ash.

But albino peacock days—like albinos themselves—had always been to me a sign of providence coming. Apocryphal, visionary, they stood against the drab design of daily brick and granite days and they shone, shone, shone.

Your losses might have stood out most clean, like beads of bone. They shone too. They were abacus counters. How hard it was to be a whippersnapper, that bright, and have to always plot strategies how to swing first one long-legged brace, then the other up the curb.

The explosion of the albino peacock, despite all my learned and mastered stage-presence, stopped my heart. Other things were heart-stoppers but not like this.

Just last night, Simone spoke to me of *the renaissance of the red apple*. Only she could speak this way. An instruction was turned into a poem. I did not know the apple had suffered a setback, almost died.

Today, seeing Maud Street with the sign "Character for Sale," once again, although we spied no albino peacock, I feel my blood iron unfurl, oracular.

"It would have been visionary," I tell Simone, "to have seen one."

But nonetheless, with autumn's resurrection of red apples, with Mother now five months safely sealed from sorrow and gone, the trees are glowing. I can count our blessings and it is in fact, *Apocryphal.* I whisper to her a moment before we swing back into our drive to take umbrage once more in the sanctuary of home.

Whether or not we have had our vision, we have our vision. I may create one for myself in dream as I made up words for the bees, in the time when I did not know precisely how the honey attracted the bee or how our parts were complementary.

In dream, for a second, I will feel how I become disentangled from things of this earth. How I glide in kelly-green shoes over a ballroom floor again, my hand in the hand of he whom I kissed when the bottle spun, and stopped at one whose mouth was full of metal. My soul, Hannah, Annike, Linea, an albino peacock we did not see— only a pariah, a freak of nature could be so lovely. Yet in my dream, for the blink of a birds' eye, in a heartbeat, will have got free.


## Shut Shop On Emotions

Children rarely shut shop in emotions. Neither would they see a peacock as a swanked up chicken. When I think of the night there was the fire in Alabama, at a farm where we were staying, and fourteen-year-old Nabeela lost her wooden leg, I draw up to the surface of my memory—which usually keeps this night in a vault—the image of her crying.

"My one good leg to dance on."

She had lost it to sarcoma and had radiation. For a year the stump was weeping. Then she had a dry socket. She began dancing lessons immediately at the Arthur Murray Dance Studio in Selma and became the fastest black girl on the floor. Color should not have counted but it did.

I stash this with other medical memories like Mara, my Irish friend, who has a cancer on her face. It wouldn't be bad but it's so near the eye and rooted. I thought back on her childhood in Ireland, the convent and how Sipsie and I had been virgins for the longest time—or so I thought, but Sipsie wasn't.

"They'll think you're out for business," Marcelle stood, arms akimbo in our Manhattan front hallway where the phone conversations went on which could never be private.

"Proud as a peacock," she'd light up a cigarette, "That's what you are, Chel."

Chel never answered back. She just left.

But it got me started thinking of and researching peacocks which, it turns out, Flannery O'Connor raised. She had lupus. Unlike me, she was not deathly ill as a child but later on— when the voice of the peacock was heard in the land of Milledgeville, Georgia. She had Catholicism. I had none. I had only the staff of a vivid imagination on which to lean. Mr. Hood was going to eat out of a vase, Flannery announced in a letter. She thought her being southern polluted her being Catholic. Her being Catholic, reciprocally, contradicted her being southern.

There is a certain hour of twilight when the nerves are in torment. Nectar drops are out of the question. Almost everything is in a state of indecision and everything is out of the question.

Like a small coal-mining town in West Virginia or Pennsylvania, the Protestant South O'Connor grew up in was "Christ haunted." The child I spoke to down South was also Christ-haunted, saying the devil had a red tail and would get me if I didn't obey my mama.

Scared as I was of Sabella, I held my dark blond head in the boy bowl haircut high and said, "Sabella Smith, no, he won't."

She spooked me but I acted brave. "You know that's a tall tale."

"No, it ain't," she screamed. "my Mama and the preacher both told me so."

I kicked a stone at my foot and walked away thinking such parents and priests were wimps.

At the same time, I was aware of the haunting, in my own life— the overwhelming sense that death could never truly happen because once my own consciousness was extinguished, other people would be lit into being. There is comfort somewhere. Or nowhere. But life carries on.

Nothing was done with perfect ease. But when I scooped up my ten jacks and red bouncing ball, or skipped my jump rope, the universe aligned. There was harmony. It encompassed those rows of shacks with secondhand lumber and tin roofs which comprised southern porches on our street, the floorboards of porches sagging like sofas, or pulled taffy.

These homes were rubber. The people sure were real in contrast. The father of my best friend, Camille, worked in the trauma unit of Selma Hospital. Burn cases, traumatized accident victims, hypochondriacs, and schizophrenics all came under his care. A series of pariahs passed before my vision— like celluloid negatives to photographs which would never make it up thru the acids in the darkroom with its red bulb to the light.

I dared in the dark to touch myself.

"You will go to hell," shrieked my Christ-haunted friend.

Haunted also, I told Camille.

She said, "Never mind. I do the same."

"Have you told your mama?"

"No, only my sister."

"Well, Sipsie knows."

Then we giggled, "Nice girls don't' touch," she echoes our teacher Miss Brown.

"Legs are like best friends. They always stay together," I echoed her and in gales of laughter we joined hands and two girls of nine going on ten ran down to the river laughing.

What we hoped to find there was an extension of our release. But guilt descended, a southern murk, a fog instead. I had not yet read

Faulkner or learned about his fictional county but would soon. Too soon.

Mother was boiling noodles when I came home that evening.

"Chel comes out of her cast soon."

"Oh."

I wondered if the leg would appear purple yellow, withered when it came out. I wondered whether I would be jealous of the attention she would receive.

"She'll need special care," Mother warned.

I must have pouted a bit because she said, "Indigo, don't puff up like a toad."

My chin quivering I ran into the dirt yard and skipped stones.

I had taught myself and rarely got to skip them over water, only over the dirt, in our own semblance of a back yard. Alabama moon rose that night, poor, not illumining golden velvet or satin earth but every piece of shrub, scrub and pebble in our yard.

I turned over the various woes of my neighbors and kin. Nabeela was outfitted with a new wooden leg, but it was never as good as the old which she had named Aunt Jane and used to thwack. The new one remained *Miss Nameless*, and she wept, hard bitter tears. I threw my arm around her shoulder because we were leaving town soon and she dared trust me with her emotions.

I thought about Camille's father, frail himself—or seeming so, a smoke or wisp of man always smoking and with a dry cough—who worked the hardest psychiatric cases in Selma.

I thought about Sipsie. Would she heal up right? That drunken surgeon on Christmas Eve could have set her leg bone wrong. Would she limp for life? I didn't think about myself and see the slammer, polio, coming. I looked in the mirror turned away knowing I was a changeling, Ingrid Bergman's daughter, not our mother's.

It has been over half a century since I played *Spin the bottle, kiss me*. The bottle is still spinning. In a profound sense, I am still waiting to be kissed. That albino peacock? Like the winter circus folk of Barnum

& Bailey whom we saw, Sipsie and I. They were indeed freaks, Ishmaels, Pariahs. But then so are all the ones I love: Hannah or Anne, Marcelle herself, a closet lesbian who must have kissed a woman on the lips at least a year before she conceived her to-be-aborted son.

I am a Christ-haunted Jew.

I rise in the Canadian night thinking how profound my needs, how frail my helpers. Doctor, and so on, are more toothpicks than crutches, the sturdy ones I would need if I were ever to walk again. But I won't. I won't even try. Flannery hobbled about in her Georgia yard on crutches, aluminum ones. I hand it to her. She brought off what I cannot.

The Albino Peacock, who might have been, was drowned in gasoline when wind whipped up flames in my dream. No faith could douse them. I nightmared and cried like a howler monkey. Did Anne, Hannah, ever scream like this in the asylums?— about Nabeela's burned wooden leg being stolen like the Bible Salesman stealing the girl's in that O'Connor story. How could one be so God-haunted and so humorous at the same time?

Constantly I want to take leave of people. Is it because I never got to kiss the children in the ward goodbye in 1951 when measles swept me away like a salty wave. Sipsie, I lie in bed again, a child hospitalized. I was too young to know the words, *This, too, shall pass*. But I knew them.

I think of the London urchin who pointed up to the stars and said, "Look at all them bedbugs."

*Forever, Hello. Forever, Goodbye.*

Tonight I can trace the white peacock in the stars.

"I seen the little lamp," said Kesia in Katharine Mansfield's story, *The Doll's House*.

Whether or not we saw the albino bird today, we saw them.

"I'd be hurt if I had feelings," Mother Marcelle often used to say.

I am always dancing even though my feet never leave the ground.

A stranger passes a shop in dreams. Summer is over. I know longer sip water thru a straw.

I ask hesitantly, "Chel, do you miss her, Mother?"

"Yes, strangely enough I do. The way things used to be."

The shop has pennies in a jar in the window. On the door the sign which catches first flakes of winter snow and moonlight, *Closed*. But behind it is not a child. South-girl, North-girl, which am I?

"Born to be torn in half," Mother Marcelle claimed.

For a child the sign reads perpetually "Open," like Flannery scattering her peacocks with her aluminum crutches.

One is thought-haunted. Even though there may be no, or few buyers for one's vision, even though the folk in this town may be as Mother claimed of "a bit emotionally thin," the child never shuts shop on emotion. My sister said our mother's eyes flew open when she died. I am certain that she saw the albino peacock then.

## About the Author

Lynn Strongin was born in New York City in 1939 and was raised in and around New York. She lived in California during the politically active sixties and worked, in Berkeley, for Denise Levertov. During that turbulent period, she also met Robert Duncan, Josephine Miles, and Kay Boyle. She moved to Albuquerque, New Mexico, in the Seventies, and to British Columbia in 1979 where, for the past three decades she has made her home, although she considers herself profoundly to be an American writer.

Lynn has published twelve books, including the anthology *The Sorrow Psalms* (University of Iowa Press), *The Dwarf Cycle* (Thorp Springs Press), *Toccata of the Disturbed Child* (Fallen Angel Press ), *A Hacksaw Brightness* (Ironwood Press), and *Countrywoman / Surgeon* (L'Epervier Press), all published in the Seventies, and *Bones and Kim: A Novella* (Spinster's Ink Press, 1980), and two new books, *Cape Seventy (Poems)* and *Crazed By the Sun: Poems of Ecstasy*. Lynn serves as Special Guest Editor for *New Works Review*. She has been nominated five times for a Pushcart Prize.

www.ingramcontent.com/pod-product-compliance
Lightning Source LLC
Chambersburg PA
CBHW051421290426
44109CB00016B/1387